NEGOTIATE THE DEAL YOU WANT

Negotiate the Deal You Want

TALKING YOUR WAY TO SUCCESS IN BUSINESS,
COMMUNITY AFFAIRS, AND PERSONAL ENCOUNTERS

BY HENRY H. CALERO AND BOB OSKAM

IN ASSOCIATION WITH

ADVANCED MANAGEMENT REPORTS, INC.

DODD, MEAD & COMPANY · NEW YORK

To my best friend, my wife, Heather
—Henry H. Calero

For further information on negotiating,
write to Box JG, care of the publisher

Copyright © 1983 by Bob Oskam, Henry H. Calero,
and Advanced Management Reports, Inc.
Copyright © 1982, 1981, 1980 by Advanced Management Reports, Inc.
All rights reserved
No part of this book may be reproduced in any form
without permission in writing
from the publisher
Published by Dodd, Mead & Company, Inc.
79 Madison Avenue, New York, N.Y. 10016
Distributed in Canada by
McClelland and Stewart Limited, Toronto
Manufactured in the United States of America
Designed by Judith Lerner
First Edition

LIBRARY OF CONGRESS CATALOGING IN PUBLICATION DATA:

Calero, Henry H.
  Negotiate the deal you want.

  Bibliography, p. 334
  1. Negotiation in business.   2. Negotiation.
I. Oskam, Bob. II. Advanced Management Reports, Inc.
III. Title.
HD58.6.C34   1983   658.4   82-25274
ISBN 0-89696-191-5

Contents

Preface

NEGOTIATE THE DEAL YOU WANT approaches negotiation as a process of communication. This is not a situation-specific guide, telling you precisely what to do when you want more money from Joe Jones or are trying to patch up differences with Sandy Smith. Too many variables operate in those particular situations for us to be able to provide an exactly tailored response.

However, by treating negotiation as a process of communication, we can help you develop ability and flexibility as a communicator. And by focusing on what makes for effective self-presentation in negotiation, we can prompt you to recognize and adopt specific attitudes and techniques that vastly increase your chances of achieving goals through negotiation. At the same time, we can alert you to behaviors to be wary of both in yourself and in those you face in any bargaining encounter.

Any problems you experience in negotiation can be attributed to questions of approach. Once you understand the process you're involved in, realize the decisive influence of attitudes you project, and tune in to habits and techniques affecting the way people perceive and respond to each other, you're well on your way to resolving difficulties experienced in particular situations. We don't guarantee we have the key to resolving every problem you may encounter; not all problems can be solved through negotiation. But mastery of the information presented here will ensure that you take maximum advantage of any available opportunity for gaining benefit through negotiation. We believe strongly that negotiation provides the best means of coordinating interests and resolving differences between people. It's the only process permitting people with different perspectives and priorities to coordinate them peacefully and anticipate a gain on both sides.

The information in this book is perhaps more particularly addressed to the business world than to coping with everyday interpersonal situations. This emphasis reflects our original intent to create a handbook of special value for those who regularly conduct business negotiations. However, the information and guidelines will work equally well in interpersonal encounters where you find yourself trying to develop a cooperative approach to resolving differences or exploiting opportunities. We've tried to make this book easily accessible to everyone. So the "you" in these pages is not just the concerned businessperson; it is also you the community member, the student, the family member, the everyday individual pursuing your daily life.

Understand that we cannot possibly address or allude to every variant of a situation entailing use of negotiation skills. We cannot cover every perspective. But we have made a conscientious effort to make you thoroughly aware of essential fundamentals and to outline as diverse a range of circumstances as is practical in a volume of this size. In virtually all cases, you can adapt information presented to fit the needs of your particular situation. You can apply it to the needs of your own perspective by adjusting or reversing the perspective given here. For example, if you are more concerned to expand your range of diversionary tactics than to guard against those being used on you, review the information in our section "Tuning into Diversionary Tactics" from a perspective of *use* rather than *defense.* A similar adjustment will expand the immediate relevance for you of other sections of the book presented from a perspective that is not precisely yours or is developed in a context of circumstances you do not wholly share.

The "Quick-Reference Problem-Solving Key" immediately following is a distillation of much of the core material in this book. It's organized to give you a quick look at guidelines to apply, or considerations to take into account in particular circumstances related to negotiation. Subject entries cover specific problems you may encounter as well as areas of communication in which problems commonly arise. More than 200 listings aim at helping you cut through to the heart of difficulties you may be experiencing in applying the negotiation process to whatever situation you face.

"Problem-Solving Key" entries are specially tailored as responses to questions we're commonly asked. Restating those questions will help you to a better understanding of the context to which any word of advice or set of guidelines applies. Page references following the subject entry provide either an expanded discussion of particular circumstances referred to or additionally pertinent remarks or observations that can help you broaden your understanding.

The "Problem-Solving Key" is not intended as a definitive index to the material in the book. It will help you home in quickly on points of presentation that apply to a problem you have or wish to avoid, but you will find that other sections of text can also provide valuable clues to improved performance in whatever situation you face. We've placed this special feature at the beginning of this book in recognition of the fact that your first concern in referring to it may well be a specific question or difficulty. The "Problem-Solving Key" will give you a quick handle on what to keep uppermost in mind in dealing with that. However, the flexibility necessary for employing that handle to best effect comes only through understanding and mastering the negotiation process.

The chapters that follow the "Problem-Solving Key" are organized to provide you both a conceptual framework and a repertory of practical insights and tactics. When you have the opportunity, review each section of the book for a more thorough, integrated view of negotiation as a problem-solving process. Apply specific guidelines as they fit your circumstances, but also develop your awareness of the principles upon which all guidelines are based. Understanding those can help you achieve the full degree of awareness and flexibility required to make you a problem solver *par excellence*.

May all your negotiations be successful!

Acknowledgments

THANKS are due Tony Whyte, President of Advanced Management Reports for his encouragement and support both in undertaking the work to produce the original copy for "The Winning Negotiator," the AMR consulting newsletter from which this book has been developed, and the work to adapt the material we've produced for use as *Negotiate The Deal You Want.*

We'd also like to express our appreciation to Ann Santee and Anne Marie Church, both of whom worked supportively with us in developing a focus for material of practical utility to negotiators on all levels. And a note of warm thanks, too, to Lindsey Biel and copyeditor Lillian McClintock, whose editorial eyes have helped shape our style for maximum clarity.

Not least, we want to acknowledge the confidence and support displayed by Jerry Gross, our editor at Dodd, Mead, whose enthusiasm for this project was instrumental in seeing it assume final book form.

HANK CALERO
BOB OSKAM

NEGOTIATE THE DEAL YOU WANT

Quick-Reference
Problem-Solving Key

(Please refer to the Preface for comments on use of this section.)

ADVANTAGE, unfair (p. 199)
What should you do when someone accuses you of taking unfair advantage of his or her position?

Stay calmly focused on your own priorities. Don't get rattled or shamed into a confession you haven't prepared yourself for; that's often the gambit in the accusation.

On the preventive side, use a periodic recapping technique to elicit concurrence from your opposite to developments along the way to agreement. That leaves him/her less room for evading any responsibility for how things get to where they are at any point.

ADVERSARY MENTALITY (pp. 209–212, 213–214, 221–222, 255, 317)
What's the best line of approach when faced with an opposite who seems to view you as "the enemy"?

Refuse to fall into the role you've been assigned. It's essential to develop some kind of cooperative relationship if the negotiation is to succeed. Follow these guidelines:

- Make it clear you view your opposite as a potential ally.
- Identify the problem to be solved rather than your opposite as the source of any difficulty.
- Avoid any tendency toward defensiveness.
- Take your opposite's ego needs into account.
- Adopt a friendly tone.
- Display an open mind.
- Avoid trickery or pressure tactics.

15

AFTERTHOUGHT INJECTION (p. 306)
What's the problem here?

Confusion. Particularly in written communications, someone may inject a comment relating to a point previously made in the middle of discussing a subsequent point. A reader can easily miss the connection between the comment and its proper frame of reference. In any communication, tie all comments to a specific frame of reference. When writing, keep all comments with your coverage of the subject, even if it means rewriting.

AGENTS, negotiating through (p. 111)
What problems should you look out for when negotiating through or with agents?

The possibility of interpersonal conflict even in a situation where goals aimed at are compatible. Be very alert to the personality factor when choosing an agent to work for you.

In facing an agent you may sometimes encounter the problem of limited authority (*see* AUTHORITY, limited) or of concessions being granted that you can't be sure will be implemented (*see* CONCESSIONS, unreliable).

AGGRESSIVENESS, displaying (pp. 134–135)
Should you rein in any tendency to aggressive behavior?

No. Aggressive pursuit of goals is to be encouraged. Just don't confuse aggressiveness with hostility. Realize you have to be sensitive to needs on the other side even when following an aggressive approach.

AGREEMENT IN PRINCIPLE (p. 253)
What's the purpose of an agreement in principle?

An agreement in principle is a joint statement of concurrence on objectives sought (although commonly on a general rather than specific level), a reaffirmation of interests held in common, and/or an agreement on a line of approach taken or to be taken in resolving any issue(s). It reemphasizes common interests/goals at points where specific differences on the issues might otherwise create a sense of division between the parties.

ALTERNATIVES, expropriation of (pp. 198–199)
Is there ever danger that alternatives you present for consideration will be exploited to your disadvantage?

It can happen with an opposite who cleverly introduces a subtle element of change while responding to what you've suggested. You don't recognize the modification until too late, if you recognize it at all. To guard against this, stay centered on your own perception of your interests; don't have someone else redefine them for you. But beware of being so defensive that you block consideration of suggested alternatives that really could be in your interest.

ANGER, expressing (pp. 126–127, 203–209, 309–310)
In negotiation, should you squelch any feelings of anger that may arise in response to the other side's attitude or behavior?

Not really. Your anger will operate beneath the surface anyway. You might just as well express it—you'll often clear up a misunderstanding that may exist or prompt a change in tactics on the other side. However, avoid attacking your opposite in response or trying to force an apology or retraction. Address yourself to the circumstance; don't draw the other side's good character into question.

APOLOGY, for a request made (p. 96)
Should you assume an apologetic attitude when presenting your opposite a request he/she may think is extreme?

Never project an attitude of apology for requesting anything. That provides your opposite too easy an avenue for rejection. The other person always has the option of saying "No." Be wholehearted in going for the "Yes" response you want.

ARGUMENT, winning
See DEBATING vs. NEGOTIATING; FAULT, determining; LAST WORD, getting in; REASONABLE vs. UNREASONABLE; RIGHT vs. WRONG.

ASPIRATIONS, high (pp. 133–134)
Is there ever a danger of setting your goals too high?

Surprisingly, the more usual problem is that negotiators fail to ask for all they might. There's no problem in starting off with high aspirations. Just don't fall into intransigent expectation that all you ask for will be granted. Be realistic about compromises that may be required to ensure your winning important benefits, even if they fall short of your ideal goals.

ASSISTANCE, need for (pp. 83–84)
What should you keep in mind in requesting assistance from another party?

The importance of fulfilling your need, above all else. That means you have to take the initiative, with an approach that wins interest and cooperation from someone who does not necessarily share your need or sense of urgency. Provide appropriate motivation to get the other party supportively involved. That means addressing his/her needs and desires effectively even as you focus on satisfying your own.

ASSUMPTIONS, making (p. 103)
Is there any particular danger to be alert to here?

While you regularly have to extrapolate needs and motives on the other side to the extent they're not explicitly expressed, you can never know precisely what's going on in your opposite's mind. Don't ever assume you know all the angles on the other side. Always keep an eye open to adjustments in outlook that provide a clearer picture of the situation facing you. That gives you flexibility, which holding to initial assumptions denies you.

ATTITUDES, counterproductive (pp. 131–132)
What commonly held attitudes work against effectiveness in negotiation?

There are many, but here are several that we see as typical "loser's attitudes" when approaching a bargaining encounter:

- Expecting things to fall into place as the result of getting a break.
- Attributing all disappointment and failure to external causes.
- Expecting formula solutions to problem situations.

- Unwillingness to admit to limited experience or incomplete knowledge.

ATTITUDE, positive
See MIND-SET, positive.

AUDIENCES, facing (pp. 310–316)
How do you ensure maximum positive impact in front of an audience?

First of all, carefully prepare your presentation. Then compose yourself for a moment or two before commencing. Put your audience at ease with an initial ice-breaking comment or anecdote. Then follow through with an organized presentation that comes across as spontaneously delivered. Don't read your speech. Be wary of body language that communicates defensiveness or distance. In handling your material, pay attention to substance, balancing generalities and specifics. Pace material for easy comprehension, building feedback breaks and signaling changes in topic clearly.

AUTHORITY, limited (pp. 174, 201–202)
How do you cope with an opposite who pleads limited authority to move to commitment on an issue important to you?

Be firm in holding to your position. Don't immediately modify your proposal or statement of goals in an effort to fall back to your opposite's range of authority. Reaffirm the importance of the issue for you, at the same time stressing motivating considerations for the other side. Then have your opposite refer back to whoever holds authority to see about winning the commitment you're looking for.

BARS AND LOUNGES as negotiating sites (p. 144)
What advantages and disadvantages can you point to here?

The advantages lie in a generally less formal, more relaxed environment for discussions. Both parties are likely to be more at ease. The disadvantages lie in multiple opportunities for distraction— from the setting itself, the service personnel, or other patrons—and in the potential that alcohol consumption may compromise discretion, cloud judgment, or impair thought processes. Particularly because of possible problems related to alcohol intake, we rarely advise a bar or lounge as a site for discussion of important issues.

BLAME, assigning
See FAULT, determining

BLUFF, risking (pp. 161–163)
What should you consider when deciding whether or not to hazard a bluff?

First consider the risk, particularly if you're including any element of threat. Is the chance of gain worth the risk? Can you afford it? Then consider whether you can carry the bluff off credibly *and* whether you're prepared for the possibility that someone might call you on it.

BLUFF, getting called on (p. 163)
What should you do if someone calls you on a bluff?

Hang in there awhile. The other side may just be testing your resolve without being prepared to go all the way in calling you on it. A lot of bluffs are exposed through a negotiator backing down too quickly.

BODY LANGUAGE, and bluffing (pp. 162–163, 240)
What should you be wary of here, either when you bluff or when you think others may be bluffing?

Anything that suggests nervous apprehension: evasive eye movement, throat clearing, hard swallowing, lip licking, flushing, nervous perspiration, etc.

BODY LANGUAGE, and offers made (pp. 170–171)
What should you watch out for here?

On your side: that body language is consistent with the image you want to project—self-confidence, expectancy, etc. On the other side: the same thing, except in application to the person facing you. Be particularly alert to any nervous gestures or gestures at odds with the mood you'd expect to see reflected in a person making a genuine, heartfelt offer.

BODY LANGUAGE, and presentations (pp. 312–313)
Are there any types of gestures you should avoid when making a presentation?

- Defensively crossing your arms, especially when fielding comments or questions.
- Pounding your fist and pointing at your audience. This makes you seem too parental.
- Nervous hand-to-head movements.

BREAKDOWN IN RELATIONS, repairing (p. 88)
What line of approach should you follow here?

Concentrate on identifying and responding to issues contributing to the breakdown. Avoid debating fault or assigning blame. Accept the need to make adjustments. Point to the benefits of any adjustment on the other side in terms of improved communication and further possible gain. Always accentuate the positive, and work to eliminate the negative by addressing its effect rather than criticizing motives or attitudes.

BRIDGE ISSUES (pp. 237, 246–247, 252–253, 319)
What are these, and how do you bring them into play?

Bridge issues are issues of relatively minor importance that can be easily resolved. They're often of strategic value in allowing a sense of agreement/cooperation to develop between parties, thus easing the route to agreement/cooperation in more difficult areas.

BUYER'S INDECISION
See INDECISION, buyer's.

BUYER'S REMORSE
See REMORSE, buyer's.

CAUCUS, calling (pp. 287–288)
When should you call a team caucus?

Whenever the need is apparent. (See reasons indicated under TEAM EFFORT, coordinating.) The team leader has the actual authority, but team members should work out signals for indicating a need to confer. There's no need to ask permission of the other side. Simply excuse yourselves politely.

CAUCUS, exiting for (pp. 291–292)
Who should leave the room for a team caucus, and where should they go?

If one side is the host and no previous arrangements have been made, the host should step out, either to go into caucus or to allow the other side opportunity to caucus privately. If previous arrangements have been made, either side may step out as necessary. Specially designated caucus areas should afford complete privacy and minimum facilities for comfortable conferring among team members.

CAUCUS, returning from (p. 291)
Who should take the initiative after a team returns to the bargaining table from a caucus?

The party that called time out should reopen discussion. The other side should listen for a statement on the issue at hand, not settle for a question as opener. They have a right to know what position the caucusing party has now taken on the issue that required time out.

CAUCUS TIME, managing (pp. 288–291)
How do you guard against caucus time being wasted?

By taking a programmed approach, limiting time in caucus to no more than fifteen minutes. Get everyone's viewpoint, without arguing perspectives. Define your present situation. Plan the next step with consideration of possible alternatives. (Hypothetical "what if . . ." questions are very useful here.) Come to a conclusion, then recap your decision to doublecheck common understanding before returning to the bargaining table.

CHALLENGES, to your position (pp. 315–316)
Is it better to attempt to bypass challenges to your position or to detail reasons for justifying your position?

Any effort to bypass challenges to your position may be read as evasion of the issues, so that can backfire. However, you don't want to get into defending your position on any grounds of merit either. That will just put you at a psychological disadvantage, and introduce considerations that are only incidental. The best response is a to-the-point, matter-of-fact reiteration of perspective without any effort to justify it in argumentative terms.

See also DEFENSIVENESS, controlling your own; SELF-JUS-TIFICATION, providing.

CHANGE, resistance to (p. 102)
What's the key to overcoming this?

In yourself: Listen with a mind already primed for the possibility of change. Consider alternatives, recognizing that change can provide added benefits for you. They are always worth exploring with that possibility in mind.

In dealing with others: Accept an initial resistance as natural. Concentrate on illustrating opportunities for positive gain, pushing persistently along that line to prompt greater openness to change.

COMMITMENT, premature (p. 196)
How do you guard against prematurely committing yourself to a final stand on any issue?

Don't explicitly commit to anything until you have a clear sense of your opposite's position on the issue. Make the taking of any final stand contingent on reaction from the other side. Don't get trapped into definitive statements or revelations until something's forthcoming from your opposite.

COMMITMENT, winning (pp. 76, 94)
What's the key consideration here?

A convincing demonstration that the action you hope to see your opposite agree to is in some way beneficial for him or her.

COMMUNICATIONS, written (pp. 304–310)
What rules of thumb should you follow to assure effectiveness in written communications?

There's a double focus here.
Pay attention to basic mechanics of style and organization:

• Keep your language easy to understand.

- Be concise.
- Give main points obvious prominence.
- Be specific about what you want/are proposing.
- Order your thoughts in an easy-to-follow fashion.

Take basic psychological considerations into account:

- Pay attention to good form.
- Address the other person correctly.
- Home in on the other person's needs and interests.
- Maintain a friendly, courteous tone.

COMPROMISE, without loss (pp. 234–235)
Is it ever possible to compromise on an issue without conceding an objective or point of interest?

On occasion, yes. Sometimes compromise works out to going along with an alternative you hadn't recognized as still providing you what you want. In that case, shifting from your declared preferred alternative exposes you to no loss, while your opposite may gain a benefit not as easily achieved or impossible of achievement through conceding your originally preferred course of action.

COMPROMISES, making (pp. 218–219, 234–235)
What are the key considerations here?

First, a recognition that benefit is obtainable through agreement with another party, even if not along the precise lines you've defined for yourself. Second, a realization that failure to achieve any agreement may leave you farther from goals than an agreement incorporating some concession on your part. With these prerequisite awarenesses, you can draw a distinction between ideal objectives and essential minimum objectives. The difference between those is your possible range of concessions. Compromise consists of offering concessions in exchange for moves on the other side toward committed agreement. Treat concessions like money: work for the best value at the lowest possible cost. Don't concede too much too soon.

See also GOALS, achieving, and entries under CONCESSIONS.

CONCESSION, first (pp. 213–214, 216–217, 218–219)
How do you keep from being the first to have to offer a concession?

Who makes the first concession has little to do with who's winning or losing. It can be to your advantage to offer the first concession. But guard against giving something away for nothing. Build in a contingency arrangement: use your concession offer to elicit some countervailing advantage. Don't get hung up on who goes first, but do plan every concession carefully, including its timing. Going first can hold the initiative for you.

CONCESSIONS, premature (pp. 135–136)
How do you keep from making concessions before you should?

Push with persistence for every goal you've set yourself. Refuse to admit defeat before all possible alternatives have been thoroughly considered, marshalling all persuasive abilities to influence the other side favorably. When it's finally clear that nothing short of concession will prompt movement to agreement, follow your plan for concessions, offering them bit by bit, not in large chunks all at once.

CONCESSIONS, quick-close (pp. 254–255)
How do you work a quick-close concession?

This is a tactic for breaking through an impasse. Present a proposition you can live with and that seems likely to tempt the other side to say "Yes" quickly. Make the concession conditional on the other side accepting it as the basis for settling the issue between you. Naturally, this is a concession you should have planned carefully.

CONCESSIONS, unequal (p. 270)
What's the usual cause of agreeing to unequal concessions?

A frequent cause is opposition tactics aimed at making you work so hard for minor concessions that the effort involved will make them appear more substantial than they are. Then pressure is put on you to make a "comparable" concession, actually one of greater substance.

Sometimes, of course, you're caught in a circumstance of greater need and may feel forced into unequal concession. Review guidelines under POWER, determining the balance, and WEAKNESS, negotiating from, to aid you in pushing for the best possible terms.

CONCESSIONS, unreliable (pp. 192–193)
How can you be certain that an opposite who almost too readily concedes an issue will actually follow through?

Where your opposite speaks for him/herself, take time to nail down how the concession offered will be implemented, and make sure that it can be.

Where your opposite acts as agent for someone else, ask for explicit confirmation from those he/she speaks for. Reiterate the positives that may aid in winning approval. Don't count the issue settled until you get reassurance that the concession is acceptable and details on how it will be implemented.

CONFLICT, dealing with (pp. 230–238)
What's the most productive line of approach for dealing with conflict between you and an opposite?

Take a programmed approach in response to any conflict that develops:

1. Consider your alternatives. Do you actually have to join the conflict?
2. Analyze the situation carefully to understand it in all its dimensions.
3. Work for a compromise settlement.
4. Review any agreement made to be sure it meets the needs of the situation.

As you go through this procedure, keep cool, don't argue, look for root causes, avoid personality clashes, choose words carefully, listen attentively, and stay open to consideration of needs on *both* sides.

CONFLICT, opposite's denial of (pp. 189–190)
How do you work through a conflict situation when the other side keeps pretending there's no problem?

Avoid argument about whether something is a problem or not. Just go immediately to a very specific consideration of alternatives— you're concerned with this or that circumstance, and these are possible solutions that fit your needs. Bypass any effort on the part of your opposite to duck out; hold to the initiative in matter-of-fact fashion. You can easily present your approach as insurance against the unexpected, thereby circumventing any effort to claim the problem you see as nonexistent.

CONFLICT, opposite's side-stepping of (pp. 190–191)
How do you deal with an opposite who continually seeks to side-step consideration of any issue that presents a threat of conflict?

By resisting any effort to distract you with side issues. Stay on the issue at hand. Consider taking the initiative with an immediate proposal for settling whatever difficulty exists. At least be firm in your insistence on dealing with the situation. Don't get sucked into justifying that insistence—that's a way of getting you off track.

CONFLICT, response options (pp. 231–232)
What's the range of response options when faced with a conflict situation?

- Pretend no threat of conflict exists.
- Accept whatever limitation is being set on you.
- Withdraw from the negotiation.
- Initiate a countering move.

In the first three cases, you're actually side-stepping the conflict. It's only in taking the last option that conflict is actually joined.

As to how to work your responses, approach conflict with a suitable problem-solving technique. (*See* PROBLEM SOLVING, pp. 235–238) Always follow behavioral guidelines to avoid contributing to a worsening of conflict.

CONFRONTATION, as a source of failure (pp. 213–214)
How do you guard against a negotiation getting bogged down in confrontation between the parties?

By dropping any inclination on your part to see your opposite as "the enemy." By recognizing that a move to concession on your part is not tantamount to surrender.

See also ADVERSARY MENTALITY.

CONFUSION, controlling (p. 267)
What do you do when the other side suddenly hits you with an unexpected development you're not even sure applies to the situation at hand?

Take it calmly in stride. The objective may simply be to confuse you. Take a methodical approach to the new situation to determine its relevance; then deal with it accordingly.

CONTRACTS, renegotiating (pp. 86–87)
What's the approach to take when an opposite isn't eager/anxious to renew a contract that's existed between you?

At the very least you have to sell yourself again.

See also BREAKDOWN IN RELATIONS, repairing; MAN-AGEMENT-LABOR NEGOTIATIONS; SELLING.

CONTROL, and speaking (pp. 99–100, 156–159)
How do you (re)gain control in the face of someone monopolizing discussions?

Actually, the person speaking isn't necessarily in control. Often it's a case of being on the defensive, trying to convince by weight of words rather than conviction. Listen for an opening on a substantive point of issue you want to address, and then step in with cogent remarks/questions of your own and follow through with your own initiative.

COOPERATION, false projection of (pp. 267–268)
How do you distinguish between genuine cooperation and illusory cooperation?

It's the difference between action and empty verbiage. Until you're assured of action, don't be too quick to prove additionally accommodating yourself. In a circumstance where someone announces warm sympathy and understanding but a lack of authority to commit to a desired line of action, insist on access to a person with authority.

COOPERATION, winning (pp. 109–110, 308–309)
How do you maximize chances for eliciting cooperation from the other side?

By demonstrating your own readiness to cooperate in helping the other side meet its needs.

CREDIBILITY, maintaining (pp. 96, 110)
What's the key consideration here?

Effective behavior consistent with your expressed objectives and with an expressed or implicit willingness to take needs/goals on the other side into account. Ability to follow through as well as intent is crucial here.

CRITICISM, as a problem source (p. 158)
What's the usual problem here?

A faulty assumption that calling the other side's motives, conduct, or objectives into question will prompt concessions. What usually develops is a more intransigent resentment that makes agreement more difficult to achieve.

CROSS-CULTURAL NEGOTIATION (pp. 323–333)
What special considerations should you take into account?

First, realize that the general process of negotiation remains the same, with reliance on persuasion fundamental. Take all the usual basics into account, both those related to the process and those related to interaction with other people holding variant perspectives. Then be alert to adjustments required in these areas of cultural difference:

• The sense of protocol to follow in addressing people.
• Orientation to time.
• Priorities generally followed in the conduct of business.
• Demonstration of good will and trust.
• Distinctions of rank.
• Language differences/difficulties.

Discover what you can of practice in each of these areas in the culture your opposite comes from. The better tuned in you are to that, the more ready you are to adjust your behavior, the easier communication will be.

DEBATING vs. NEGOTIATING (pp. 214–215)

How do you guard against debating the issues when you should be negotiating them?

Some effort to sway the other side into seeing things your way is natural. However, your overall orientation should show an awareness of fundamental differences between negotiation and debate:

NEGOTIATION	DEBATE
A win-win line of approach	A win-lose line of approach
Readiness to consider compromise	Resistance to compromise
Search for a common ground/position	Defense of position
Listening for needs and feelings	Listening for rebuttal points
A spontaneous back-and-forth exchange	A structured back-and-forth exchange
Equal emphasis on questions and statements	Emphasis on statements
Efforts to convince the other side of common interests	Efforts to convince the other side of greater comparative merit
Strategic use of disclosure	Unwillingness to make disclosures

DEFENSIVENESS, controlling yours (pp. 125–126, 156–158, 210–212, 236, 259, 264–265, 266–267, 316)

What are the key considerations here?

First of all, a projection of a sense of self-assurance. (*See* SELF-ASSURANCE, projecting.) When responding to any question raised or challenge posed, provide the most direct, succinct response you can. Don't engage in excessive explanations, overselling, or self-justification.

DEFENSIVENESS, in an opposite (pp. 126–130)

What can you do to moderate any inclination to defensiveness in those facing you?

Present yourself as a potential ally rather than an adversary. (*See* ADVERSARY MENTALITY.) Show common courtesy in listening to what the other person has to say, and maintain an attitude of personal respect. Be tactfully frank. Show whatever personal consideration you can. Drop any tendency on your part to defensive behavior.

DEMAND vs. SUPPLY, imbalances in (p. 323)
What adjustments are recommended when negotiating a purchase in a situation of limited supply?

Refocus on traditional considerations for winning a sale rather than on those for making purchase decisions, as in this case the traditional pattern has been reversed.

DEMANDS, acceptable vs. unacceptable (pp. 220–221)
Is there any meaningful distinction here?

There is only this: It's unrealistic to expect others to be cooperative in pursuit of your priorities at the cost of their own. Since priorities vary so widely among all parties, what's acceptable or unacceptable can differ radically from negotiation to negotiation. An important part of negotiation is sorting out what's acceptable to both sides. Don't get caught up in judgmental debates about what's acceptable or unacceptable in any absolute sense. Keep it in the context of your situation vis-à-vis that of your opposite, relating demands to needs and priorities on both sides without labeling those in judgmental terms.

DEMANDS, as fundamental (pp. 83–85)
Is the presentation of demands fundamental to negotiation?

Not necessarily, although demands are at the basis of most negotiations involving differences between parties. It's quite possible to negotiate without voicing demands as such. Joint efforts in the face of a common threat, exploring opportunities for mutual gain, and desire for influential favor are examples of preconditions to negotiation that need involve no demands on either side (although they may). However, every negotiation presupposes some sense of need.

DESPERATION, sense of (p. 269)
What's suggested for keeping any developing sense of desperation under control?

Tune into possibilities that exist for you even when you're in an apparently weaker position. (*See* WEAKNESS, negotiating from.)

Recognize that power is a relative perception; look for a power advantage you may be able to bring into play. (*See* POWER, determining the balance.)

Take a calm, methodical approach to any situation you see as presenting you with uncomfortable difficulties. (*See* PROBLEM SOLVING.)

Be alert to any tactical maneuver to stimulate a sense of desperation in you.

DEVELOPMENTS, unexpected
See CONFUSION, controlling.

DIFFERENCES, cultural
See CROSS-CULTURAL NEGOTIATION.

DIFFERENCES, gauging (pp. 251–252)
What's a good technique for determining how far apart two parties are on any issue?

Review both the points of agreement and disagreement as specifically as you can. If at an impasse, do this recapping aloud, thus allowing both sides to determine that differences are real rather than apparent and to confirm that areas of agreement do exist. It may help to chart out areas of agreement and disagreement in a visual medium so that they stand out clearly.

DIFFERENCES, settling (p. 101)
What do you recommend as a first line of approach here?

Concentration on identifying areas of common interest you can develop to achieve an initial positive momentum toward agreement. Don't limit your focus to points of difference, or you may never get beyond those.

DIFFERENCES, and third parties (p. 197)
How should you react to an opposite's efforts to involve a third party in conflict between you?

Hold to the issue as it exists between you and your opposite. Make no statement of position on a situation involving a third party that has no direct relevance to the issue between you and your opposite.

DISENGAGEMENT, painless (pp. 87–88)
How do you accomplish this?

Negotiation isn't always necessary, but where negotiation is involved, avoid long explanations or justifications for your decision to disengage. Concentrate attention on arrangements to ease dislocation on either side, without getting pulled into argument or recrimination.

DISTRUST, of your opposite (pp. 219–220)
How can you protect yourself in a situation where you do not trust your opposite to honor commitments made?

Tie the elements of agreement as strongly as possible to important motivational factors influencing your opposite. That will ensure that the force of self-interest works for you here. You can also make it explicit that breaking the agreement cancels benefits achieved through the agreement.

DOUBT, overcoming (pp. 94–95)
How do you keep an opposite's focus on doubts from killing any chance of agreement?

Respond as matter-of-factly as possible to objections raised, always stressing the potential for positive gain. Once you've done that, hold off on any effort to argue away doubts—that only sets the focus back on them. Push ahead for commitment as the only route to benefits desired, while remarking that possible negatives have been considered and taken into account so that risks are minimal.

"DOUBTING THOMAS," shunting out (pp. 98–99)
How do you handle someone on an opposing team who keeps pressing negatives as a counter to positives you've identified?

Keep to the positives. "The Persuader's Helper" is a particularly useful tactic here: Subtly enlist the support of someone else on the other side whom you've observed reacting more to the positives.

EAGERNESS, as a problem source (pp. 268–269, 271–272)
How do you guard against an eagerness to conclude agreement compromising your pursuit of priorities?

Stay focused on real gains rather than promised gains. Don't get prompted into concessions on the basis of vague assurances that these can provide grounds for agreement.

See also CONCESSIONS, premature.

EGO NEEDS, in an opposite (pp. 81, 126–130, 210–211)
How do you deal with intrusive ego needs on the other side?

With calm, matter-of-fact self-assurance. Avoid making it a contest of who defers to whom. Stay focused on the issues and address yourself to those. If you show yourself indifferent to subjective interpretations of rank or prestige, the other side is very likely to deemphasize those as well (pp. 216–217). However, don't dismiss out of hand every indication of ego needs on the other side; distinguish between those implying any distinction of rank or superiority over you and those that are really basic to everyone. You can gain valuable good will by taking basic ego needs into account, and it doesn't require any concession on issues or approach to them that could work to your disadvantage.

ENTHUSIASM, controlling (pp. 134–135)
Is there any danger of getting carried away in enthusiastic pursuit of objectives?

There are two dangers: (1) that your enthusiasm will cause you to overlook some element of concern that should be taken into account seriously, and (2) that you'll be so wrapped up in pursuit of your own objectives that you fail to take needs and priorities on the other side into account.

EXPECTATIONS, and indecision (pp. 275–276)
What's the connection here?

Where expectations are tied to idealistic hopes, the individual concentrates on a search for ideal situations/solutions. These rarely exist. In the meantime, bona fide opportunities for benefit are passed over because they are not perfect. Until there's an assessment of options in real terms, meaningful decision is virtually ruled out. Don't focus on ideal expectations to the exclusion of consideration of practical realities.

EXPLANATIONS, as a source of difficulty (pp. 156–158)
Does an effort to provide explanation for a position you hold ever expose you to added difficulty?

It can. Explanation in response to a specific question or to clarify a position taken is routine and expected. But where explanations amount to an attempt to justify positions or explain rationale in great detail, they'll be read as defensive efforts and dismissed as such. As a general rule, people don't want lengthy explanations of why you feel as you do; they just want enough information to understand how what you're feeling affects them in relation to issues between you.

EYE CONTACT (p. 104)
What rule of thumb applies here?

Maintain *comfortable* eye contact in exchanges with your opposite. It's normal for listeners to look at a speaker more than vice versa. However, a convincing speaker does make regular eye contact. A drop-off in eye contact is often an indication of untruth or evasiveness in what's being said.

FACTS, reliance on (pp. 79, 93, 98, 136–137)
Can you generally rely on a simple, direct presentation of facts to make your case for you?

Definitely not. Facts by themselves rarely make a convincing case. More essential is that you tune into needs, which are as much based on emotional outlook as anything else. The manner of your presentation is also very important—it has to be more than a rote recitation of facts.

See also entries under MOTIVATION and NEEDS.

FAILURE, reasons for (pp. 213–222)
Barring the obvious problem of irreconcilable differences on the issues, what other factors can contribute to failure in negotiation?

- Confrontation instead of negotiation.
- Debating rather than negotiating differences.
- Lack of clearness on what the issues are.
- Focus on ego needs rather than on resolving issues.
- Suspicion of motives on the other side.
- Emotional/irrational reactions to difficulties encountered in devising a common approach to the issues.
- Unwillingness on either side to compromise.
- Distrust related to previous bad experience.
- Totally unacceptable opening demands on either or both sides.
- Personality clashes.

FAULT, determining (p. 232)
How do you determine who's at fault in any conflict situation?

You're better off not trying to make an objective determination here, since it's really a subjective perception. You're only likely to get into unproductive argument. Instead of trying to determine fault, address attention to resolving the existent difficulty through agreement on remedial steps to be jointly taken.

FEEDBACK BREAKS (p. 314)
What are these, and what do they accomplish?

A feedback break is a brief self-interruption in a presentation, used to explicitly test for audience awareness/receptivity. It's helpful whenever you've covered an important point to ask whether those listening to you have understood your conclusion and how you arrived at it.

FEELINGS, your opposite's (pp. 100–101, 238)
How do you tune in to feelings in those facing you?

Primarily through attentive listening, with an eye open to unvoiced reactions that may be evident and an ear tuned to nonverbal sound clues as well as to any choice of words in an articulated response.

FEELINGS, personal (pp. 81–82, 96, 203–209)
How do you keep your own feelings under control?

Recognize what feelings arise in connection with different phases of a negotiation. Accept them as natural. Rather than trying to suppress them, work through them with whatever line of action is appropriate in connection with that phase of the process.

Where strong feelings arise as a result of provocative behavior on the other side, recognize that it's perfectly acceptable to express those. However, in expressing them, direct yourself to the situation that exists; don't respond with a personal counterattack.

See also ANGER, expressing.

GAIN, obtaining (pp. 76, 84–85)
Can you always count on negotiation to provide you some gain?

There is never a guarantee of gain, but negotiation as a process has the potential for expanding your opportunities for gain considerably. Much depends on the relative positions of the parties; much depends on your skill. Do keep in mind that *gain* is a relative term. Sometimes keeping losses to a minimum in a difficult situation may amount to gain; on other occasions you may be able to contemplate possibilities for achieving major benefit in relatively leisurely fashion.

GENERALITIES vs. SPECIFICS, striking a balance (p. 314)
What's the trick here?

Recognize that generalities are only good for indicating a subject area and broad considerations relative to that. They're not good as definitive statements of position intended to detail a commitment requested or proffered. When it comes to commitment, it's important you be specific: what's being committed to and precisely what operative conditions apply.

In detailing specifics, be sure they're tied together in some sort of evident organizational framework so that both sides understand them in the proper context.

See also ORGANIZATION, logical; SPECIFIC, getting.

GOALS, achieving (pp. 133–134)
What's the recommended first step for initiating movement toward goals?

Start by expectantly asking for whatever it is you want. Don't inhibit yourself here—you cut yourself off from any chance of achieving a preferred goal if you censor yourself before anyone else tells you "Yes" or "No." But make clear to yourself in advance what the difference is between ideal goals and minimum acceptable goals. That way you'll be able to plan concessions that may be required to win a benefit you want that isn't ideal but is within reach.

See also COMPROMISES, making; EXPECTATIONS, and indecision.

GOALS, hard-nosed pursuit of (pp. 152–154)
Is this required for maximum chance of success in negotiation?

No. Persistence is advisable, but you should always consider and address the other side's needs as well as your own. The hard-nosed negotiator typically shows lack of sensitivity to those, with a resultant loss of effectiveness in motivating cooperation.

GOOD WILL, limitations of (pp. 113–114)
Can you count on good will to pull you through most difficulties encountered in working for agreement with an opposite?

Good will can tip the scales in your favor to some extent, but you can't count on it to outweigh the effects of practical realities. So while it's to your advantage to cultivate good will, always look for ways to work considerations of reality to advantage as well—those related to resources, time, ability, adaptability, convenience, etc. Often one or several of those determine whether you achieve the agreement you want, the presence—even the absence—of good will notwithstanding.

GOOD WILL, maintaining (pp. 113–115)
What are the key considerations here?

A demonstration of trustworthiness/reliability and a projection of respect and regard for the other side and its needs/objectives.

GOOD WILL, regaining (pp. 114–115)
How do you accomplish this?

By responding with immediate positive focus on areas where negativity has intruded. This requires open acknowledgment of any difficulty that's led to estrangement between the parties and a readiness to assume responsibility in a readjustment of relations.

GUILT, invoking (pp. 244–245, 250–251, 255–256)
Is it ever to your advantage to invoke guilt on the other side?

As long as your efforts aren't so blatant that they're read as a deliberate attempt to lay a guilt trip on your opposite. When faced with a threat that endangers the potential for agreement, it may help to express regret that relations have been clouded as a result of the threat. You can also note interests all around (including those of third parties) that will be injured as a result of agreement being stymied. Avoid an accusatory tone in any effort to work this tactic to your advantage.

GUILT, plays on (p. 272)
How can you tell if someone is trying to lay a guilt trip on you?

You can just feel it! There's all this emphasis on what the other side has done for you, or stress on injury others will suffer if you don't concede a particular point. The element of positive appeal to your needs is missing or deemphasized. Respond as you would in controlling any impulse to defensiveness (*see* DEFENSIVENESS, controlling yours).

Note that one guilt-inducing tactic occasionally employed is that of offering you an unsolicited benefit/service, then returning thereafter to ask your consideration in some way. Don't respond out of a sense of obligation to return the favor. Weigh each situation on its own relative merits, and respond according to needs or objectives you have that will be met.

HARD-LINER, shunting out (pp. 97–98, 145–146)
What can you do to shunt out a hard-liner on an opposing team?

You can try the tactic of "The Persuader's Helper" to enlist the support of an opposing team member who's demonstrated greater receptivity to your perspective and proposals. Sometimes you can unobtrusively effect a division of opposing personnel during a recess period and then lobby those whose support you feel a chance of winning.

HARD-NOSED vs. PERSISTENT (pp. 152–154)
How do you draw a distinction?

By reviewing conduct in terms of readiness to address needs and priorities on both sides, not just on one's own side. The hard-nosed individual tends to see things unilaterally and push demands from just his/her perspective. The persistent individual takes a bilateral approach, pushing hard for objectives but in terms that reflect awareness of two perspectives to be considered.

HONESTY, and disclosure of information (pp. 97, 127–128)
Does adopting a policy of honesty require full disclosure of all information from your side?

No. All it requires is that you not deliberately misrepresent facts or otherwise deceitfully mislead your opposite.

See also INFORMATION, disclosure of.

HOSTILITY, dealing with
See ADVERSARY MENTALITY.

HOTELS, as negotiation sites (pp. 142–143)
What advantages and disadvantages attach to use of a hotel or motel as a site of negotiation?

Advantages include a sense of neutrality attached to the site. The range of meeting facilities may be greater than elsewhere available. Both sides are away from any interruption or distraction from the day-to-day conduct of office business. It's often easier to ensure discretion vis-à-vis noninvolved personnel on either side.

Disadvantages can include expense, poor service, or surroundings that are not optimally comfortable.

HUMOR, as a negotiating tool (pp. 137–139, 167, 243–244, 312)
What advantages are possible; what problems should you be alert to?

The advantages of humor are: (1) it's a great self-teaching device; (2) it's particularly good for winning or holding a listener's attention; (3) it's a very effective way of making a point; (4) it's great for breaking tension.

You can get into problems with humor that (1) is at someone else's expense; (2) betrays a lack of sensitivity to social values held by an opposite; (3) appears to dismiss or slight an element of presentation that's seriously intended as a basis for meaningful discussion.

As a general rule of thumb, keep expressions of humor to spontaneous good-natured remarks or jokes that neither denigrate anyone or subject them to humiliation in any way.

IMPASSE, breaking through (pp. 249–257)
What are the steps to follow to push a negotiation through impasse?

First, try simple tactical steps:

- Stress mutal interests.
- Point to negative consequences in any failure to reach agreement.
- Take a recess from discussions to release tension build-up.

If these don't do it, take a few minutes to verify explicitly what points of agreement and disagreement exist; then consider further possible alternatives:

- Defer the issue in favor of another where agreement seems more likely.
- Discuss the range of available alternatives for resolving differences.
- Go for an agreement in principle.
- Disclose additional information.
- Take a hypothetical approach to possibilities suggested.
- Throw out a quick-close concession.
- Appeal to an "ally."
- Play on feelings.
- Change the setting in which you're negotiating.
- Issue a threat.
- Call it quits.

INDECISION, buyer's (pp. 273–276)
What stumbling blocks usually contribute to buyer's indecision?

Unrealistic criteria relative to an ideal price, often expressed in bargain-hunting terms. Also, such a focus on ideal expectations from the item/service sought that no decision based on a realistic evaluation of achievable benefits is ever made.

The key to overcoming buyer's indecision is to keep both your needs and market realities squarely in view. Don't chase after a once-in-a-lifetime bargain unless you have the leisure for that.

INDECISION, and making offers (pp. 280–281)
How do you break through any mental impasse when it comes to deciding what offer to make an opposite?

Come to a clear conclusion on what your essential needs are and what you can afford to offer/concede to meet those. Then begin with exploratory offers conceding less than you can afford to—you may not have to pay "full price" for the benefit desired.

See also COMPROMISES, making.

INDECISION, seller's (pp. 278–279)
What stumbling blocks usually contribute to seller's indecision?

Either a subconscious unwillingness to actually part with the property in question, or an exaggerated determination to get top price.

Getting past seller's indecision is a matter of reassessing the initial decision to sell in terms of any need that fulfills. Where the need is real and compelling, go for the best offer obtainable within the realities of the situation.

INFORMATION, disclosure of (pp. 103, 154–156, 254)
What guidelines should you follow here?

Recognize that sometimes you will have to provide the other side more information in order to prompt them to concession, compromise, or other decision that leads to benefit for you. But be thrifty with your informational assets. Follow a policy of incremental disclosure, providing additional detail bit by bit rather than spilling it all at once. That protects you from disclosing more than you need to in order to prompt movement to resolution of issues.

INGREDIENTS, missing (pp. 306–307)
How do you guard against failure to present elements of information
important to the communication of a message to an opposite?

By taking an organized approach to the presentation of all information. Avoid any assumption that what's obvious or automatic for
you will be so for anyone else. Detail everything pertinent to
achieving understanding by the other side, whether or not it appears evident to you. But avoid throwing in incidental details that
do not contribute a necessary element of understanding, or an
important one may get lost in the crowd.

INTEREST, getting (pp. 92, 94)
How do you accomplish this?

By immediately holding out the prospect of meaningful benefit to
the other side in whatever you propose for their consideration.

INTERRUPTION, as a problem source (p. 164)
What's the most common shortcoming where interruptions are con-
cerned?

Butting in with a remark or question while an opposite is in the
middle of outlining an offer or proposal. Listen for *all* the details
before you voice a response.

INTIMIDATION, resisting (pp. 191, 197–198, 262, 317–318)
What's the approach to take in resisting intimidation?

Continue quietly firm in pursuit of your objectives. Refuse to be
scared off; don't let yourself get baited into a shouting match. Stay
as cool and calm as you can. It's okay to express your feelings about
the other side's behavior, but do this in a controlled fashion (*see*
ANGER, expressing). Maintain your sense of self-respect and dignity even when you're negotiating from a weaker position. Giving
in to an effort to intimidate you only accentuates any disadvantage
you're under.

ISSUES, resolving differences on (pp. 215–216)
What's the first step toward successfully resolving differences on the issues between you and an opposite?

Coming to a clear definition of what those differences are. Until you've pinpointed what it is that separates you with regard to any issue difference, you can't readily move to refocus or realign pertinent perspectives. Take care also to identify areas of agreement, so that you can push positives there—never narrow your focus just to differences separating you from an opposite. Then proceed through the negotiation process, addressing needs on both sides.

See also DIFFERENCES, gauging.

JARGON (pp. 183, 304–305)
How do you cope with an opposite who insists on use of specialized terminology you find hard to follow?

Insist on having any term you don't understand defined clearly. Indicate your preference for everyday language that's easily understood by using such language yourself.

"KILLER" STATEMENTS (pp. 94–95)
What's the best response to these?

"Killer" statements are those last-minute reintroductions of negative concerns that have provided any difficulty earlier in the negotiation. Don't question or challenge them. That usually results in a further flood of negativity. Respond rather with a self-confident, positive statement noting that the point of concern has already been considered in previous discussion and put into manageable perspective.

LABOR CONTRACTS, negotiating
See MANAGEMENT-LABOR NEGOTIATIONS.

LAST WORD, getting in (pp. 206–209, 236, 246–247)
Is who gets the last word in of any significance in resolving differences?

Efforts to get a last word in commonly exacerbate and prolong conflict between parties. They typically reflect a determination to prove the speaker "right," as if some contest existed on that level. Instead of trying to get in a last word, take the initiative with getting in a first word—introduce an alternative for consideration, present a proposal, etc. Address the issue(s) without arguing right or wrong, without trying to prove yourself or your perspective somehow superior.

LISTENING, for greater comprehension (pp. 100–104)
What can you do to ensure picking up the important information in whatever is being said?

- Take notes.
- Repeat key words and phrases to yourself mentally.
- Minimize the possibility of distraction from the speaker.
- Maintain a comfortable eye contact while following remarks.

LISTENING, while talking (pp. 100–101)
How do you accomplish this?

By observing and attending to reactions of those who make up your audience. Note body language: does it indicate interest, indifference, defensiveness, skepticism, etc? Note sound clues: murmurs of approval, groans of disbelief, mutters of disagreement, etc. When speaking, don't rely so much on presentations that are fully written out or rehearsed to the last word. Concentrating on your lines makes listening difficult. Speak from notes if possible, so you can develop a more spontaneous flow and observe your audience's reactions more attentively.

LOCATION, changing (p. 256)
Is it ever to your advantage to request/suggest a change of location for a negotiation in progress?

Location does exert some psychological effect, particularly where you're in a home team–visiting team situation. A change to neutral ground can put the visitor(s) more at ease; it can result in the home side becoming more conciliatory and ready to compromise. When the parties are at an impasse, this is one adjustment that can prompt renewed movement.

LOCATION, choosing (pp. 140–148)
What criteria should you follow here?

Weigh the pertinent practical and psychological considerations.

- How many people will be involved?
- What's the range of possibilities on location?
- What kind of support facilities are needed?
- What time constraints are there?
- What are the related needs/preferences on the other side?
- Where will you feel most comfortable?
- What need for privacy/discretion is there?
- What can you and/or your opposite afford?

LOSS, assuming (pp. 257–259, 261, 263)
Should you ever just throw in the towel if it seems you have no bargaining chips?

Never assume you have no way to win some advantage. Always pursue the issues. By pressing for advantage, you may win it. You can't win anything by giving up.

See also WEAKNESS, negotiating from.

MANAGEMENT-LABOR NEGOTIATIONS (pp. 86–87, 317–320)
Are there any special guidelines for contract negotiations between management and labor?

The same general considerations apply here as in any other negotiation. We advise particular emphasis on:

- Avoiding any stress on the adversary nature of the interparty relationship.
- Keeping statements to third parties (especially the press) as neutral as possible.
- Keeping personal abuse and/or intimidation efforts to a minimum.
- Maintaining disciplined unity in any team negotiation.
- Side-stepping any challenge to your authority to deal with the issues.
- Avoiding use of ultimatums.
- Resisting any urge to walk out when the going gets tough.

- Handling less sensitive, noneconomic issues first.
- Going for a package deal.
- Keeping all involved parties fully informed of progress made.

MANIPULATION vs. NEGOTIATION (pp. 77–78, 97, 212)
Why bother to negotiate differences if you can manipulate the other side into doing things your way?

Negotiation is more likely to lead to a mutual relationship characterized by commitment in areas where cooperation is desired. Manipulation may achieve short-term objectives, but long-term commitment is unlikely. There's a much greater chance of problems developing in follow-through phases with manipulation than with negotiated agreement.

MERIT, proving
See RIGHT vs. WRONG; SELF-JUSTIFICATION, providing.

META-TALK (pp. 169–170, 186–189)
What is it, and how do you work around it?

Meta-talk is a manner of speaking in which there's a hidden, often contradictory meaning behind a statement made. If you take a meta-talk statement literally, you'll actually be misled as far as the real message goes.

You can recognize meta-talk by your own habits here: when and why do you take this approach to communication? Also, be alert to any inconsistency between what's said and how it's said. If someone too insistently makes a point you wouldn't have thought it necessary to emphasize, that can be a sign of meta-talk.

Working around meta-talk is as simple as keeping things on a specific level, with follow-up questions and proposals of your own to clarify and further develop the situation.

MIND-SET, positive (pp. 110–111, 130–137, 311–313)
What's necessary for getting this to work for you?

A strong sense of direction with respect to goals pursued. Readiness to take responsibility for your own actions/decisions. Readiness to see an element of opportunity in any problems that arise. Curiosity about and a readiness to explore the unknown.

MOTIVATION, discovering (pp. 93–94, 181–182)
How do you go about ascertaining what will motivate an opposite to make the commitment you're looking for?

Consider the record—what motivations appear to have been operative in any similar previous situation? Consider the present situation—what benefit do you see possible for the other side? And then ask what motivational consideration would prompt movement to a commitment you'd like to see. And throughout the negotiation stay alert to indications that an element of motivation you haven't considered—or even that your opposite hadn't considered—can be brought into play.

MOTIVATION, possibilities (pp. 181–182)
Are there any motivations of significance besides the obvious ones of money and power?

Consider the possibilities on this list:

Enhanced prestige
Increased security
Competitive advantage
Protection of reputation
Saving time
Conservation of assets
Added work satisfaction
Keeping up with the times
Avoiding effort

Contributing to the public welfare
Expansion of information resources
Avoiding trouble
Avoiding criticism
Greater public visibility
A chance to display individuality
Opportunity to exert influence

MOTIVATION, providing (pp. 93–94, 111, 181–182)
What's the key consideration here?

Tuning into your opposite's needs, then demonstrating a compatibility or alignment of interests with yours in respect of those. Show that in helping you your opposite helps him/herself.

NEEDS, balancing (pp. 77, 108–109)
How do you ensure a focus that achieves a balance between the needs you want to fulfill and those on the other side you have to address yourself to?

Through working to coordinate those along lines of common interest, either actual or potential. Give priority to your own as far as pursuit of objectives goes, but always draw in a consideration of those on the other side. Be explicit in your identification and pursuit of common or complementary elements on both sides.

NEEDS, different (pp. 77, 260)
Does it matter if needs are very different on either side?

It's not essential that they be the same or even roughly similar. What is important is that you find a way to establish compatibility. Avoid drawing any distinctions between needs in terms of right or wrong; don't try to force needs on both sides into a common mold of identity.

NEEDS, identifying (pp. 77, 82–90, 108–109, 237)
How can you even be sure that the other side has any needs?

By the simple fact that they are in discussion with you. If there were no potential seen for meeting any needs on their side, they wouldn't be there. Review possible preconditions and probe to establish what objectives are operative on the other side.

See also MOTIVATION, discovering.

NEEDS, incompatible (pp. 77–78, 237)
How do you reconcile them?

You probably won't be able to if they are truly incompatible. But a full exploration of alternatives may lead to a discovery that the incompatibility is more apparent than real. You may find you can outline areas of compatibility neither side previously recognized and move to agreement through those.

NEEDS, objective vs. subjective (p. 77)
What's the distinction here?

Objective needs are those that grow out of actual problem situations facing one. Subjective needs grow out of desires and/or goals one sets for oneself. Either type can provide impetus to cooperation with a second party.

NEGOTIATIONS, international
See CROSS-CULTURAL NEGOTIATIONS.

OBJECTIVES, achieving
See GOALS, achieving.

OFFERS, final (pp. 167–171)
How can you tell whether an offer presented as final really is?

By questioning the offer. Probe for more information. Note speech and body language clues. Efforts along these lines often result in a follow-up offer that provides better terms. If the offer is really final, you'll find your persistent efforts to win a restatement come to naught. Don't take it for granted that an offer is final just because your opposite says so.

OFFERS, responding to (pp. 163–167)
What guidelines should you follow here?

Always:

1. Listen to be sure you hear and understand the complete offer.
2. Repeat the offer to check your understanding and possibly elicit a restatement in return that provides more latitude for response.

Then consider your further options: acceptance, rejection, further questioning, ignoring it, postponing response, probing for more information, modification of the offer, substitution of another offer, apparent indifference, praise for the offer, a comparison with other offers, and/or a refusal to take it seriously. You can pick one of these or several, but be judicious in your choice.

OFFICES, as negotiating sites (pp. 141–142)
What considerations attach to selection of an office as site for a negotiation?

The usual practical considerations of physical space and comfort, of course. Also the easy availability of support personnel. However, you want to be alert to any difficulties that may arise from any home team advantage when the choice is between the office of either party. Problems may arise from the distraction of day-to-day business affairs being carried on around you. If there's a particular need for discretion, that's sometimes less easily satisfied in an office location.

OPPONENT, untrustworthy
See DISTRUST, of your opposite

OPPOSITION, misreading the (pp. 179–184)
How do you guard against this most effectively?

By taking these facts into account:

1. Others can see the world only from their perspective, which is never the same as yours.
2. Others form opinions based on their own experiences, not on appreciation of yours.
3. Others are not necessarily motivated by what motivates you.
4. Others are not necessarily interested in all you have to say.
5. Others may react negatively to you even when it appears counter to their own interests to do so.

ORGANIZATION, logical (pp. 305–307, 313–315)
How do you ensure that your presentation of perspectives comes across in an easily comprehensible fashion?

Through careful preparation. Adopt an ordering principle that is readily apparent: a step-by-step discussion where any process is involved; a chronological review when going over developments over a period of time; a priority-ranked coverage of issues where distinctions of importance are meaningful; a response to questions in the order of their initial presentation. Be explicit as to what ordering principle you are following, and then adhere to it consistently.

See also AFTERTHOUGHT INJECTION; INGREDIENTS, missing.

OUTBURSTS, emotional/irrational (pp. 197–198, 218)
What's the best response to these?

Let the outburst run its course while you keep calm. Stay focused on the issues. An emotional/irrational outburst is often a tactic for throwing you off balance. As long as you don't let yourself get provoked into a shouting match, the outburst will subside before long.

OVERSELLING (pp. 95–96, 157, 313)
How do you avoid any tendency toward this?

By giving the other side a chance to express and define its interests, taking any opportunity to close that presents itself as a result. Be alert for openings to settlement of the issue or conclusion of the sale. Don't concentrate on anticipating or meeting every possible objection that may be raised to your presentation. Your focus on countering the negatives will be read as reflecting your own insecurities on whatever position you've taken or proposal you've made.

PERCEPTIONS, tuning in to your opposite's (pp. 179–182)
Is there any key to ensuring that you tune in to your opposite's perception of the issue promptly?

The best you can do is start with the recognition that your opposite's perceptions will not be the same as yours. Then listen attentively to his/her presentation of viewpoint. Keep your efforts to understanding and working to influence his/her perceptions in your favor. Don't get into trying to prove yours "better" or "right."

PERFECTIONIST, as opposite (pp. 199–200)
What's the best response to someone who's never satisfied with how things are being worked out?

Be as calm and organized as you can in presentation and discussion of alternatives. Use a recapping technique to win concurrence at different phases of your exchange—that will somewhat commit your opposite to interim points of agreement on the way to settling issues and thereby allow less leeway for criticism. Where the language of agreement is what's picked at, keep on as direct and clear a level as possible. Avoid getting pulled into debates on semantic distinctions.

PERSONAL ABUSE, responding to
See ANGER, expressing; FEELINGS, personal; INTIMIDATION, resisting.

PERSONALITY CLASH (pp. 221–222, 236–237)
How do you negotiate with someone you can't get along with?

It may prove impossible to negotiate with someone who has strong negative feelings about you. However, you'll probably find you can get along with most people well enough to negotiate. It's not important that you like each other, just that you be able to identify some area of common need or interest. Don't emphasize personality differences. Matter-of-factly deal with the situation between you without getting involved in personal recriminations. Resist any effort to bait you into any ill-considered response along those lines.

PERSUASION, applying (pp. 91–95, 326)
What are the basics here?

1. Getting the other side's interest.
2. Eliciting the other side's understanding of your situation.
3. Providing motivation for the other side to act supportively.
4. Overcoming any doubt the other side may have relative to the advisability or cost of support.
5. Winning an explicit statement of commitment.

PERSUASION, problems related to (pp. 95–97)
What particular difficulties are you likely to create through a poor approach to the challenge of persuasion?

Turning your opposite off through any of the following: overselling, an overly apologetic attitude, passing the buck, expressions of impatience, an attitude of rudeness or arrogance, a display of dishonesty, underestimation of your opposite's intelligence, resorting to trickery manipulation.

POWER, determining the balance (pp. 148–151)
How do you do this?

Power is as often a perception of relative position as it is an objectively determinable advantage. Who has it or is seen to have it can depend on a multiplicity of factors:

• Availability of material resources.
• Weight of authority.

- Degree of self-sufficiency.
- Influential friends.
- Information resources.
- Degree of adaptability.
- Relative freedom from constraint.
- Determination to prevail.
- Readiness to take risks.

An apparent advantage on one point can often be cancelled out by shifting focus to another factor. The power balance shifts according to either party's ability to use relative advantages in any area to achieve total advantage.

PRAISE, as a problem source (p. 297)
Are you ever likely to get into trouble for praising your opposite's cooperative attitude/efforts?

You can overdo it. Overstated praise at times arouses suspicion that you're trying to cover something up. It comes across as flattery and suggests a possible ulterior motive.

PRECONDITIONS, for negotiating (pp. 82–90)
What are these and what influence do they exert?

Preconditions are the circumstances that prompt you into negotiation with another party, and what they are affects your relative position and hence necessarily governs the line of strategy you have to develop. The range of preconditions includes:

- A need for assistance.
- The experience of a common threat.
- A possible opportunity for gain.
- The opportunity to conclude a sale.
- A purchase requirement.
- A contract renegotiation.
- A desire to disengage from a relationship.
- A breakdown in relations.
- A last-ditch effort to salvage something from an extreme situation.

PROBLEM SOLVING (pp. 115–120)
What's the recommended approach for working through problems that arise in negotiation?

We highly recommend Robert Olson's four-phase DO-IT technique:

1. Define as precisely as possible what your problem is.
2. Open your mind to as wide a range of possible solutions as you can.
3. Identify the best solution.
4. Implement your decision.

PROBLEMS, defining (pp. 116–117)
How do you go about defining exactly what problem you're up against in any situation?

Follow this three-step approach from Olson's DO-IT technique as described in his book *The Art of Creative Thinking*:

1. Narrow in as closely as you can on what specifically causes you difficulty.
2. Write out at least three two-word statements regarding its effect on you; then pick the most accurate combination.
3. List objectives you hope to achieve by a solution; then consider the obstacles that exist there.

This approach gives you the most specific possible sense of the problem and difficulties to overcome in achieving a solution.

PROBLEMS, specific solutions to (pp. 118–119)
How do you arrive at the best solution to a problem?

First by considering as broad a range of possibilities as you can. To achieve this, ask others for input; list all ideas that occur to you, even if they seem a bit ridiculous; work out comparisons with other situations you've observed. Then evaluate all solutions you've put on your list in terms of the considerations pertinent to the situation—time, cost, effort, etc. The solution that meets the most demands inherent in your situation is the one to go for.

PROCEDURE, for negotiations (pp. 79–80, 324)
Is there a set procedure to follow?

The nature of the process requires following a step-by-step "ritual" approach.

- Make introductions.
- Present an overview of objectives sought and your feelings about those.
- Provide pertinent background detail.
- Define specific issues/points of concern.
- Work to obtain maximum advantage from the encounter.
- Fall back to compromise positions to win the cooperation desired.
- Conclude agreement on what each side is to do.

You have to take the steps in order, and considerations of practicality and common courtesy apply all along the way.

PROMISES, broken (pp. 176–177)
Can you ever give a good reason for breaking a promise?

You can cite *force majeure,* unanticipated circumstances beyond your control. You can't do what's been rendered impossible. But recognize that some difficulties can be anticipated or guarded against. The only obstacles that provide you a bona fide excuse are those you couldn't possibly have anticipated.

PROMISES, and expectations (pp. 171–173)
Are you likely to encounter any difficulty relating to promises as long as you hold back from explicit commitments in any area?

You may. Promises aren't simply a matter of explicit commitment. You can contribute to a build-up of expectations in such fashion that you'll be thought to have made a promise even if you haven't stated one outright. Implicit promises you don't keep can cause just as much trouble as explicit promises you don't keep.

PROTOCOL, following (pp. 328–329)
Are there any special rules of protocol to follow in the conduct of negotiations?

There is a universal line of procedure to follow. (*See* PROCEDURE, for negotiations.) There are no formal established rules of protocol, except when it comes to diplomacy. Simply apply everyday rules of common courtesy, and recognize that it's generally in your interest to project cooperative intent.

When negotiating across cultural lines, it is a good idea to check what general rules of protocol may exist in the other culture with respect to business and/or social encounters.

PURCHASE DECISIONS (pp. 86, 320–322, 323)
What are the key considerations here as far as another party (the seller) is concerned?

- Clearly identifying your needs/desires for yourself, to begin with.
- Clearly communicating those to the seller.
- Ascertaining the other side's ability to fulfill your needs/desires.
- Consideration of other possibilities for fulfilling needs/desires more completely or on better terms.

QUESTIONS, asking (p. 125)
Should you ever squelch an impulse to ask a question for clarification of your opposite's perspective/position?

No, that's how you develop information you need for making considered decisions. You may even reap a side benefit: added good will through the other side's appreciation of your evident concern to understand its position.

QUESTIONS, fielding (pp. 315–316)
Are there any reliable guidelines to follow when fielding questions from an opposite?

There are only these general guidelines: Never ignore or dismiss questions posed, although you may defer responding to those that present a note of challenge before you complete a presentation. Answer immediately those that request clarification or definition of issues/terms you're dealing with at the moment. Avoid a defensive response to any question asked, but refuse to be sidetracked into irrelevant side issues. Be calmly matter-of-fact in response to anyone trying to win points at your expense.

QUESTIONS, as a problem source (pp. 158–159)
When are questions apt to lead to difficulty?

When they haven't been carefully planned for cumulative impact
—poorly asked or coordinated questions reflect a weak line of
strategy. When they are used to call motives or behavior on the
other side into question along judgmental lines—that gets you off
the central issue(s) and introduces a strong note of argumentative-
ness.

REASONABLE vs. UNREASONABLE (pp. 93–94, 98)
How do you convince an opposite he or she is being unreasonable?

This is another judgmental determination that just contributes to
unproductive argument. Don't argue about what's reasonable or
logical with respect to the taking of a position. Focus on your
objectives and how, through appeal to the other side's self-interest,
you can motivate movement to a commitment that serves you
both well.

RECAPPING (pp. 241–242, 243, 252, 293–294, 296–297)
What advantage does this technique provide you?

Recapping, an out-loud summary of what's been covered and decided up to any given point, is the prime technique for double-
checking understanding on the status of affairs up to that point. It's
useful for defining precisely what areas of agreement have been
established, what areas of difference remain. In using the technique, be sure you win the explicit assent of the other side to
statements you make in recapping.

RECREATIONAL ACTIVITY, and negotiation (p. 146)
Are they compatible?

They can be, where the shared enjoyment of the activity leads to
easier communication between people working to establish
agreement with each other. But to the extent that competitive
considerations affect either or both parties, it may be advisable to
select another environment for a discussion of issues.

REMORSE, buyer's (pp. 276–278)
How do you keep any tendency to buyer's remorse under control?

By taking a realistic, methodical approach to purchase decisions from the very outset. If you're already committed to a purchase, look to the realities of your situation—don't stay hung up in the feeling of remorse. Review the benefit obtained, considering long-term convenience and gain as well as immediate need. Develop a methodical approach to payment problems you may see, working up alternatives as necessary or possible. If you think you paid too much, do some comparative pricing. If it turns out you paid too much, see if you can get a refund; if you can't, accept the price paid as part of the lesson learned. Should it be essential to get out of the deal, negotiate your way out as best you can, *if* you can. Otherwise explore what alternatives exist for getting someone to take your purchase over from you.

REMORSE, and offers made (pp. 280–281)
How do you keep any tendency toward experiencing remorse at an offer already made under control?

Focus on benefits gained, needs satisfied. If you've miscalculated and conceded more than you had to, accept it as a lesson learned—unless you also miscalculated on your ability to follow through. In that event withdraw your offer as promptly and gracefully as you can. Keep in mind that it almost never helps you to renege on an offer made.

REMORSE, rejector's (p. 282)
What can you do if you realize you ought to have accepted an offer you've already rejected?

Try for it again. However, the price will very likely go up unless you can finesse re-eliciting the offer as something of an afterthought, asking for it at a lower cost to you. The unexpectedness of that sometimes works to keep the price down.

REMORSE, seller's (pp. 279–280)
How do you keep any tendency to seller's remorse under control?

By a clear, methodical approach to sales decisions from the very outset. If you've already concluded a sale, regard it in the light of whatever benefit you've gained. Or if you're convinced you erred badly, consider negotiating for repurchase of the property/item. You can often work out a buy-back arrangement, but generally that will raise the price.

RESISTANCE, stubborn (pp. 191–192)
How do you elicit movement from an opposite who's mulish in resistance to any efforts to develop compromise solutions to outstanding differences on issues?

A carrot-and-stick approach is probably best. Play the motivational angles as flexibly and insistently as you can. Reiterate benefit possibilities while noting that no benefit is achievable as long as there's no movement to compromise. Make any benefit accorded the other side contingent on settling all the issues between you.

RESTAURANTS, as negotiation sites (pp. 143–144)
What are the advantages and disadvantages of restaurants as negotiation sites?

The greatest benefit is in the less formal, less structured environment a restaurant provides, which encourages a more open, friendly discussion than other, more official settings, such as offices or hotel conference areas. The disadvantages relate to the ever-present possibility of interruption and distraction, including food and/or service that may be poor. However, you can somewhat guard against problems here by care in selecting a restaurant where you can be relatively free of distractions and where service is efficient and unobtrusive and food is of good quality.

RIGHT vs. WRONG (pp. 78–79, 210–211, 214–215)
How do you prove one or the other?

You shouldn't be focusing on this. It's an incidental, subjective consideration. The point of negotiation is coordinating interests to mutual advantage as much as possible, not proving one set of interests morally superior.

RISKS, opposite's fear of (pp. 94–95)
How do you work around an opposite's fear of the risks involved in any proposed joint commitment to action?

By showing that you've taken those into account and then stressing the positive benefits to grow out of the joint commitment. Don't go to the extreme of trying to prove no risk whatsoever exists. Rather, put it into perspective as an acceptable chance to take, given that the possibilities have been anticipated.

RUMORS, responding to (pp. 263–265)
How do you contend with an opposite who tries to use the force of rumor to put you on the defensive?

Respond with matter-of-fact statements that are brief and to the point. Don't start defending yourself or making long explanations. That just plays into your opposite's hand.

SELF-ASSURANCE, projecting (pp. 107, 124–126, 262)
What do you advise for developing and projecting a sense of self-assurance?

Recognition of the importance of preparing well for any bargaining encounter. Once in negotiation, a free exercise of the right to ask questions as they arise. Regardless of the circumstances of the negotiation, always keep sight of the reality that you are as worthy as your opposite. Drop any tendency to view yourself or your position defensively. Behave with calm courtesy; speak frankly.

SELF-JUSTIFICATION, providing (pp. 243, 262, 266–267)
Do you ever have to present justifiable reasons for objectives pursued or positions taken?

You're not on trial in a negotiation. The proper focus is on how priorities on your side can be aligned with those on the other side. There's no need to explain objectives/positions taken in any terms of right or wrong. You need only review them in light of whether or not they truly address your needs well. In negotiation, "why" questions should relate to evaluation of goals and alternatives in terms of concrete benefit desired or achievable. Don't feel obliged to respond to those that implicitly challenge your motives on judgmental levels.

SELLER'S INDECISION
See INDECISION, seller's.

SELLER'S REMORSE
See REMORSE, seller's.

SELLING (pp. 85–86, 320–323)
What are the key considerations for effectiveness in this area?

There are two: (1) pinpointing motivation, i.e., identifying a need, objective or subjective, that will prompt a purchase decision; (2) convincing the prospective buyer that you're well or best placed to meet that need. The first requires careful preparation and attentive listening during presentation and discussion. The second requires effective employment of the art of persuasion.

See also OVERSELLING.

SEXIST BEHAVIOR (pp. 97, 179–180, 184)
Aside from obvious discriminatory conduct, what should you be alert to here?

Any remarks or behavior betraying a disposition to assume either gender more capable, better, or more to be taken seriously than the other. Men should particularly beware of projecting the attitude that it really is or should be "a man's world."

SEX-RELATED DIFFERENCES (pp. 76–82)
Are there any rules of thumb to keep in mind when negotiating with men as opposed to women, or vice versa?

While many people report observing differences in behavior between men and women negotiators, these are on a very general level and do not necessarily appear consistently in all men and women. As a general rule, treat every person as a distinct individual in his or her own right, without projecting upon them characteristics attributed to sex roles. Follow the same approach in developing a relationship with either gender, adjusting that to take individual differences into account as necessary.

SILENCE, and initiative (p. 159)
Does who breaks a silence after a proposal has been made have anything to do with who holds the initiative?

Not really. You win or lose the initiative through *how* you respond more than through *when*.

SPECIFIC, getting (pp. 305–306)
What's the most common problem here?

Sometimes the problem is being too specific. At times, especially when refusing an offer, it's just as well to respond in general terms—attempting to outline specific reasons can lead to argument you'd rather avoid.

On other occasions the problem is that you think you're being specific when you're not. This particularly crops up in references to things that can be quantified: a person will use terms such as "a lot," "soon," "certain," "some," etc. without indicating what that means in a particular context and think he or she is being clear. When you want a clear understanding about money amounts, time factors, problem situations, requests for change, etc., make as specific a statement as you can.

STRATEGY, developing (pp. 80–81, 82–90, 120–122)
Where do you begin?

Identify the preconditions that prompted your entry into negotiation; identify those operative on the other side as best you can. That will provide you a sense of position relative to the other side and clues on the approach to follow in resolving points of difference or exploiting opportunities for benefit that may exist.

STRATEGY vs. TACTICS (pp. 120–121)
What is the distinction here?

It's a fairly simple and clear one: Strategy is the general "game plan" you devise for achieving your objectives; tactics are the specific moves and maneuvers taken in implementation of that general plan.

STRATEGY, and applying tactics (pp. 121–122)
How do you ensure particular tactics won't compromise your general line of strategy?

Through carefully planning both in advance, with a recognition of the distinction between the two. Tactics have to be supportive of strategy and should be planned for cumulative impact. Don't make adjustments in use of tactics without first considering how that adjustment will affect your ability to pursue a planned line of strategy. When you make an adjustment in strategy, make corresponding adjustments in tactics for implementing that strategy.

STRENGTH, negotiating (pp. 152–159)
Are there any common misconceptions to be wary of here?

Yes. In particular a mistaken conviction that

- The strong negotiator is inevitably hard-nosed and uncompromising.
- The strong negotiator is habitually secretive.
- The person doing all the talking has the advantage.
- The person who first breaks silence after a proposal is made loses any advantage of initiative.

STRESS, contributing factors (pp. 223–225)
What should you review when trying to home in on what's contributing to stress in a negotiation?

Review your perception of self and of goals you've established in terms of your own value judgments, your expectations, your sense of self-image, your view of reality, your impulse to idealism, and your emotional needs. Then look at influences around you: others' expectations, conflicting goals, communication difficulties, interpersonal relations, resource limitations, and time pressures. All of these will influence you to some degree, but the experience of stress generally grows out of particular difficulty in just one or two areas. Identify what the most troublesome factor is in your situation, then apply problem-solving techniques to work through that. If more than one factor is involved, establish how these interact to build stress in you. Don't focus on external influences only. You're part of the process, and to the extent you experience stress that proves hard to manage, you're also part of the problem.

STRESS, eliminating (p. 222)
How do you eliminate stress in negotiation?

You can't eliminate stress. The disparity between what you want and what you get, the fears and anxieties related to uncertainty of outcome, are inevitable concomitants of the negotiation process. The focus should not be on eliminating stress, but on managing it.

STRESS, managing (pp. 226–230)
What is the key to managing stress successfully?

Self-awareness in particular. Identify signs and sources of tension within yourself so you're alert to how you contribute to the difficulty you experience. Develop a realistic sense of your abilities, and tune in to your self-expectations. Consider use of stress-reducing techniques like meditation before going into negotiations. Review external influences and how you can adjust to them. Always keep in mind that stress has a positive side: it prompts creative adjustment to situations for which you need new solutions in order to resolve matters satisfactorily.

TABLES, conference (pp. 141–142)
Is there any need to be concerned about details related to a conference table employed in bargaining sessions?

Recognize that shape can exert a subtle psychological influence. Rectangular tables tend to emphasize the division between opposing parties more than round tables do.

TACTICS, applying (pp. 120–122)
How do you decide what tactics are appropriate for trying to influence the other side?

By first developing a clear statement of goals and devising a line of strategy to follow in an approach to those. Then evaluate possible tactics in terms of their compatibility with strategy and for achievement of cumulative impact. Be sure you take personality factors into account as well as situational ones. The same tactic can have a different effect on different people.

TACTICS, diversionary (pp. 265–272)
How do you recognize an opposite's efforts to sidetrack you with diversionary tactics?

For starters, maintain a clear focus on your objectives and how any exchange with your opposite moves you closer to or blocks you in movement toward those. Be alert to any maneuver that appears aimed at

- Putting you on the defensive.
- Confusing or disorienting you.
- Promising cooperation that doesn't materialize.
- Playing on your eagerness to settle.
- Playing on your sense of desperation.
- Playing on your greed.
- Making a planned concession seem hard won.
- Stalling for time.
- Impressing you.
- Softening you up for a quick kill later.

Where efforts along these lines obscure a sense of progress toward objectives, where they're made with no reference to needs you have, you can generally safely assume you're being plied with diversionary tactics.

TEAM COMPOSITION, changes in (p. 295)
How should you handle changes in team composition during a negotiation?

Very routinely. If on your side you require the special talents of someone not originally included, pull that person into the process. As a rule, it's useful to announce any planned changes of personnel so that the other side can make any necessary preparation for response to the new perspective introduced. In your first encounter in which the new team member is included, it's generally advisable to introduce him or her by name and title. When the other side introduces a change in team composition, always take time to ascertain who that person is and what role he/she plays in the organization he/she is part of.

TEAM EFFORT, coordinating (pp. 285–293)
How do you keep team members effectively coordinated throughout long bargaining sessions?

By planning general strategy and individual assignments in pursuit of that strategy in advance. Then by prudent use of caucus breaks to absorb new information, to consider any member's awareness of a significant change in circumstances, to review an offer that's been made, to review/adjust strategy and/or tactics, to pull an out-of-hand team member back into control, and/or to take new goals into account.

TEAMWORK, ineffective (pp. 284–285)
What are the usual causes for a breakdown of team effectiveness?

Any of the following can create problems:

- Autocratic team leadership.
- Refusal to respect authority lines established within the team.
- Failure to maintain a common front.
- Failure of individual team members to assume their responsibilities.
- Personality rather than team focus.
- Overt sympathy for the position of the opposing team.
- Oversensitivity to ego needs on the part of team members.

TELEPHONE NEGOTIATIONS (pp. 299–303)
What approach will provide you maximum effectiveness in telephone negotiations?

The same kind of preparation and attention to details of situation and interpersonal communication as you'd follow in any negotiation.

Plan your telephone session so you're not interrupted or distracted during your conversation. Engage in a bit of preliminary small talk when first you get on the phone. This gives you a sense of your opposite's everyday speech pattern; you'll be more alert to changes in tone thereafter.

Be explicit, airing any uncertainty or question that arises. Resist urges to hang up in frustration during moments of impasse. You can recess discussions easily, but be sure you can reestablish the connection without difficulty. Don't short-cut discussion in your eagerness to get off the phone. Take notes during discussion to keep track of issues presented and how they're resolved.

THREAT, shared experience of (p. 84)
What line of approach should you take in getting help?

Stress common interests in the area of a need for relief, and focus on the mechanics of effective cooperation. Providing motivation is secondary to demonstrating the advantages of the approach you'd like taken in resolving the problem. The element of motivation is already present in the precondition.

THREATS, acquiescing to (pp. 248–249)
Is there any way to salvage something from a situation where it appears you have to concede under the pressure of a threat?

Avoid a panic-inspired concession. Respond in a calm, reasoned fashion, taking time to evaluate alternatives. Your evident self-control may win you some latitude for response. Also, a refusal to be panicked by a threat may actually serve to expose a bluff that you didn't dare call.

THREATS, calling (pp. 247–248)
What's the recommended line of approach for calling an opposite's threat?

To begin with, act on the basis of a considered decision, with all possible risks taken into account. Then calmly announce your decision, making two things clear: (1) You will not give in on the point at issue and are prepared to risk the consequences threatened; (2) you'd still rather work for a negotiated settlement of differences. Making the second point is important, because it leaves a bridge for the other side to use in backing down without losing face.

THREATS, issuing (pp. 161–163, 256, 318)
What should you take into consideration in deciding whether or not to influence an opposite through a threat of any kind?

You have to weigh the risks involved. Ask yourself:

- Is your objective worth the risk?
- What will you lose if you're called on your threat?
- Are you prepared for that eventuality?
- Is your timing appropriate?
- Can you present the threat credibly, or will it be regarded as a standard bluff tactic?
- Is the threat itself credible?

THREATS, redirecting (p. 245)
How do you manage this?

Show in convincing fashion how the action threatened will actually operate to damage interests on the other side. Point to any inevitability that the same difficulty that prompted the threat will arise with anyone else, if the threat is one of withdrawal.

THREATS, responding to (pp. 239–249)
What guidelines should you follow in deciding on response to a threat?

Take a moment to consider the threat: is it real; is it credible? Let the words sink in before you give any response. Perhaps your opposite misspoke him/herself; perhaps you'll get a restatement that introduces some qualification. Then as a first articulated response, repeat or rephrase what you just heard. You may have misunderstood it; your opposite may have second thoughts, either backing down or moderating the threat.

Always follow that sequence of response. Then review your plan and select whatever further response(s) fits in best with your position and strategy.

TIME, in caucuses
See CAUCUS TIME, managing.

TIME, and stalling tactics (pp. 270–271)
How do you tell when an opponent is stalling?

Through perception of a repeated interweaving pattern of apparent cooperation that almost gets you somewhere but then runs into delay . . . over and over again. This is a particularly difficult tactic to counter. Persist with strong pushes for positive commitment; emphasize benefits possible for the other side. Tie benefits the other side seeks to a commitment to final agreement on all issues.

TIME ORIENTATION, differences (pp. 329–330)
When are you likely to encounter problems growing out of a different perspective on time?

Whenver there's an unequal sense of urgency on the two sides. (*See* TIME PRESSURES; TIME, and stalling tactics.) Also when negotiating with an opposite from another culture where general attitudes toward time differ from those common in your culture. Make an effort to determine what any difference in this area may be in advance, and adjust accordingly.

TIME PRESSURES (pp. 151, 202)
How do you ensure getting the best deal in the face of pressures to conclude negotiations within a brief time frame?

By getting right down to business. Stay focused on your priorities; don't let yourself be pushed into glossing over important issues or into making quick, unconsidered concessions. The trick is to avoid getting sidetracked into consideration of incidentals or any debate on the merits of positions taken on either side. A well-organized, carefully prepared approach is essential to assure priority interests are all addressed. Be succinct in presentations and responses, but don't short-cut consideration of priority interests.

TIME-WASTING, avoiding
See CAUCUS TIME, managing; TRANSITION, from day to day; and other entries under TIME.

TRANSITION, from day to day (pp. 293–298)
How do you keep from repetition of efforts in negotiations that extend over a period of two or more days?

At the close of each day (1) recap what's been discussed, agreed upon or settled, etc., being sure to obtain your opposite's explicit concurrence on each point; (2) set up a schedule for the next day's discussions; (3) indicate any personnel changes that may be made. Then, on the next day, begin with (1) an introduction of any new personnel on either side; (2) a concise restatement of benefits looked for in agreement; (3) a summary of progress made so far, obtaining your opposite's explicit concurrence on each point. If no disagreement surfaces with respect to these points, go on to the next issue immediately. Otherwise first resolve the specific point of difference that's become apparent.

TRUST, building (pp. 105–113, 331)
What's the best way to go about this?

Pursuing objectives with attention to

- Openness in discussion in all issues/opportunities.
- Projecting a sense of honesty.
- Displaying self-confidence.
- Building on positive past experience.
- Showing receptivity to the other side's needs.
- Demonstrating cooperative intent.
- Considerations of credibility.
- Displaying a positive mental attitude.
- Clarity in expression of motives and motive compatibility.
- Demonstrating acceptance of the other side.
- Displaying an ability/willingness to let go of preconceived notions.

ULTIMATUMS, issuing
See THREATS, issuing.

ULTIMATUMS, responding to
See OFFERS, final; THREATS, responding to.

UNDERSTANDING, checking for
See FEEDBACK BREAKS; QUESTIONS, asking; RECAPPING.

UNDERSTANDING, getting (pp. 92–93)
How do you elicit the other side's understanding of your perspective/position?

You elicit a willingness to consider and understand your perspective/position by showing your own willingness to consider those of your opposite. After that, it's a matter of clear communication.

WEAKNESS, negotiating from (pp. 257–263)
What can you do to keep some range of flexibility when in a weaker position vis-à-vis your opposite?

To begin with, avoid focusing on your sense of weakness. That will block your view of any alternatives you may have. And don't adopt a defensive mentality—that only emphasizes your sense of weakness. Address the other side's needs in a positive effort to expand your alternatives. Pursue the issues; don't just concede them. Project an attitude of self-confidence as you push for a win-win solution.

See also CONCESSIONS, premature; DEFENSIVENESS, controlling yours; LOSS, assuming; POWER, determining the balance.

WIN-LOSE GAMES, countering (pp. 194–203)
What's the key consideration here?

Calm, clear-headed pursuit of your objectives coupled with an awareness of patterns commonly pursued in an effort to victimize you with a game-playing tactic. Games frequently employed by manipulative negotiators include: The Bear Trapper; Let's You and Him/Her Fight; Uproar; Cornering; Cry "Rape!", Blemish; Now I've Got You, You S.O.B.

Two games that appear to have a lose-win result can also expose you to the possibility of loss: Wooden Leg; The Harried Worker.

WITHDRAWAL, threatening (pp. 231–232, 248, 256–257, 318)
Is it ever in your interest to threaten withdrawal from a negotiation?

Not if the precondition on your side contains a need you can't readily fulfill without the other side's cooperation. However, if the other side's needs are more compelling than yours, you may be able to prompt a concession this way. But recognize the risk involved and weigh whether you want to take it. Recognize that a threat to withdraw sometimes adds to conflict rather than operating to cut through it.

See also THREATS, issuing.

WITHDRAWAL, threat of (p. 245)
What's a good line of response to an opposite threatening to withdraw from a negotiation?

A convincing citation of possible benefits lost as a result of that action. You might also indicate that the precipitating difficulty would have to be faced with any third party your opposite might otherwise refer to.

WORD CHOICE (pp. 183–184, 210–211, 237)
What rules should you follow to keep word choices from exacerbating differences between you and an opposite?

Avoid words loaded with a negative emotional/judgmental content. Resist any temptation to characterize attitudes or behavior in your opposite in absolute terms of good or bad or right or wrong. And refuse to get pulled into any name-calling.

1
Understanding
What It's All About

PROBLEMS faced in a negotiation commonly revolve around details relating to procedure, personality, perspective, and approach in dealing with another party. There are many aspects to each of these, and flexibility on your part is required for favorable adjustment to whatever combination faces you.

As you might expect, there is a substantial range of specific guidelines and techniques for meeting varied problem situations, and many of them are discussed in this book. But resolving problems is not just a matter of matching up Problem No. 21 with Resolution Guideline No. 21 in some master catalog of answers to bargaining difficulties. That's both too complicated and too simplistic: too complicated because it suggests having to memorize a chart of potentially hundreds of problems and matched proper responses; too simplistic because it's based on the faulty assumption that problems constantly repeat in a totally predictable fashion. They don't. Every problem has its own elements of uniqueness. Sometimes what seems the same problem requires different answers at different times.

We've built a problem-solving reference key into this book, which we think will prove useful to you. But we're also working here to move you beyond looking up the answers. If you can memorize the various guidelines presented and apply them in the appropriate context, good for you. However, we hope you will go beyond that to adopt a manner and method of communication that naturally makes for effective performance. That's less a matter of memorizing than of seeing the underlying grid on which all the guidelines hang. That's why we think it important to begin with general observations on what it's all about.

WHAT'S INVOLVED IN NEGOTIATING

A major part of minimizing problems is simply arriving at an understanding of what's involved in negotiation. It's not the total incompatibility of the parties on whatever level, but the failure on either or both sides to understand what is at the heart of negotiating that dooms many efforts at agreement.

Winning Agreement

This is absolutely fundamental. It seems almost too obvious to emphasize, but there are implications here that are too frequently overlooked. First of all, there's the fact of approach to a second person or group. You're dealing with someone else, and thus with a set of perspectives and priorities different from your own. Second, you want something from that person/group, and you want them to agree to give it to you. (It needn't be something material.) Third, you're not prepared or in any situation to use force. Somehow you have to talk your way through to the commitment desired. That means lines of communication must remain open and clear.

You want agreement because it holds a benefit for you if everything works out right. You can't win agreement except through dealing with the other side. The other side has to be persuaded to go along with providing you a route to the desired benefit.

THE IMPORTANCE OF A WIN-WIN ORIENTATION

It's at this point that a key concept enters the picture—a win-win orientation to the negotiating process.

It's simple logic. The most convincing way to win agreement is a demonstration that providing you what you want will get your counterpart what he or she wants, too. Conversely, you're least likely to win agreement when you make it appear gains on your side will be made at the other side's expense. (*Gain* is a relative term, of course. In an encounter between two parties to a conflict, minimizing losses can be the gain projected for either side.) If these bits of common sense are kept in mind, everything else involved in negotiating follows naturally.

Meeting Needs

Needs are at the root of all negotiations. And the needs on both sides must ultimately be compatible on a practical level. If there are needs on one side only, why is the other side there? The very fact that two parties sit down together for discussions is evidence that each has some need it wishes to have met, even if not ready, at first, to admit a specific need.

Note, however, that need does not always grow out of problems that both sides are desperate to resolve. Often that is the case with only one of the parties to a negotiation; sometimes it is the case with neither.

When we speak of needs, we include both those that arise objectively (out of actual problem situations) and those that arise subjectively (out of goals either party has set itself). For example, an opportunity for profit through cooperative endeavor can be exploited through prompting interest in financial gain. Desire for profit creates the need there, impelling one or both parties to negotiate.

Needs are not necessarily the same for the two sides, nor is it important that they should be. What is essential, if the negotiation is to have any chance of success, is that the needs be or become compatible. You are off track if you take the position that bargaining is a process of getting the other side to adopt your priorities. That implies one party subordinating its position to the other. You're setting up an "I win–you lose" equation, which doesn't readily lead to agreement. Your proper aim is to demonstrate that the priorities on each side converge on a practical level. Then you can plot out a common course of action to suit both sides' needs, which may remain widely disparate.

INCOMPATIBLE NEEDS

There will be occasions when two parties enter into negotiation with incompatible needs, perhaps because the incompatibility is not immediately evident. That makes reaching agreement virtually impossible.

Occasionally the nature of the needs on one side are such that they can be satisfied even though no agreement results from the bargaining sessions. One party may deliberately enter into a negotiation with the intent of winning advantage at the other's expense. It may be just a psychological advantage—gratification of some need to exercise influence, for example. It may have roots in a public relations gesture insincerely intended. Or it may be that one party's needs were informational, while the other hoped for some commitment to mutual action. So, although as a rule we speak of negotiation as a process of moving to agreement, it's important to recognize that the process is at times initiated without agreement being the end one or other party has in mind. When that happens, it's not negotiation in good faith; it's a manipulation.

Coordinating Different Priorities/Perspectives

Negotiation is a *mutual act* of coordinating areas of interest. As these are rarely identical for both parties, this is customarily accomplished through developing compromises that ensure benefit to both. One party dictating to the other is not negotiation. One party manipulating the other with no concern for the other's needs is a cynical travesty of negotiation.

You may raise the objection that dictating and/or manipulation can work to get another to do what you want him/her to do. Of course that's true. But put yourself in the other person's shoes for a moment. Are you going to like the way you were treated? Are you going to be enthusiastic and supportive about whatever was decided on? Aren't you going to figure out some way to squirm out of this situation? You're certainly not going to deal with this person again if you can avoid it. You might even feel yourself biding time—until you can zap it right back to the so-and-so's!

Doesn't the advantage of an agreement built on meeting needs on both sides seem pretty evident now?

In resolving problems between the parties, it is not essential that one side prove itself right or wrong. The question of right or wrong is usually beside the point. Where's the answer to that one, anyway? Take a note from Harry Reasoner, one of America's most seasoned news reporters:

. . . there are two keys to understanding most stories. One is that there are always at least two sides to any story. The other is that the world doesn't have many real villains, very many real bad guys, if you define a villain as a person who *thinks* of himself as a villain.*

At the heart of negotiation is the (unspoken) recognition that each side is entitled to its own priorities. The whole art of negotiation lies in persuading a second party to make a commitment you want because it is in the other party's interest, too.

Neither party's view of its priorities need be considered static. An effort to change the other party's priorities may in fact be at the basis of a negotiation. But that change has to be prompted by stimulating a reconsideration of perspectives, not by invoking concepts of right or wrong or better or worse. If one side takes as its objective getting the other to confess error, the likely result is that differences are going to be emphasized rather than resolved.

Gathering Information

Negotiation is more a learning process than a form of instruction. Both parties are engaged in discovering each other's views and needs. Both are exploring possibilities for combining energies in a new way. Each is gaining a sense of reality about its own expectations or particular wants. The moment one party attempts to play out a teacher-pupil relationship vis-à-vis the other, you're back to the situation where one set of priorities is being touted as superior.

Gathering information is part of what you're doing when negotiating, but that does not make fact finding the essence of negotiation. Fact finding is but part of the process, used to help define issues, establish needs, and clarify positions taken. The essence of negotiation always remains the effort to forge mutual agreement. Fact finding is best viewed as the basic research tool for establishing and following a sense of direction for winning agreement.

Engaging in a Ritual

There's no defined etiquette or set of Robert's Rules for specifying what's correct at particular steps along the way to winning agree-

*Harry Reasoner, *Before the Colors Fade*, Alfred A. Knopf, 1981.

ment, but there isn't any way to avoid following an established sequence of steps. That makes negotiation something of a ritual. To make it work you have to take each step in proper order:

1. Introduction of the parties to each other;
2. Presentation of a general overview that indicates initial goals and feelings on each side;
3. Review from the perspective of both parties of the pertinent background leading to the negotiation;
4. Definition of the specific issue(s) existing between the parties and comprising points of difference or opportunity that each feels need to be addressed;
5. Engagement in conflict, with each side pressing its perspective and questioning elements of the other's perspective (but in terms of actual advantage, *not* in terms of right or wrong);
6. Fallback and compromise, identifying areas of common interest and adjusting positions to facilitate achievement of common interests in other areas;
7. Agreement, with both parties settling on a single statement of how the common interests that have been identified will be pursued.

Following these steps is a critical post-negotiation phase, in which each party acts to implement its part of the agreement.

You have to follow the ritual to successfully complete the process, no matter with whom you're negotiating. A consumer negotiating an appliance purchase goes through each of them, if in very abbreviated form. The steps can be very abbreviated in simple exchanges. They can get quite involved in encounters between spokespersons for major organizations, and particularly involved in exchanges between political leaders. You can simplify or complicate the ritual. You can't skip steps or shuffle them around and expect to get results.

Planning Strategy

Because negotiation is a goal-oriented process, it's implicit that each side develop a line of strategy for moving in the direction desired. Preparation and planning are essential. Tactics—the moves employed in pursuit of the strategy selected—have to be consistent and cumulative in their effect. They also have to fit effectively into the ritual of exchange between the two parties. It doesn't matter if the strategy and tactics adopted prove incomprehensible to others. The important thing is that they provide a sense of direction for the party applying them.

Dealing with People

Always remember that negotiation is a process between people. That makes it subject to all the vagaries and inconsistencies that are part of human nature. However, that also makes it subject to all the pleasant surprises people can present each other. Those involved on both sides come to the encounter as more than proponents of a perspective they officially represent. They also come as individuals in their own right. Don't ever forget they are concerned with their own feelings of self-worth, security, status, pleasure, etc., as well as with "official" business at hand. You have to take personal needs and prejudices constantly into account. Fortunately these often provide opportunities for coming to agreement more readily. It's shortsighted to think of them only as complicating factors.

Controlling Yourself

Feelings play a major part in determining how you act and react in a negotiation. You may be tempted to view everything exclusively in terms of maneuvering and influencing whomever you're up against, but you're integral to the process, too. Your disposition affects your chance for success as much as anything else does.

You can't keep everything on one level, as far as your feelings go. The way a negotiation naturally develops affects how you're involved, emotionally as well as in terms of position. Fortunately, the ritual nature of negotiation always makes for some predictability with regard to what potentially troublesome feelings you will likely be dealing with and when. It also provides cues for action to take you through each stage. Follow through as deliberately and calmly as possible on the action level. You'll generally find you can keep these feelings under control.

Kaye Raymond of Kaye Raymond Associates in Sydney, Australia, offers the following chart identifying what unsettling feelings commonly surface at various stages of a negotiation and what general action line, effectively pursued, serves as a tool of control.

STAGE	FEELINGS	ACTION KEY
Prenegotiation	Aggression Apprehension Fear	Prepare strategy
Entrance (Ritual steps 1, 2, 3)	Anxiety Tension	Establish communication/ rapport
Commencement of confrontation (Ritual steps 4, 5)	Stress Frustration Anger	Begin bargaining tactics
Turning Point (Ritual step 6)	Fatigue Uncertainty	Adjust position(s)
Conclusion (Ritual step 7)	Relief Easing of tension	Compromise

In addition to the feelings that arise in connection with difficulties you anticipate at various stages of a negotiation, there are those that come up in response to personalities and attitudes on the other side. Your success depends on keeping those under control, too. Chapter 5 specifically aims at helping you with difficulties there. Here we'll just cite a general rule of thumb: Controlling yourself is primarily a matter of maintaining and projecting a positive attitude.

Keep these general points firmly in mind: Negotiation is about winning agreement through the force of persuasion. That's accomplished through meeting needs and coordinating interests on *both* sides. It involves gathering information. It requires a natural, step-by-step (ritual) approach, with strategy planned and applied to get to the goals that have been set. And it is always to some degree subject to the influences of personality.

PRECONDITIONS FOR NEGOTIATING

Preconditions to negotiate? What are they? Quite simply, they're whatever it is that prompts you to enter into the negotiating process.

Is that all? you may ask. Certainly anyone going into a negotiation knows what he or she wants to achieve.

Yes and no. Most people are clear on specific goals they're trying to achieve through negotiation. What we're talking about, however, are the circumstances that govern the position in which either party stands relative to the other. Often there is such focus on the desired end of the bargaining process that those present lose sight of their actual position relative to the other party. Allow confusion to enter in here, and you'll find it difficult to devise a manageable strategy for winning an agreement supportive of your objectives.

The Preconditions Identified

Let's look at what the preconditions affecting bargaining positions are. You will probably find a number of these self-evident, but beware of dismissing further consideration of them for that reason. Even with those that seem most obvious, it's still all too easy to slip into a strategy or tactics not fully commensurate with what actually brought you to negotiate.

A NEED FOR ASSISTANCE

You face a problem or situation that adversely affects you and that the other party can aid in solving.

The point to keep foremost in mind here is that *you* are experiencing the adverse effect. *You* want relief. So *you* have to take the initiative.

If the other party with whom you are negotiating is contributing to your problem, then somehow you have to motivate him/her to change whatever activity or inactivity is troubling you. If the same difficulty also exercises some adverse effect on your counterpart, then the motivation will already be present to some extent. You will still have to demonstrate that what seems a solution for you will also prove a solution to the other side. And in a case where you see the other party as a necessary factor in the solution of your difficulty, even though it has not contributed to that and does not necessarily feel a need or desire to become involved, you must provide an incentive for involvement.

The particulars of your situation will always have an effect on your line of strategy, but you have to keep it generally tailored to fit the precondition. You can't forget your need for assistance in pursuing details related to particular goal elements. You may not feel it desirable that your opposite have full knowledge of the extent of your difficulties. *You* must nevertheless keep the reality of your position ever in mind.

A SHARED THREAT

You and the other party face a common threat from the same source.

The situation here is distinguished from that preceding by an awareness that *both* of you need a solution to a problem that affects you similarly. It is pretty definitely established on both sides that a cooperative approach on meeting the threat stands the greatest chance of success.

Motivating your partner is less at issue here than agreeing on the mechanics of cooperation. You still have the need for relief, but now you have that in common. Your strategy should be to build on your common interest. Focus on your ally's need for relief, integral to the precondition here, as well as on your own. You thereby more readily avoid any subsequent dispute as to the mutual advantage of any course of action suggested or taken. Stay aware that any third party who constitutes or represents the common threat will aim at coming between you and your opposite with the object of "divide and conquer" in mind.

A POSSIBLE CHANCE FOR GAIN

You simply want to check out, on a general level, whether there may be an opportunity for benefit or further benefit in some relationship with the other party. You don't have a particular need you want the other to fill.

This kind of situation allows a negotiator considerable flexibility, because there's no sense of urgency attached to the process. There's no critical issue. Participants are likely to be in their best humor if both share the same precondition. (Different things often bring each party to the bargaining table.) The fact that you have nothing to lose, maybe something to gain, that you do not feel yourself in any kind of adversary position, will contribute a positive feeling to the whole experience. The one thing to guard against is deceiving yourself.

Sometimes people go into a negotiation with a false sense of this precondition. They're not ready to admit that some problem is really the reason for meeting with the other side. When that happens the other party had better brace itself for a difficult time, because not until the real issue is identified and acknowledged is there going to be significant movement toward achieving resolution of the problem. Granted it's sometimes a tactic in negotiation to sidle up to a desired goal without betraying your full motives. But in this case we're talking about kidding yourself, not the other party.

DESIRE FOR INFLUENTIAL FAVOR

You want to get the other party favorably disposed to your interests. You want to develop some kind of assurance that the other party will, at some probably yet undefined point, use his influence on your behalf. No present difficulty, no anticipated threat may be involved. But there is an implicit recognition of potential need.

Your tactics have to be appropriate and effective for winning favor. It's made considerably easier, of course, by the absence of specific demands at this moment.

You may find some who react negatively out of expectation that specific demands will be forthcoming from you before long. They don't care to respond to what they imagine those demands will be, so you in effect run into a blank wall. But most people are ready to take a more open attitude, reacting with friendliness toward friendliness, not concerned with possible demands until they are made. They'll deal with the difficulties if and when they come up. If by that time you have had the opportunity to present a better understanding of your situation and yourself, that may very well influence events to your benefit. You won't then have to negotiate separately for support. This is exactly the dynamic involved in lobbying activities.

There's nothing dishonest in following through on this precondition. The honesty or lack of it lies in *how* you follow through. Bribery is dishonest, as is coercive threat. Entering into an open exchange of ideas with an eye toward winning someone's good favor is the essence of democratic freedom.

A SALES OPPORTUNITY

You're selling. You want to develop a sense of need in the other party for a product or service you can provide.

Selling is the process of motivating others to buy. You often have to provide an important part of the motivation. So in this situation you first have to spend time probing the other side's circumstances and attitudes. Then you have to convince them that employing your product or services will result in a wanted or needed improvement.

During both the probing and the convincing, you have to retain your credibility. If you lay your finger on an experienced want or need but then can't bring your prospect to believe you're best able to satisfy it, you haven't met your precondition. If you have to depend on the prospect to point to and keep in sight the need your product or service is to fill, you'll also find your effectiveness low. Sales personnel in particular have to develop an ability to read people, to know when to emphasize a point, when to remain silent. And they must always conduct themselves so that the focus of the negotiation remains on how *they* provide the best answer to the needs of the other party.

A PURCHASE REQUIREMENT

You want someone else to provide a product or service you feel you need. Now you're buying.

The first thing to do in this situation is to clearly communicate your needs or desires. Then you want to ascertain that the other party really is equipped to satisfy them. This is always important. Sometimes the party you are turning to won't be able to provide exactly what you're calling for, and yet will still be eager to sell you.

Another consideration is whether a party who can satisfy you is the only one who can. Your strategy in negotiating a purchase can vary considerably, depending on whether you have a choice of people/organizations to go to. If you need something that only one or a far-flung few can provide, you will be much more cautious in risking bargaining tactics that may prove abortive.

Usually there's a multiplicity of supply sources, so you find buyers customarily requesting a range of information from possible suppliers before entering into final negotiation with any one of them. Those negotiations are always influenced by the knowledge on both sides that a third party may be standing by ready to cater to the buyer's needs in the event the present supplier cannot or will not come to a desired commitment.

A CONTRACT RENEGOTIATION

You want to renew an expiring contract or agreement.

This is the precondition that brings labor and management together regularly in companies or industries employing unionized personnel. It is what brings two companies together periodically when some kind of formal service relationship exists between them. It is what motivates key executives to negotiate with their board of directors when tenure or terms of work have been spelled out in an employment agreement.

The tactics appropriate in particular circumstances under this precondition can vary considerably. If both parties want to renew, then the subsequent negotiations should be characterized by an immediate sense of mutual interests. This doesn't mean that either party should forgo pursuit of its individual interests, nor that efforts by either side to win an advantage automatically demonstrate lack of good faith. But whatever maneuvering either side indulges in, neither the general line of strategy nor specific tactics should be allowed to create an atmosphere that hinders working together again.

Unfortunately this is precisely the problem that crops up in many a labor-management negotiation. Both sides get so involved in pursuit of intermediate goals, or both sides get so caught up in devising tactics to win advantage over the other, that the fact of mutual interest recedes into the background. The parties exchange recriminations that may push them farther apart than when they started to negotiate. Occasionally you read of companies going out of business because labor-management relations have become so acrimonious that the initially shared precondition ceases to be considered at all. Both sides lose—badly.

Where the precondition exists primarily on one side, the situation is roughly parallel to the selling precondition. You'll find yourself having to stress that you have up to now filled the needs of your opposite and that *you* are best situated or equipped to continue doing so. To the extent your opposite is prepared to acknowledge the quality of your service, product, etc., you may have leverage for winning renewal of your relationship on terms you find favorable.

A DESIRE TO DISENGAGE

A relationship has existed that you now wish to dissolve.

This doesn't always require entering into a negotiation. If a service arrangement with someone has proved unsatisfactory, you can often terminate that simply by giving notice. In some cases you can let a relationship lapse without even that formality. But in a surprising number of cases this precondition makes negotiation necessary. If you're dissolving a formally established business partnership, you'll find you have to come to an agreement on the disposition of assets or on responsibility for various debits that may remain.

With this precondition, the negotiation is less likely to focus on the dissolution itself than on the manner of its accomplishment. A negotiation that is badly conducted probably won't keep you from achieving dissolution, but will affect how painless or painful that may be for you or for your opposite.

Sometimes relationships that are dissolving are characterized by such hard feelings on one or both sides that conduct in a negotiated settlement is deliberately offensive and vindictive. This is true in business and in divorce—and unfortunate in both instances. Perhaps some satisfaction is achieved by seeing someone who has become "the enemy" suffer, but more often than not mean-spirited behavior in this kind of circumstance creates victims on both sides.

A BREAKDOWN IN RELATIONS

This is one of the most delicate situations a negotiator can face. Unless bargaining is conducted with a considerable tact, the risk of not meeting this precondition is substantial. You're working to salvage a foundering relationship, and the wrong move(s) can set you farther from your objective than when you started. You have to deal with the specific issues that have contributed to the deterioration of your relationship without getting hung up in defensive or fault-finding exchanges. You have to be ready to acknowledge your own possible responsibility for an uncomfortable situation—always, a difficult thing for the average person to do—and then act accordingly. If, for example, you are a temperamental boss faced with the threatened departure of a valuable employee who finds the manner in which you exercise authority hard to take, you have to avoid a response that smacks of your customary authoritarianism.

A LAST-DITCH SALVAGE EFFORT

You want to save what can possibly be saved in an extreme situation.

The very nature of this precondition is such as to draw into question whether negotiation can accomplish anything at all. The other party has the upper hand to such an extent that your leverage is close to or at nil.

But negotiation isn't only a question of exerting leverage. It involves the ability to influence behavior as well. And even in the most extreme situation, there is often some opportunity to influence the other party's behavior so as to moderate the threat posed.

The Other Side's Preconditions

Any combination of circumstances can coalesce in one fashion or another into a precondition for negotiation. But in order for negotiation actually to materialize, a precondition has to exist on both sides. You can't bargain for assistance if no one is interested in your problems; you can't sell if no one wants to buy; you can't save your job if no one's open to persuasion that maybe you should be allowed to keep it.

Quite often the precondition that exists on one side is different from that existing on the other. In some cases, such as buy-sell situations, that is essential for meeting either precondition. At other times the difference allows for a compatible pursuit of separate interest.

Take the example of one party with a problem entering into bargaining with another party primarily interested in checking out opportunities for profit in a relationship with the first. Immediately you see the importance of recognizing what precondition exists on both sides. In this example, the strategy of the first party has to focus on persuading the second that an opportunity for profit exists in working to resolve the problem the first party has. If you only talk up assistance needs here, you're in trouble. The other party is waiting to hear of a chance to make money.

There is an alternate approach possible here. You can concentrate on communicating your precondition in such terms that the other party adopts it. It amounts to a presentation something like this: "I need help with this problem. You want to know what the advantage to you is in providing that help. Well, if you consider . . . you'll realize that this state of affairs really presents you with a problem, too."

In order to meet your precondition, you have to focus on your own need; otherwise you won't be able to keep track of your own interests. But you have to be able to communicate in terms of the other side's needs; i.e., accurately identify or refocus the precondition that pulled them to the bargaining table and address that. Otherwise you won't win the cooperation you want.

Incompatible Preconditions

Sometimes you will find incompatible preconditions pushing parties to negotiate. Say one side wants to salvage a foundering relationship while the other wants to see it dissolved. Unless the first can find a way to refocus the second's precondition, or vice versa, chances are there will be a lot of fruitless exchange. The result could well be a painful separation rather than either a reconciliation or a clean parting of the ways. Or in other cases of incompatible preconditions, the relative positions of the parties might enable one to emerge with a sense of having won at least something, but the flaw introduced by the incompatibility might well prove problematic at a later date.

The whole matter of what preconditions are and how they interrelate is basic to negotiation. It should be easy to determine the precondition on your side. Determining it on the other side may not be so easy. Things are not always what they seem. Circumstances are subject to change, and often for reasons that are not evident or logical. Then once you've identified the preconditions, you have to accent the point of compatibility. How you do that depends substantially on what they are—reality always limits what choices are available.

Make it a point to look on both sides for operative preconditions *before* you get involved in the actual ritual of negotiation. You've probably always had some sense of their influence. Become fully conscious of that, and you'll find you have a more defined sense of direction at the very outset of exchanges with the other side.

2
Taking Basic Considerations into Account

To BE effective as a negotiator, you have to understand what the process is all about. Then you have to recognize that there are basic considerations in every negotiating encounter. Failure to take these into account inevitably leads to problems. You may think a problem grows out of obstacles thrown up by an opponent. But the real problem may be that you haven't taken some basic considerations into account in your approach to that person.

THE ART OF PERSUASION

When you enter into negotiation with someone, you always bring your own perspectives on the issue(s) with you. You have ideas on what course of action either of you can or should take relative to the existing situation. You have a sense of available and preferable options.

Say the point of your discussions is improvement of a present unsatisfactory condition. You almost certainly have defined for yourself what the problem is and what the best way to eliminate it is. The fact that you're in a negotiation is already an indication of what's involved: getting the other side to join with you or act for you in dealing with the difficulty. To achieve that you have to talk them into it. To get it done right, you have to talk them into doing it in a fashion that protects and/or promotes your interests.

The Elements of Persuasion

The challenge facing you is to persuade the other side to share your perspective. Somehow you have to convince them to listen to you, to understand the elements that shape your perspective. You want them to accept that this understanding provides appropriate motivation for action on their part along mutually determined lines. You want them to commit themselves and/or their resources to the designated line of action.

GETTING INTEREST

Appeal to the other party's needs is at the heart of all persuasion. You must telegraph a signal that says first, "Hey look! Listen!" and immediately thereafter, "It'll be worth your while—there's something in this for you." Work to overcome or reduce distractions that vie for your opposite's attention. As fast as you can, tune in on fears: to overcome those that are obstacles, to reinforce those that would prompt action suited to your ends. Stress the benefits that can only be achieved through the suggested course of action; play down any doubts that they can be so achieved.

Because you're working to involve the other party's interest, you have to do more than just state your own case in support of any proposal you may have. You must also listen for what your opposite has to say. The thrust of your initial effort is to elicit a receptive attitude, so selling what you have to offer is important. But often a negotiation gets off to a bad start because one party is so eager and determined to make its case that the other party is provided no opportunity to set out its needs or perspectives. You have to know those in order to be truly persuasive. If you are determined that the ideal solution to your Problem A is to get your opposite to undertake Action X, listen for a clue to what will actually impel your opposite to take Action X. If it turns out he will take Action X only if convinced that Condition B exists, you will be a poor persuader if you continue to speak only in terms of Problem A—particularly if Condition B is somewhere operative or can be seen as imminent. Your opposite will correctly deduce that you are limited to seeing things from your own perspective, and his interest will wane accordingly.

GETTING UNDERSTANDING

The old rule of thumb holds here: *To get understanding, prove understanding.* Proving understanding is important for sustaining interest. Once you've shown an awareness of and readiness to consider the other side's needs, you can generally count on them to be willing to listen to your point of view.

Again, a reciprocal exchange is essential. Take the Problem A–Action X sequence we used above. You've listened to your opposite and discovered he'll undertake X only if Condition B exists. If Condition B is demonstrably operative, you have only to point that out and then work from there.

But it's rarely that cut-and-dried. Generally you'll have to go on to extract elements of commonality between your needs and your opposite's needs. Translate your understanding of *his* perspective into a statement that works to support your *needs*: "I know you feel everything hinges on any threat that might arise from B, which doesn't seem to be operative now, but note how this aspect of A can impact on you in a fashion similar to B."

Negotiation is not a unidirectional process: you talk; the other party listens and is then swept into a supportive position by the sheer force of your logic. It doesn't work like that. It's an exchange, not a force-feeding. The objective is to come to an agreement, not to win debating points. You want enthusiastic support to the degree possible, not some kind of intellectual concession. To get that, you have to show your understanding that needs exist on the other side, too.

PROVIDING MOTIVATION

We've actually begun our discussion of this element in reviewing the previous two. Keep in mind that the elements here are not a step-by-step sequence to be mastered in one-two-three-four order. Each of these elements comes into play continuously. Providing appropriate motivation is part of getting interest—pulling positive attention to you. And you don't get interest just once and then count on it for the balance of the time you're dealing with your opposite. You have to *hold* it. Likewise, you continually have to work for understanding; you have to provide continuing motivation.

A couple of cautions: First of all, rein in any tendency to an attitude of "Be reasonable, see it my way." Reason is much less frequently a motivating factor than we like to think, probably because reasonability is so subjective. Similarly, don't assume that a flood of facts will turn the trick. Facts alone rarely influence one to act in any prescribed manner, and you are devising a prescription for action. You may support your position with facts, but the motivation still lies in the answer you provide the other party to the question "What's in this for us?"

Winning commitment is simply a matter of credibly following through on the line of motivation. Not that that's always easy. It can take a lot of effort to get the other side to respond the way you want them to. Monitoring the reaction to your citation of benefits is crucial. In particular, listen carefully for reactions that indicate obstacles or possible alternate avenues toward achievement of your goal.

There will always be questions and frequently objections to deal with. Respond to those in a manner that reinforces your promise of benefit to be achieved. See questions or objections as opportunities to work closer to the other party's sense of priorities. They may indicate obstacles, but you should know where the obstacles lie. Also, you'll get readier commitment if you deal with them right away; otherwise they'll be around to trip you up later, maybe just when you thought you were in the clear. It's also psychologically advantageous to be seen as one who deals openly and effectively with obstacles. It makes you seem a natural ally in whatever joint venture you and the other side are embarking on.

OVERCOMING DOUBT

You won't always be able to completely identify an opposite's interest(s) with your own. Some doubts may remain in the other side's mind. Often the only way to get around them is to get the other party to accept that some risk is inevitable. Of course, you work to minimize the force of any doubts, but your opposite is apt to stress them. And he may well be tempted to follow the old convention of "When in doubt, don't."

Fielding Killer Statements. Your opposite, hesitating at the sight of a risk remaining, may throw out what we call a killer statement: "My people will never go for this"; "My partner is against this kind of arrangement"; etc. He uses the statement to avoid taking an uncomfortable risk.

When responding, it's best to avoid asking a question like "Why won't your people go for this?" or "What does your partner have against this kind of arrangement?" That just introduces an opportunity for the other side to go through a recitation of fears and/or unfavorable precedents. Refocusing on those can so reinforce doubts that your opposite consequently shies away from the desired commitment.

By this time you should know what doubts exist on the other side. You don't want to see fears that arise in connection with these build up into an insurmountable obstacle by allowing negativity to hold the floor just when you're pulling for positive commitment. Far better at this point to speak out positively in favor of the commitment requested: "Your people will be pleased to find that we've anticipated the situation so it's unlikely Condition B or Y can interfere with your priorities."

Note that you don't try to persuade the other side that absolutely no risk exists. What you do is put it in a perspective that makes it seem acceptable, that makes it clear it's been considered in such fashion as to render it unlikely to be detrimental. Your focus is on the probable, mutually desirable consequences of what is being committed to. You reinforce the positive mind-set you've been building up all along.

Preventing Problems

It should be obvious that a certain element of diplomacy is intrinsic to the art of persuasion. After all, if you make the other person look or feel stupid or foolish, he's not going to find much interest in prolonged discussion with you. Even if it happens that your opposite needs you more than you need him, you improve chances of having things go your way more completely if you take his ego needs into account.

Here are specific guidelines for minimizing any danger of creating problems that interfere with effective persuasion:

Avoid Overselling Your Opposite. If you assume your proper task is to keep talking until the other guy gives in, you'll have a rough time of it. Your opposite will wonder why you're so desperate to conclude agreement that you won't allow him an opportunity to discuss the issues from his perspective. It works out to a negotiator's variation on "Methinks the lady doth protest too much."

Unless you pull your opposite into *full* consideration of the benefits from his angle, he'll probably react with suspicion that you're covering up something that could be a problem for him. If you keep harping on alleged benefits when substantive questions are raised, rather than dealing with those questions, you'll also wind up arousing suspicion.

Don't Apologize for What You're Asking For or See As Possible. It's just common sense. You want wholehearted support and participation from the other side, so you've got to show your own wholehearted conviction. Start with an "I hate to ask you to do this" attitude and you'll immediately communicate to the other side that there's something uncomfortable or disadvantageous about what you're asking for. You'll have started with a signal that you expect a negative response, and you may very well get it.

Own Up to Your Own Responsibilities; Don't Pass the Buck to Someone Else. It's simply a point in maintaining credibility. If your tack in discussing any problem you have is always to lay the blame for it entirely on someone else, your opposite is going to question both your sense of judgment and your ultimate preparedness to share risks in whatever venture you want him to join in. Although many people find it hard to admit their errors in judgment—the logic being that if you indicate a past weakness, your opposite won't feel able to rely on you in a case of future need—the more common reaction is actually enhanced credibility. Of course, in admitting error you ought also to indicate clearly that you've learned to avoid making the same mistake again.

Exercise Self-Control When You Get Impatient. Lose your temper and the predictable reaction will be a defensive one that sets you back even further. When an unrealistic (to you) amount of time is devoted to a point of issue you feel has already been covered, try a combination of recapping and positive motivation: "We've seen [agreed] that . . . and the advantage that provides you is . . ." Don't come out with an exasperated remark like "I can't understand why you people are so hung up on . . . !" You'll only prompt a flood of defensive reasons, the recitation of which will leave you dealing with more negativity than the obstacle that initially frustrated you.

Avoid Rudeness and Arrogance. So basic a point it shouldn't require explanation, but still so much of a regular problem, particularly when parties view each other in an adversary context (as happens all too frequently in contract disputes between labor and management), that the rule bears repeating. And avoid the gaffes that can trip you up if you don't keep the other side's sense of dignity in mind. If you're a man, for example, don't condescendingly call a woman opposite "Sweetie."

Cultivate an Attitude of Honesty. You don't have to turn all your cards over before the game even starts, revealing all on your side. You do have to avoid deliberately misleading your opposite on points of issue that affect his anticipation of advantage in coming to agreement with you. A liar may be persuasive in manipulation of facts, but the persuasiveness lasts only until the lie is found out. Then it's irretrievably lost. And an agreement that is built on misrepresentation is one established on the very shakiest of ground.

Don't Underestimate the Other Side's Intelligence. They may know something you don't know. There may be an element in their perspective that can actually be made to work to your advantage.

Even if neither of these considerations is operative, it's almost impossible to mask an attitude of condescension successfully. If your words don't give you away, your intonation or body language will. Ultimately your attitude says, "I know what's best for you better than you do," and hardly anyone will go for that.

Avoid Maneuvering Your Opposite into a Corner So That You Can Spring a Trap on Him. Springing a trap may get you a response you're angling for, but it will also destroy whatever trust you've built up. Trust is fundamental. An agreement reached through trickery will last only as long as it takes the other side to maneuver out of it. There won't be the sense of commitment that ensures your getting the cooperation you want.

Persuasion in a Group Context

It's easier to persuade one person than two or more at the same time. With more than one, there's a diversity of egos to contend with.

Besides that, a group often includes at least one person who has staked out a role for himself as a sales-resistant Doubting Thomas. His ego finds satisfaction in blocking agreement. His harping on negatives can extend sessions seemingly forever and hold the focus of fellow team members on those rather than on positive results to flow from agreement.

In a group context, observe who responds positively to elements of your presentation and who assumes the position of resistance. Then work your persuasive abilities so as to get those who respond positively to deal with the Doubting Thomas. Use the tactic we call "The Persuader's Helper" to maneuver around him. To the extent possible, turn over the task of convincing those who are unsure or wary of the alleged benefits of an agreement to whichever person on the other side shows himself most favorably included.

You can do this fairly easily. Suppose the team facing you includes (doubting) Tom Jones and (more open) Cynthia Smythe. As just the wrong moment (for you), Jones pipes up with an objection: There's no sure way to control costs. Smythe has appeared more open on that score all along, at one point even remarking offhandedly that their cost-accounting procedures have proven very effective for anticipating problems in cost-control areas. Rather than taking on Jones directly, get Smythe to deal with his objection: "Of course that's a legitimate concern, but I recall Ms. Smythe remarking that your cost-accounting procedures could prove helpful as a control there. Ms. Smythe, could you outline for us what safeguards are built into those?" Ms. Smythe becomes the Persuader's Helper here.

Again, beware of relying too heavily on facts and reasonableness. By themselves, they are rarely the key to carrying the day. You have to tune into the emotional context of the situation, too. Equally important, you have to give evidence of your own emotional conviction in suggesting a course of action. You've probably had occasion to laugh at a remark like "Don't confuse me with facts; just tell me what I want to hear." It comes right back to our initial point: the key to persuasion is to tie in what you want with what the other side wants or needs. That will always include at least some emotional element.

Persuasion is the negotiators' primary tool for getting what they want. Master it in all its many subtleties and you'll not only find negotiations going your way more readily, but you'll find yourself interacting more easily with another party who's become convinced it's also going his way.

THE ART OF LISTENING

Too many negotiators are poor listeners. About 70 percent of the time we observe them failing to pick up on opportunities presented by an opposing party for concluding a discussion of issues more quickly and/or more favorably. Instead of listening for clues indicating the direction to an advantage that can be gained, they stay wrapped up in their own part of the discussions.

Hank Calero uses videotapes to train business negotiators. When workshop/seminar sessions are replayed, their preoccupation with just their side of the issue(s) is painfully evident even to them. Once the pressure to perform is off, they catch much of what they previously missed. Suddenly it's clear what ordinary, attentive listening could have accomplished.

People are taught to speak, read, and write properly; they aren't taught how to listen. For the most part, that's something they're expected to pick up by themselves. Fortunately, many do. Unfortunately, just as many don't.

In negotiation you get others to share and support positions you hold on any issue by talking them into it. In order to make a convincing case, you have to ascertain what they consider desirable gain, so that you can make use of that knowledge. You won't discover that by continual talking; you have to shut up and listen, too.

Points to Remember

The Person Speaking Is Not Necessarily the Person in Control. Very often that person is on the defensive, explaining and justifying a position, trying—sometimes desperately—to convince the other side of the benefit of accepting a particular position. The other side, playing the silent role, should listen attentively for where the presentation or argument is unsound, illogical, impractical, impossible, irrelevant, etc. That's important for keeping control of the situation; it's important for winning whatever benefit may be presented by the person doing the talking. Because it's so important, listeners must also beware of jumping to a premature conclusion that they have heard all the evidence required for an accurate evaluation of the situation. That, in fact, is a characteristic fault of the poor listener.

Listening Is a Bilateral Process. It's not just a matter of remembering that each side must have its turn to present its viewpoint while the other side listens. There's a step beyond this that many negotiators fail to take: learning to *listen while talking.* That can be very difficult for people who rely on rehearsed presentations: they're so concerned not to blow their lines that they don't keep an ear tuned for telltale reactions to what they're saying. A murmur of approval, a groan of incredulity, a sigh of relief, a mutter of disagreement can all provide clues on how to follow up on a point important to you. You will also more quickly be aware of whether your opposite is really listening to you. It won't matter how brilliantly articulate you are if he's not.

Listening Is More than Just Hearing. It Includes Watching. Awareness of others' reactions depends in part on learning to coordinate eyes and ears. Comprehension is easier when you face those addressing you, or vice versa. It's easier because you can observe body language cues at the same time you hear what's being said. At times, in the absence of a vocalized response to something you may be saying, your eyes become your primary listening tools.

As for the spoken language, there's more involved than just understanding the meaning of the words used. You must also *listen for the expression of feeling* behind those words. It helps to ask yourself at times, "What is the speaker feeling?" rather than thinking only in terms of what is being said. This is important whether you're on the receiving end of things or making the presentation and trying to monitor reactions to that. When someone else speaks, inflection can sometimes tell you as much as the words used. Pace of speech can also carry an important message. (But avoid jumping to premature conclusions about what a particular speaking style means with any one person. The range of speech patterns among people is great. What may indicate uncertainty or insecurity in one speaker, for example, may indicate only a process of thinking out loud with another.)

Learn to *listen for content or central theme.* It's easy to feel inundated by a flood of facts—details of costs, recitations of technical specifics, even introduction of tangential issues. Keep a note pad handy for jotting down themes as they're presented. It's an easy, effective listening aid that can save you from drowning in a sea of secondary facts or empty rhetoric.

In line with listening for content, *listen with an open mind*. It's natural to carry expectations or prejudices with you into a negotiation. The problem is that frequently you wind up hearing—even listening for—just those points in the other side's presentation that confirm a prejudice or appear to substantiate an expectation you hold.

When two parties with sharp differences come together, it's almost inevitable that each side will at first respond primarily to areas of disagreement with the other. Because of the focus on those—after all, each is expecting the other to be difficult, obstinate, unrealistic, obnoxious, etc.—they are too likely to overlook or ignore areas of possible agreement. You can bet this is the exact situation when one side responds to another's statement of position with "I (We) totally disagree with you on everything you've just said!" It's probable, of course, that there will at times be differences which prove difficult to reconcile, but unless each side listens for an indication of some common ground, they're going to have a hard time reaching that common ground.

Hank Calero recalls a negotiation in which a spokesman for one side was so suspicious of and hostile to the other side that eventual agreement seemed out of the question. There were snorts of skepticism and numerous negative interjections. Finally came the moment when even those could not adequately express his rage. He yelled out to the chief spokesperson on the other side, "You stupid ass!" The man thus verbally assaulted looked back with a disarming smile and quipped, "Now that we finally agree on something, let's see what else we can agree on." A wave of laughter from both sides broke the tension. The unexpected riposte successfully jolted the heretofore hostile negotiator into focusing on possibilities for agreement, which had existed all the time.

Listening Impediments to Override

In his excellent communications guide, *Getting Through to People,* Jesse Nirenberg outlines five human characteristics that impede communication between people. These particularly come into play when diverse viewpoints are being presented. In each case, the problems arise because some block has been set up against hearing what the other party has to say, i.e., because of faulty listening.

1. Resistance to Change. Except on rare occasions, humans resist change. There's the uncertainty of the unknown, the possibly uncomfortable break with routine. When presented with either the threat of or opportunity for change, the common first reaction is to be only selectively attentive to what is said. People tend to listen first for what confirms their view of the way things are or should be.

It's naively optimistic to enter into a negotiation aimed at resolution of substantial differences with the expectation that a clear presentation of your viewpoint is going to result in a rapid conversion of the other party. Your slant on the issues may ultimately carry the day, but first your opposite has to accept the possibility that change can be for the better. Before you can convince him of your "better" way, he has to be convinced there *can* be a better way. You have to get him to open up to an acceptance of possible change.

On the other hand you may be the one hard to convince that your stand on the issues isn't the only correct one. That is your resistance to change. Try to listen with a mind already primed for the possibility of change. You will hear things that otherwise your mind screens out simply because of your human preference for the familiar. Remember too that you can be open to the *possibility* of change without immediately committing yourself to it. We're talking about developing an attitude here, not about adopting change for the sake of change.

2. The Tendency to Think One's Own Thoughts Instead of Listening. An example of this can be found in a circumstance as mundane as the making of introductions. Many of us are so busy evaluating new social or business acquaintances when first introduced that we don't really listen for their names. We're busy sizing them up, making judgments based on our assessment of how they look, sound, dress, etc. Even the most elementary information goes right past us—an hour later we're embarrassed to realize we can't recall the person's name, although we may very well be able to describe in detail what we liked or didn't like about the way he or she looked.

Monitor yourself sometime. You may be chagrined to find how

often you can't recollect the last point of substance made in an oppo-site's presentation. Perhaps, at the time it was made, you were reflect-ing on an incidental detail or mannerism that caught your attention, or thinking only of what you planned to say next. Or you may have been "absent" altogether, dwelling instead on some personal matter that came to mind.

3. Wishful Hearing. People are all too apt to hear what they want to hear rather than what is actually being said. The consequent prob-lems are obvious: disagreement and argument later about what was said. Stay attentive to the fact that another viewpoint is being pre-sented, rather than holding your focus just on your own. You'll pick up on important points you'd otherwise miss or possibly consider a reflection of what you yourself think and feel when something else entirely was intended.

4. Making Unwarranted Assumptions. An unwarranted assumption is thinking something is so when it isn't. Listening to what another party is saying while holding onto an unwarranted assumption that colors interpretation of what you're hearing can be a prelude to disaster.

5. Habitual Secretiveness. It's common for people to want to know or influence others' business without letting those others know any-thing about their own business. In negotiation, participants often give in to the temptation to push for commitment from the other party without providing information necessary for making that commitment.

There is a delicate balance to be achieved here, of course. You may not want to play your hand prematurely; it may be important to retain confidentiality on some point. But beware of simply trying to get something for nothing. The other side will be listening for infor-mation that can help them come to a conclusion on the point at issue. If you are too coy with information from your side, you are apt to find before long that the other party has stopped listening. When that happens, the movement toward agreement stops as well. Listen for indications that your opposite needs more input from you at crucial points.

Tips for Better Listening

Listening is 50 percent of negotiating. Any negotiator who focuses energies primarily on speaking and making articulate presentations is doomed to be only half effective, if that. Always keep in mind the general points of emphasis given above; in addition, here are a few easy, practical tips that will very quickly improve your listening ability.

Take Notes. This keeps you on track of what is being said and how points follow and tie in with each other. Use key words and phrases, word maps, or any other system that works for you.

Repeat Key Words or Phrases Mentally. This can be especially helpful if you're faced with a speaker who seems glib; it can also help with a slow speaker. Unless you actively search out and repeat the key concepts such speakers articulate, you may jump to the conclusion they really have nothing to say. That can be true, but you may be surprised at how often it's not.

Minimize Distractions. This means distractions of all kinds: phone calls, interruptions, things that catch the eye (aquariums, scenic vistas, etc.). Good listening requires concentrating on the interaction at hand.

Maintain a Comfortable Eye Contact. In his book *The Psychology of Interpersonal Behavior*, British psychologist Michael Argyle emphasizes the degree to which eye contact facilitates comprehension of what another is saying. We've observed that ourselves. Argyle also points out that eye contact can introduce a note of embarrassment or discomfiture, especially when one party glares at the other with evident hostility. It can happen as well when one party gazes with open adulation at the other during a presentation. "Comfortable eye contact" is the key consideration.

Argyle additionally observes that people who are listening tend to look at the speaker more than the speaker tends to look at them. A convincing speaker, however, does make regular eye contact with his audience. As a rule, eye contact drops off noticeably when a speaker is being untruthful or otherwise evasive.

In any negotiation, resolve to be a good listener as well as an articulate spokesman for your position. You will find yourself experiencing a greater sense of self-confidence throughout the discussions and are less likely to feel lost at any point. You'll not only comprehend issues and statements of position more readily, you'll tend to be more to the point when it's your turn to speak.

BUILDING TRUST

Trust is central to the negotiating process. Without it negotiation is just talk with little prospect of resolving issues: neither side will be prepared to commit to any course of action that depends on the other's cooperative participation. Only the belief by both sides that the negotiations are being carried on in good faith, and that an agreed-upon settlement will be honored can give real momentum to the discussion of issues.

It's more than the mere presence or absence of trust. Trust can exist in degrees. Trust can be built up painstakingly in the course of long bargaining sessions or be destroyed in a moment of ill-considered or deliberate negativity.

We usually judge the extent to which a party is trustworthy by observing various elements of behavior. Most of us do this instinctively throughout the course of any discussions, and many negotiators have remarkable intuition when it comes to deciding whether or not to trust others.

Contributory Factors

It's important to develop an awareness of what builds or diminishes trust if you want to avoid problems in that area. We've isolated significant contributing factors here to give you a better understanding of why you react as you do when others invite your trust. They will help provide insight into any difficulty you may be having getting others to trust you.

OPENNESS

Don't confuse openness with gregariousness. Don't equate it with that ingratiating manner so many salesmen have, being too quick to smile, to shake your hand, pat you on the back, and generally act outgoing and likeable. (The object, of course, is to get you to relax and be receptive—to think of them as friends who have only your best interests at heart.)

This kind of behavior sometimes complements openness, but of itself it doesn't constitute openness. You know when you've been played up to by some jovial type who really has no genuine concern for your interests. Somehow you can sense when the other person is simply manipulating you for his own self-serving ends.

Genuine openness is more than the projection of an attitude of eager friendliness. It is expressed in a desire to address all aspects of any difficulties that exist, as well as to respond to opportunities. It indicates a commitment to review issues from all perspectives and not to hide doubts or mixed feelings behind a false front of perpetual good cheer. Consequently, each side, recognizing the other as being "up front" in the course of discussions, feels more secure and has a clearer sense of place when it comes to evaluating progress or formulating alternatives for resolving difficulties.

HONESTY

"Ask a man if he's honest—if he says yes, you know he's a crook," Groucho Marx once quipped. You cannot get others to believe in your honesty by claiming to be honest. Honesty isn't simply verbal expression, it's a quality proven through conduct.

Honesty can be simply defined to mean fairness, straightforwardness, integrity, truthfulness, and sincerity and, above all, it absolutely precludes misrepresentation of fact (without, necessarily, telling all in an emotional rush of words.).

It's puzzling how difficult some people find it to be honest. Dishonesty makes things so much more complicated.

A dishonest person attempts to sell others a view that he himself does not hold. To be persuasive, he also has to demonstrate behavior consistent with this false view of things. And yet, because he necessarily has to deal with the facts of life as they are, he also has constantly to take those into account. He is always having to balance between falsehood and truth.

Some manage this balancing act better than others. Many, however, create so much or such complicated disparities between fiction and fact that the inconsistencies between them threaten constantly to become evident. When that happens, as so often it does, the result is loss of credibility at the very least.

Then there are those who, in working to cloud others' vision of the truth, manage to confuse themselves as well. By some process of transference they come to believe their own distortions, and in so doing complicate their own situation immensely. When such a person sits across the bargaining table from you, the inconsistencies that are evident or that you intuitively sense in his behavior make you suspicious. Not only do you not trust this person, you'd like if possible to avoid dealing with him altogether.

SELF-CONFIDENCE

The reaction to someone who's behaving with evident nervousness and uncertainty about what he's doing is hardly ever positive. How can you trust someone who doesn't seem to trust his own capability or authority? You don't know that he'll stay committed to any decision he's prevailed upon to make—he might suddenly conclude it wasn't the best decision for him after all. You don't feel assurance that his input is of a quality to influence decisions you're being asked to make.

It's not unusual to see some nervousness at the beginning of a negotiating encounter, particularly among those whose experience in bargaining is fairly limited. But usually the individual involved gradually adjusts to the situation; he begins to feel more at ease in the role he's playing. As this adjustment is perceived, others present feel reassured that they're dealing with a person who is in control of himself, who can therefore concentrate his best energies on the task at hand.

Self-confidence builds with experience. Initial nervousness displayed by a negotiator doesn't necessarily impede development of trust—as long as a sense of self-confidence emerges progressively— but starting out with a clear attitude of self-assurance contributes to a more immediate feeling of trust. After one of his seminar sessions several years ago, Hank Calero had someone come up to him saying, "I knew this was going to be a great seminar just by the way you walked into the room this morning. You looked so confident that I just sat back and relaxed."

POSITIVE PAST EXPERIENCE

A decision to trust is based considerably on past experience. You're almost certain to be disposed to trust someone you've had good experience with in the past. Even if major issues separate you, there's a conviction that you both will work energetically and sincerely to resolve them in a manner that takes everyone's interests into account. That's how it happened before. It makes sense to trust it can work out that way again.

Conversely, if the other person previously proved stubborn and obstructive toward you, that will have left its aftertaste. Now, even if the issues separating you are relatively minor, in all probability you'll enter into exchanges suspicious and distrustful of the person facing you. (Of course, it works both ways. What will the other side's experience of you have been?)

Positive past experience builds good will. The differences between a negotiation in which parties are dealing with each other for the first time and one where past association has resulted in a reservoir of good will is obvious. Where good will exists, it's easier all around. The incidence of game playing is less; the bargaining process more secure. Even a radical difference in negotiating style between the parties proves no obstacle to progress in resolution of issues.

RECEPTIVITY TO THE OTHER SIDE'S NEEDS

You've probably learned by now that you're not likely to get something you want from another unless you ask for it. You surely know the importance of convincing that person you *ought* to get what you want.

Which brings us back to the art of persuasion. People expect you to be articulate in expressing your wants. You may impress them with that, but you won't begin developing trust until you show yourself concerned with their wants as well. A receptive ear to statements of need on their side creates potential for generating trust.

However, you can take it a step farther. You can show yourself ready to consider needs that aren't directly stated. Sometimes you can do this simply by anticipating the other party's needs from what you know of their situation. But it often requires an additional something—an interpretive skill, learning to read between the lines. (For more specifics on this, see our discussion of meta-talk in Chapter Five.)

Negotiation alternates listening with talking—at least it should. You build trust by listening and responding in positive fashion to what your opponent says he wants and needs. You generate greater trust if your ears are sufficiently sharply tuned to catch references to needs that aren't immediately explicit. You're not expected to forgo achievement of goals on your own side to prove that you perceive and are receptive to those of your opposite. In fact, that kind of self-effacement is as likely to arouse suspicion or evoke contempt as win trust. But if you show yourself concerned to help the other party win their goals to the extent possible while working to achieve your own, you'll almost certainly find the process moves more easily for you.

COOPERATION

This can be viewed as a logical extension of receptivity to the other side's needs. After all, you can't very well be genuinely receptive if you don't mean to follow through with cooperative action. We cite cooperation as a separate factor to highlight it, not to suggest that there's some division that makes it possible to be receptive while holding off on cooperative action in a search for resolution of issues.

How do you get others to be more cooperative? *You* become more cooperative and watch to see what effect it has on the other party. It's only a slight variation on "To get understanding, prove understanding."

Perception of cooperation is often warped by perspective. This is one of the first things apparent in reviewing videotapes from Hank Calero's negotiating workshops. When asked how many of them feel they've been cooperative in a mock negotiation, the overwhelming majority of workshop participants inevitably respond with self-approval. When asked how many feel their opposites have been cooperative in the same session, the number drops dramatically. Generally speaking, less than 20 percent rate their opposite as cooperative.

Review of the videotaped sessions provides those who see themselves as cooperative with a valuable lesson. Relatively little cooperative behavior is evident in the filmed encounters. The participants have obviously concentrated on preserving and enhancing whatever advantage they held over the opposition, without thinking of the ultimate greater advantage to be gained through attacking issues jointly. The videotape betrays the self-delusion negotiators regularly fall victim to. There's generally less emphasis on coopera-tion than you might expect. Are you realistic in your assessment of how cooperative you are in a bargaining encounter?

CREDIBILITY

Every negotiator makes statements concerning priority interests, about what is or is not possible, about what his or her side will or will not do in a given circumstance. Although it's in the nature of negotia-tion to build a certain leeway into remarks reflecting a preferred position, in order for dialogue to be meaningful each side's state-ments must also be seen to reflect honest intent and the ability to follow through on that intent. If one's statements don't ring true, then those on the other side will naturally be skeptical or distrustful of proposals or promises made.

Credibility is, of course, closely tied to a perception of honesty. Someone who's seen as dishonest has no credibility. But it includes something more than honesty. Strange as it may seem, there are occasions when an honest negotiator lacks credibility. Through awkwardness in presentation, through an evident miscalculation of fact, because those for whom he or she speaks are seen as unlikely to prove supportive, the other side will not give full credence to remarks made. It can be as simple as an obvious discrepancy between stated good intentions and a perceived ability to follow through on them. A negotiator concerned to establish credibility has to present an honest face, but also has to do more. He or she has to project an *ability as well as a willingness* to live up to promises or commitments made.

POSITIVE MENTAL ATTITUDE

Some people consistently reflect a negative outlook on things, even when they're supposed to be working for positive achievement. Others, picking up on the vibrations, become vaguely uneasy. The fear develops that perhaps some negative factor pertaining to the issue at hand isn't being openly presented. Or the cynical outlook may be taken as a form of personal denigration, whether it actually is or not.

A negative outlook generates its own peculiar energy. An opposite party often doesn't know what's in the mind of a cynic, and yet will sense the negative energy. And that impedes development of trust. Consider: people go into a negotiation looking for positive gain. Negativity in the other side, from whatever source, just isn't consistent with that goal. How can you fully trust someone whose attitude doesn't jibe with the supposed aim of the endeavor in which he's involved?

CLEARLY EXPRESSED, ACCEPTABLE MOTIVES

We might use the word *honor* here, but that raises too many judgmental considerations. Then, too, there is always the possibility that parties seen to be without honor by others negotiate with trust among themselves. In that case the motives each has are compatible with and acceptable to those with whom they're dealing.

Leaving the question of collusion among criminals and terrorists aside, a sufficiently wide diversity in values exists in general society so that two respectable, law-abiding parties may still not concur with or concede to each other's motives. For example, one party's profit motive may be distasteful to another. There can be charitable motives as well as vindictive intentions that an opposite will not wish to endorse or share in pursuing.

What about hidden motives? One side knows the motives impelling it to act clash with preferences or principles on the other side. So it presents its case in terms of motives it knows the other side will readily endorse and cooperate in pursuing. This happens all too often in politics. Usually the underlying motive surfaces sooner or later. Trust evaporates.

ACCEPTANCE

The absence of acceptance implies that one thinks the other party somehow deficient, less worthy. If you think that of an opposite, you almost certainly won't rate his or her interests and priorities to be of as much import or concern as your own.

In a negotiation involving intermediaries (bargaining agents), there are two levels of acceptance to consider. At the first, the two sides face the question of mutual acceptance as parties equally involved in the same process. At the second, the interacting agents face that question. It happens frequently enough that two compatible parties who accept each other are represented by individuals with difficulty in this area. The problem of establishing trust between the individuals in this circumstance can stymie the development of good relations organizationally. And yet there may be no question of either individual's honesty.

Acceptance is recognized through an intuitive "knowing." An alert negotiator senses acceptance or the lack of it and trusts his or her instincts when it comes to that.

When we say "let go," we mean to let go of old habits, hangups, judgments, etc.

A career woman puzzled her friend of many years with her readiness to listen to advice and opinions from a business colleague who had once steered her very wrong. "Why do you listen to John so seriously?" she was asked. "That other time you listened to him nearly cost you a lot of money."

"Well," she replied, "to begin with, I have to take responsibility for my own decisions and actions. All he was doing was telling me the way he saw things. And after they turned out the way they did, he came up to me and said, 'Fran, I can see where I was taking the wrong approach to that situation. I'm still ready to provide suggestions on how some things might best be handled, but I want you to recognize that sometimes I may be wrong.' How can I not at least listen to a person who's got that kind of sense?"

Show yourself willing to be convinced there's a better way and ready to reevaluate your own position on issues and personalities. Others will be more likely to trust you. They won't see you as forever wed to your own view of things. They'll feel a greater potential empathy existing between you.

Humility is central to an ability to let go. By humility we mean a freedom from overbearing pride or arrogance; we don't mean to imply you should scrape and bow to your opposite. You don't have to defer to him or her at every turn. All you need do is recognize you're not perfect, that the other person's perspective on things merits as much consideration as your own and will sometimes prove superior in the context of dealing with a particular problem or opportunity. There's a bumper sticker that reads, "It's hard for me to be humble when I'm so great." That's the problem with some negotiators. Hold to the realization that no past record of success guarantees you're better than an opposite you're facing now.

FAITH

You could include this under "a positive mental attitude," but it bears separate mention as well. Here we're talking about faith in the negotiating process. "Negotiating in good faith" commonly describes the actions of parties with the demonstrated commitment to the process necessary for the development of trust on both sides.

Certain types of feeling and behavior are essential to the development and promotion of trust. Anything that works positively contributes to the potential for gain. At the same time, conscious attention to appropriate behavior for building trust reduces the danger that you'll wind up struggling to assert your interest in an adversary relationship. Pulling together in the same direction always makes for better results than pulling against each other because of lack of trust.

MAINTAINING GOOD WILL

Good will is an intangible quality, but it can lead to very tangible results. Present, it always facilitates exchanges between people. Lack of it invariably makes relations less comfortable, less smooth. Where business is involved, good will can provide a meaningful competitive advantage. One usually prefers to deal with a friendly, familiar face rather than with someone unknown. (You might see this as a positive side to the general human trait of resistance to change.)

Qualities of Good Will

As an intangible, good will is paradoxically strong and fragile at the same time. It has a tremendous positive effect where it exists. In many cases it can actually counter factors that could influence affairs in another direction. As long as the parties involved demonstrate mutual respect and a certain pleasure in relating to/working with each other, a sort of magnetic attraction exists between them. This creates an environment for preferential treatment, at least up to a point.

But good will can be destroyed in a few seconds. Any breach of trust can do it, since good will cannot exist where there is no trust. It can also be torpedoed by differences developing in the area of expectations either party has of the other. One of the fastest ways to torpedo good will is with remarks reflecting resentment at or suspicion of the way one's opposite is acting. The reaction is likely to be, "Well, if that's the way you feel about it . . ." The relationship may survive, but it will generally assume a different tone.

Good will has its limitations, too. It cannot override all other considerations. Practical realities do have to be taken into account. That's especially evident in business. A strong bond of good will may exist between two companies, but considerations pertaining to a competitive position vis-à-vis others may still lead to established links being deemphasized and alternate links outside the relationship being pursued. All else remaining equal, however, people would rather do business with someone they like who has provided good service previously than with someone unknown or less pleasant to deal with.

The fragility and limitations of good will do not preclude voicing disappointment or discussing difficulties that may arise between the two parties. In fact, such expression can often serve to strengthen the good will existing between them. The key is to introduce difficulties or disappointments in a manner that avoids recrimination. Every relationship requires its adjustments from time to time. If those are handled with an open, direct approach that demonstrates a continuing underlying mutual respect, adjustment need not disturb the overall quality of the relationship.

Regaining Good Will

Good will is a positive attitude. So long as the variables in a relationship are approached in a positive manner, there's little danger that it will evaporate, even if the variables include problems on one side or the other. It's negativity that proves destructive. Introducing a negative attitude where previously a positive attitude had been evident diminishes or destroys good will.

Whichever side allows negativity to intrude should take immediate remedial action once there's recognition that existent good will has been drawn into question.

Remedial action goes beyond a simple salvaging of an agreement or business order immediately at issue. An agreement or order is often fairly easy to salvage simply because both parties have already invested time and energy in it. Neither is going to be eager to start the process of getting to that point all over again with someone else. However, *salvaging an order or agreement when good will has been drawn into question does not automatically save the good-will relationship itself.* Next time the disillusioned party starts on a project from the ground up, the old enthusiasm to link up with the previously favored partner may be lacking.

It's important to address any threat to good will immediately. Immediate open acknowledgment of any misunderstanding usually works to promote a further flow of good will. Whatever offense was taken isn't given time to fester. The irritation is soothed before it turns into lingering resentment. The openness with which you deal with a problem that's arisen between you and an opposite adds to your credibility. The momentarily offended or disillusioned party goes away feeling more positive than ever, because evidence indicates you are alert to the specialness of the relationship and genuinely value it.

Good will is the strongest psychological supporting factor for achievement of a win-win resolution of whatever is at issue.

Good will has to be cultivated. There isn't a separate set of guidelines for achieving it. If you practice the art of persuasion effectively and pay attention to what's involved in building trust, you'll establish good will at the same time. Just don't ever take it for granted once it has been established.

AN ORGANIZED APPROACH TO PROBLEM SOLVING

A primary difficulty for many negotiators is that they're charged with a problem-solving mission but have no organized approach to problem situations. An organized approach to what you're doing is fundamental.

An outstanding book by Robert W. Olson, *The Art of Creative Thinking* (published by Barnes & Noble), presents a variety of methods for dealing with such difficulties.

We see particular value in Mr. Olson's DO-IT technique for successfully dealing with problem situations. DO-IT stands for DEFINE-OPEN-IDENTIFY-TRANSFORM. Each of these is a step in approaching problem situations so as to arrive at the best possible solution. They go directly to the heart of what is involved in problem solving—facilitating the marshalling of creative talents through organization of one's general line of approach to any situation requiring change. Most of us need aids of this sort for organizing our thought processes.

The plus in the DO-IT technique is that the steps outlined automatically pull you past your usual way of looking at things. That facilitates building *new* solutions to problem situations, as opposed to feeling limited to old, familiar solutions that aren't entirely satisfactory.

Here are the steps Mr. Olson sets out in telling us to DO-IT. (We've added some commentary of our own in each case.)

Define the Problem

Most of us spend too little time defining the problems we find ourselves grappling with—according to Mr. Olson, "usually only a few seconds." We don't consider a situation carefully enough to get a clear understanding of all the elements involved. Instead we are likely to seize on the first expression that appears to encompass the particulars facing us, and then decide that identifies the problem.

Take time to understand the actual nature of the problem you face. It will save having to deal with the effects of a poor solution later on. As Olson says, "Many of us come up with solutions in search of a problem. To most of us, it is easier to come up with solutions than it is to define a problem." Solutions that don't tie in directly with the real problem are as likely to complicate as simplify matters.

Olson sets out a three-part process for getting to the clearest possible definition of a problem.

1. MIND FOCUS

Inquire what's behind the problem you see. This may lead you to a broader statement of the problem or get you to an underlying problem behind the original problem. Then try to subdivide what you see as the problem into smaller problems. This may lead to a narrower interpretation or a more specific restatement. In either case, what you're doing is focusing your mind much as you do when you use a camera range finder—turning the lens first one way, then the other, to get as distinct a view as possible before snapping the picture—defining exactly what you're contending with.

2. MIND GRIP

Write down *at least* three very brief statements of the problem's effect on you. Then select the combination of words that best represents the precise difficulty you want to solve. For example, you may be short of money right now. Three possible statements of difficulty might be: "can't take on new expenses," "can't meet current obligations," "threat of loan foreclosure." Which of these states the most pressing situation existing as result of your problem?

3. MIND STRETCH

List the goals, objectives, and/or criteria you want the solution to the problem to satisfy. As you do so, think also of the obstacles that must be overcome in order for these to be met. This will indicate further dimensions of the problem that have to be faced in arriving at a suitable solution.

Once you've defined what your problem is and what its effect and dimensions are, move on to the next step.

Open Up to Ideas

Consider the possibility of a wide range of solutions. Delay judgment on any of these as practical and feasible (or impractical and unfeasible) until you've noted down all the solutions that may be available. Here again Olson suggests a three-part process to aid in the stimulation of ideas relating to a problem's solution.

1. MIND PROMPT

Ask other people with diverse backgrounds, knowledge, and intelligence for their view of solutions to the problem you've defined. Use their ideas to stimulate further ideas of your own.

2. MIND SURPRISE

List even ridiculous, laughable, and/or "impossible" ideas for solutions. Use these to trigger more reasonable, possibly usable solutions to your problem.

3. MIND FREE

Stimulate fresh ideas by forcing comparison of similarities between your problem and things that aren't necessarily logically related to your problem.

The point of each of these recommendations is to get you past a conventional approach to things to a way of looking at them from a new perspective. That's the key to creativity. It's important not to dismiss anything immediately. Allow yourself to fantasize about each solution. That will prompt you into making new connections, moving from the realization of your present position to the visualization of a variety of possible routes for escape.

Once you've laid out as wide as possible an array of solutions to be considered for possible adoption, move on to the next step.

Identify the Best Solution

Consider your resources, both in terms of material and time. Consider your ability to deal with the side effects that may be inherent in any solution. Be realistic about adjustments that will be required on your part.

Weigh your alternatives carefully. You will have opened yourself to the possibility of a variety of solutions to no avail if you then take the next step hurriedly and accept as the best solution the first one that appeals to you.

Why does a particular solution appeal to you? Because it seems to meet the problem you've identified head on, or because of those that are at all feasible it seems the least complicated? (Sometimes the least complicated will be the best choice, but the decision that it is should be made with awareness of what makes it preferable.)

Make a chart listing each of the solutions you've noted as possible. Then across the top enter in sequence the various considerations pertinent to the situation: time involved, cost involved, personal effort demanded, immediate effect, long-range effect, possible side effects, risks. This will give you a grid within which you can identify factors of import to you and rate each solution against all the others to arrive at a "score" indicating the solution that works best for you.

Of course, you have to weigh the various factors in terms of *your* abilities and priorities. If, for example, the solution must be operative within a stated time, you can quickly check off those that meet the time requirement. But don't immediately cross out those that don't meet the time requirement. First work out your total checklist of factors to be considered. It may be that a solution that doesn't meet the time requirement would be the best solution in every other respect. Stop to see if there's some way you can finesse the time factor so you can win the other advantages you want. In any event, this charting approach makes identification of the best solution a more organized, rational process than most people follow in this aspect of problem solving.

When you've identified the best solution for the problem facing you, the final step comes into play.

Transform Your Decision into Action

First break the solution into its component elements. Work out a schedule of implementation for these. Then accept and undertake whatever effort and expense (in time, energy, or money) is required to put your solution into effect. Be realistic. There will always be some effort and/or expense required; there will often be some element of risk. But if you've thoroughly reviewed all your alternatives, you will already have defined those factors and prepared yourself to face them once you've reached this stage.

A lot of people get hung up at the last stage of problem solving. They know that a problem exists, and they're prepared to devise possible solutions, even to pick out the best solution. But when it comes to committing a solution to action, they freeze. Those are the people who then have to deal continually with the frustrations occasioned both by the problems facing them and by their own fear and inability, or unwillingness, to move beyond those problems. They assume the role of victim, complaining of situations for which remedy can usually be found.

Negotiators cannot afford to take on the role of victim in this way. Implicit in the negotiating process is the readiness to search for solutions to problem situations. It's precisely because problem solving is so integral to negotiation that it's important for every negotiator to be organized and exhaustive in approaching problems.

The involvement of a second party further necessitates development of creative abilities. The goal, when faced with a problem that exists between two parties, is to fasten on a solution that meets needs expressed from *two* different perspectives. It is all the more important therefore to devise a means of going beyond the limitations of conventional approaches to dealing with a problem; otherwise you never get beyond the limits of your own perspective.

In addition to adopting the DO-IT technique for individual use, recognize its suitability for joint application at the bargaining table. It's important for the parties to define the issues between them as clearly as possible. It is to the advantage of both to be open to a consideration of as wide a range of solutions as possible.

Olson's DO-IT technique requires discipline and realism. You have to work at the technique in order for it to work for you; it doesn't get results by itself. You have to break old habit patterns first, and that's not always easy. But the results that can flow out of application of the technique will often spell success for you. So DO-IT.

PLANNING STRATEGY, APPLYING TACTICS

You may have expected a look at the basics of negotiation to lead off with a discussion of strategy and tactics. That's where most people think the primary focus belongs.

There's no question that strategy and tactics are basic elements in any negotiation, but we think they're often overemphasized. Somehow the impression develops that negotiation is nothing more than working a variety of ploys to maneuver an opposite into a desired commitment. More fundamental considerations are slighted in favor of a kind of "game" theory that concentrates attention on techniques for "playing" the opposition rather than on understanding the nature and psychology of the negotiation process itself. To us, that's putting the cart way before the horse. Until you understand the art of persuasion, the importance of listening, the essentials of building trust and maintaining good will, you can't negotiate effectively, no matter what your line of strategy or arsenal of tactics includes.

Distinguishing between Strategy and Tactics

When it comes to actually applying strategy and tactics another difficulty sometimes arises. Many negotiators confuse the two. And because of that confusion, often there's a missing link in the bargaining process. Someone who finds that a particular tactic isn't working may wind up changing a strategy that is sound. Someone following a line of strategy that doesn't work may wind up shifting tactics without really solving the problem of poor strategic planning.

The difference between strategy and tactics is really quite simple: *Strategy is the overall game plan* that one follows in a campaign for achievement of goals; *tactics are the specific maneuvers* used in pursuit of strategy. The tactics have to complement the strategy, but depending on the situation, you can use any of a number of tactics while pursuing the same strategy. You cannot have two strategies in effect at the same time, although you can develop a plan whereby a new strategy is substituted for one that seems not to be working. You can also devise a strategy that incorporates more than one guideline element, but the elements do have to be compatible.

Let's take a sample situation. You're an employer about to lose a valued employee. Standard corporate policy does not allow a salary review except on an annual basis. Your employee has a job offer from a competing firm and won't be eligible for review for another six months. You consider two strategies for dealing with the employee in an effort to keep him on the staff: (1) to convince him that his own long-range interests are best served by staying in your employ, or (2) to throw every possible obstacle in his way to discourge departure. Tactics under the first strategy could include playing on his sense of loyalty and security, tailoring his present job to "fit" him more comfortably, pointing to long-range financial opportunities in his present situation. Under the second strategy, tactics could include pointing out problems that would arise in the other company, a refusal to supply favorable business references, and/or a threat of legal action to preclude use of information obtained in your company to benefit your competitor.

The Importance of Cumulative Impact

In this situation (highly simplified), it's fairly clear that you'll create a difficulty for yourself if you want to follow the strategy that emphasizes the rewards for staying with your company but then go on to threaten a lawsuit if your employee does leave. That tactic is not consistent with your strategy. If you adopt the viewpoint that any maneuver that looks as though it could get you to the goal wanted is suitable to your situation, then you're in trouble. Each tactic has its own impact. The point of strategy is to obtain a cumulative effect, where each tactic's impact contributes to moving your opposite in a desired direction. If your tactics have the effect of combining a caress from one hand with a slap from the other, you'll find that one impact cancels out the other.

Whenever you go into a negotiation, devise a plan of approach—a strategy—for getting what you want. Then make sure that the individual steps you take—the tactics—work to build a cumulative impact in the direction you've decided will work best for you. If one tactic doesn't work, there's often a compatible one that will. Beware of employing a tactic that's not in line with the approach you've decided to follow—unless you're going to change strategy, which may be advisable in some circumstances. But then be certain your new strategy is carefully thought out and that your subsequent tactics work consistently to support it.

As for how to decide what strategy to pursue, recognize that as a question to be approached with the DO-IT technique. Define the situation facing you as clearly as possible. Open yourself to consideration of alternative approaches. Identify which best suits your needs. Then implement the line of strategy selected.

3
Developing a
Negotiating Personality

NEGOTIATION is a bilateral process. It's easy to focus on the difficulties that arise as a result of problems other people present. The fact is your involvement is half the process, so potentially you can present as much of a problem as the person facing you, and not only for him. It may very well be that you're creating problems for yourself.

Up to this point we've presented guidelines to help you in any circumstance where a faulty understanding of the general process or of its basic elements can lead to trouble. You can also lead yourself into difficulty by failing to realize how self-presentation contributes to or detracts from your bargaining power. Your personality is integral to the process. How you come across can win you advantage or disadvantage, and that may be completely unrelated to the issues at hand. To avoid or resolve problems related to your participation in the process, it's essential you recognize what aspects of your personality contribute to them and which contribute to achieving agreement.

THE TWO DIMENSIONS OF PERSONALITY

In negotiation, the more comfortably the spokesmen on each side interact with each other, the more likely it is that their energies will be devoted to achieving a win-win settlement. To the extent they are suspicious of or hostile toward each other, an added impediment to agreement exists. Personality conflicts only serve to contribute to the development of an adversary relationship that makes agreement difficult.

Establishing a comfortable personal working relationship as

negotiators for opposing sides doesn't mean deemphasizing issue priorities on either side. On the contrary. When mutual respect is firmly established, spokesmen can feel less inhibited about exploring differences. Discussions aren't so apt to lead to a defensive response that makes it hard to work through sensitive areas. Each side may actually find it easier to press its priorities if it is confident that the other side wants to understand those priorities and take sensitivities into account. The eventual move to compromise and accommodation works more smoothly. The personalities of the bargainers operate in a complementary fashion, eliminating the troublesome distraction of personal suspicions and dislikes.

For some it's virtual second nature to project what is commonly termed a winning personality (and nowhere is that term more appropriate than in a negotiation). Others find it very hard to do so.

The Internal Dimension: Self-Assurance

A major distinction between those with a natural winning personality and those who have difficulty in this area lies in the differences in attitude within oneself. Those with an easy ability to get along with others characteristically display a sense of being at ease with themselves. They are self-assured. Because they are self-assured, they are relaxed with others. They're not hard at work trying to cover up or compensate for insecurities that plague them. Being more relaxed makes them easier to be with, makes having to deal with them less of an ordeal from the very beginning (although there's always a period of adjustment) and eventually downright agreeable.

Nobody can make you self-assured. That's a quality you have to develop within yourself. However, following the next two points of advice can make that easier for you in the context of negotiation.

1. Always Do Your Homework. To begin with, make sure you know all the issues and priorities on your side. Work to come to an understanding of the rationale for objectives you're being asked to pursue. If you know the rationale as well as the stated objective, you may be able to achieve an underlying goal through adoption of an alternative course of action from that initially proposed. Second, familiarize yourself as much as possible with the issues between you and the other side. Develop a good overview of the general situation facing you. Then you won't feel nervous about being called on once bargaining starts. You'll be as informed as anyone there, short of knowing what the other side is thinking at any given moment. And there's a tool for learning *that* to some degree: asking questions.

2. Always Feel Free to Ask Questions. Prepare yourself as thoroughly as possible in advance for a bargaining session. But don't take that to mean you have to comprehend immediately every aspect of every issue or perspective you're hit with and should cover up any failure in that area.

Don't feel apologetic for asking to have something clarified for you. Questions pack a powerful one-two punch. First you benefit by obtaining information you need to help you in your deliberations. Then you benefit by reaping good will through the overt effort to understand someone else's situation. Everybody wants to be understood. We've seen instances where parties were unable to come to agreement because the differences of perspective on the issues were too extreme, and yet they left the bargaining table with a genuine good feeling for each other. Both were convinced the other side had at least done its best to understand them.

By applying these two points of advice, you'll be helping to provide yourself with a basis for self-assurance. Both offer useful information about what you're there to do. Remember that the worst mistakes in a negotiation are generally made by those who don't have a clear picture of the overall situation. Pretending to know something creates more potential headaches than acknowledging you need something clarified. By doing your homework and feeling free to ask questions at any time, you run much less risk of making a foolish mistake. And that contributes to your self-assurance.

THE IMPORTANCE OF SELF-ESTEEM

There is more to developing self-assurance—but it isn't a matter of simple technique, which the previous two points essentially are—the establishment of a solid sense of self-esteem. This isn't accomplished in some simple one-two-three sequence. It can come as a result of a moment's clear insight, or it can take a lifetime to develop. All we can do here is encourage you to realize that *you are as worthy as the next person.* With that attitude you'll be able to forgo defensiveness on occasions where you might otherwise fear coming under attack.

When others jab out at you in their irritation or frustration, you can respond with conciliatory patience, bearing up under any intimidation or disparagment from the other side. You can even turn it to your advantage with a disarming refusal to get defensive.

But you can't easily turn personality to your advantage if you don't have a positive attitude about yourself. Recognize your worthiness, whatever the situation that faces you. Recognize also the impossibility of perfection; you'll make an occasional mistake. Everybody does. But by keeping your eyes and ears open, by using your talents to pick up information rather than trying to prove how much you already know, you'll be able to catch most mistakes you do make.

The External Dimension

Sometimes you may not find your opposite as relaxed as you are. If his self-assurance doesn't match yours, seeing you acting calmly and purposefully in your pursuit of goals may initially unnerve him and heighten his sense of insecurity. His first reaction may be increased defensiveness. However, you can usually moderate defensiveness or suspicions fairly quickly.

COURTESY

Common courtesy is fundamental. Simply apply the Golden Rule—treat others the way you'd like them to treat you. Think about the basic decent conduct you hope to experience from anyone else.

Listen to What the Other Person Has to Say. Give him the chance to speak his piece; try to understand "where he's coming from." Don't cut him off before he's made his point. Give an indication that you're sensitive to the point being made, even if it happens that you're not in agreement with it or don't want to go into it at length. Doublecheck your understanding with a question or a paraphrase of what you think you heard. (It's surprising how often we hear something that's significantly different from what the other side thought it said.) The result can often be a valuable insight into perspectives on the other side of the bargaining table. And you'll increase the likelihood your opponent will listen to what *you* have to say.

Maintain an Attitude of Respect For Your Opposite at All Times. Exercise patience, even if you find yourself vexed at what you see as obstinacy or obtuseness. When you take exception to something said to you or about you, do so without projecting hostility or vindictiveness. It does not serve your interests to escalate an uncomfortable exchange into an extended series of acrimonious charges and countercharges. That only moves you farther away from agreement. Showing respect consistently for your opposite is the surest means to winning respect for yourself.

Does that mean you can't sound off or take exception to obstructions posed by the other side?

No, it doesn't. But there's a way to do so and still demonstrate basic personal respect. The key lies in attacking the situation rather than the person. Express your feelings in terms of the circumstance affecting you: "I find it discouraging to see no progress being made here." Avoid personalizing your frustration as in: "You people are deliberately complicating the issues here, without showing the least cooperative intent!" A personal attack prompts angry, defensive response that adds to the problems. "You people" are still those persons you have to continue to work with to solve your problems as best you can.

Honor Minor Courtesy Commitments You've Made. Be on time for meetings. Follow through any time you've promised some consideration, however insignificant that may be. People routinely make judgments about your credibility and trustworthiness on the basis of what may seem to you negligible points of behavior. Someone who experiences even a slight inconvenience as a result of your thoughtlessness may not be ready to risk the chance of major inconvenience in deferring to you elsewhere.

HONESTY

Honesty supplements common courtesy in winning personal respect from a negotiating opposite. Frankness simplifies things immeasurably in any communication situation.

Sometimes, though, frankness can provide a momentary discomfort. Speaking your mind can put someone on the spot. At times that's unavoidable. However, as long as you observe rules of courtesy, the damage will always be less than if you get into a personal attack in the process of expressing your feelings.

Have the good sense to *employ tact in exercising frankness.* Recognize that there are times when it's more politic to hold your tongue.

Too many negotiators justify an ill-timed negative remark with the excuse of exercising candor. Stifle the urge to frankness just to satisfy an impulse arising out of momentary irritation.

For those who fear a policy of honesty means "telling all," *honesty does not require that you disclose all information* you have at your disposal. What it does preclude is misrepresentation of facts you're presenting or deliberate misleading of the other side as to your intentions.

CONSIDERATION

Common courtesy and honesty are minimal requirements for prompting a favorable response to you as a fellow participant in the negotiating process. You can go a step farther to make the exchange with your opposite as comfortable as possible—*extend "extra" personal consideration.* Acknowledge personal likes and dislikes on your opposite's part.

This is especially easy and appropriate if you're hosting the negotiation. It can be as simple as keeping coffee and refreshments on hand, or providing a substitute for someone who doesn't drink coffee. If you're handling lunch reservations, take your opposite's preferences in cuisine into account. Play the role of host with evident pleasure and concern for your opposite's comfort and convenience. Do it gracefully and without fuss. Your intention is merely to put everyone at ease, not to bribe the other side into a concession on the issues.

If you don't have the advantage of being the host, you can still be alert to putting your opposite at ease. Maybe it's no more than a routine exchange of pleasantries, rather than remaining stony-faced and silent until actual bargaining begins. A little friendliness can go a long way. But keep it real—don't start slapping backs all around and playing up to your opposite with a false effusiveness. You'll gain no points for friendliness; you'll lose them for your phoniness.

Pay attention as well to indications of discomfort. If you observe that a nonsmoker facing you has been sitting downwind from cigar or cigarette smoke, take a moment to rearrange the seating.

Being considerate needn't affect your commitment to the priorities you're pushing in discussion of the issues. Don't concede a point at issue just so the other side will think you're a nice guy. That can backfire, anyway. The other side may see you as something of an insecure chump instead. Pursue your goals vigorously; weigh your concessions carefully. Be firm about what you're there to achieve. Once in a while interpersonal tensions will build as a result of your pursuing objectives tenaciously. In those moments, realize it's frustration with the situation that's giving rise to these.

Don't take expressions of frustration personally, reacting as if you've been judged unworthy. Maintain your positive approach in the area of personality. Things will get back on course much sooner than if you get defensive in return.

Your personality is the strongest asset you have in a negotiation, if you keep a focus on the positives. Develop your self-assurance. Be sensitive to the ego needs of those with whom you negotiate. It'll be easier to keep lines of communication open, and that's essential if you're to achieve your goals in the process.

THE ROLES TO PLAY

There's more involved in being a good negotiator than the development of just one talent. It may sound as though effective performance at the bargaining table requires only one thing, the ability to negotiate, but that's hardly a one-dimensional skill. By the time you've gone through the list of all that's involved, you've realized that the good negotiator is really a sort of composite personality.

To begin with, a negotiator has to be a *psychologist*, with an understanding of what turns people on and off. He has to be able to read others—through what they say *and* what they don't say, and through their body language. He has to be able to discern when they are exaggerating, hiding information, lying, and telling the truth. He has to recognize when someone is primed for agreement. He should be able to subtly influence behavior on the other side in a desired, positive direction.

He has to be something of an *intelligence agent*, collecting pieces of data and pulling them together into a coherent pattern. Conclusions must be drawn, frequently from bits of information that seem trivial. He has to pump the other side with great discretion for clues on which priorities are paramount and which are secondary. And he must continually probe for indications that strengthen the bargaining position he's in.

The negotiator has to develop skills as an *interrogator*. He should have an ability to elicit information of importance to the development of his case so that the person questioned isn't tipped off to how evidence is accumulating for later use. A negotiator should prove adept at asking tough questions without it appearing he's being hard-nosed in taking a position against the other side.

And that means he also has to be something of an *actor.* The really accomplished negotiator can play an assigned role so believably that his audience is convinced he's become the character he's playing. The danger lies in his getting so wrapped up in a specific role—as when playing "bad guy" in a team practicing the "good guy–bad guy" tactic—that he forgets to drop it at the appropriate moment.

Because negotiations so frequently hinge on interpretation of figures, a good negotiator often has to serve as something of an *accountant,* dealing with debits and credits, computing potential profits, uncovering hidden costs. He has to recognize when numbers make sense and when someone's fudging to make a bottom line seem better than it really is.

The negotiator often finds himself acting as a *personal confidant,* a party to confidences that must not be disclosed. In order to build and maintain the trust that is essential to negotiating success, he has to be as prepared to keep his mouth shut as he is to open it for pursuit of his own interests. He must learn to recognize when it's time to do which.

At times he acts as *educator,* teaching his opposite what objectives are possible of achievement, instructing in the means of achievement. On other occasions he becomes a *diplomat,* speaking tactfully to build bridges across differences that separate his side from the other. And frequently he uses his talents as a *humorist* to break a tension between parties.

A negotiator in action seems like half a dozen or so people inhabiting one body. It's not a case of psychotically split personality; it's just a good negotiator doing his job.

THE MATTER OF ATTITUDE

Attitude is an important part of personality, operating on two levels. The first is a general level of overall outlook or approach to challenges posed, not just in a negotiation, but in all areas. Effective negotiating behavior is very much tied to how you approach and handle *every* problem and opportunity life presents you. The second level at which attitude operates relates specifically to the negotiating process itself. Your frame of mind, as it relates to what you're doing throughout bargaining sessions, contributes an energy that can mean the difference between achieving goals or leaving an encounter empty-handed.

General Attitude

On the level of general attitude, we've found it useful to speak in terms of distinguishing winners from losers. A negotiator who instinctively takes what we call the winners' approach to situations as they arise primes himself for winning in bargaining encounters.

It's a matter of mind-set. If you sometimes find yourself wondering if you've developed the mind-set that makes for a winner instead of a loser, reflect on your attitudes in the following areas:

GETTING A BREAK

Losers are continually looking for a break. That's all they need. Once they get their break, everything else will fall into place. Winners know you can't sit back and wait for a break. You have to work for what you want, with a clear sense of direction established. If an opportunity comes along, you'll know from having this established sense of direction how to take advantage of it—how to build it into a break. The loser doesn't work to establish a sense of direction, he wants things mapped out for him. So he rarely recognizes an opportunity when it does arise. If he does sense that an opportunity exists, he's not organized to take advantage of it.

To the extent there are such things as breaks, they don't come packaged with simple directions to follow for success.

TAKING RESPONSIBILITY

Winners recognize their responsibility for their own actions and decisions. They learn to make adjustments in their own decisions and actions when situations become threatening or counter-productive. Their change provides energy for a change in the situation, often for the better. Losers look outside themselves for explanations of why things go wrong. Failure occurs because of an outside influence over which they have no control. Since they have no control, as far as they're concerned, they see no rationale for adjusting their own behavior to better effect. And they typically remain victims rather than serving as agents for change.

EXPECTING FORMULA SOLUTIONS TO PROBLEM SITUATIONS

Losers are convinced there's some fail-safe formula that can be developed to solve all problems. Winners know that the only way past a problem is to deal with it, not to apply some formula that will make it—and all others—go away. Winners recognize the inevitability of problems and learn to view each one as a unique opportunity for change as well as a difficulty to be surmounted. Losers view problems only as headaches and look for ready-made solutions they can take like aspirins. They keep trying to apply the same solution to different problems, missing the element of opportunity each problem presents.

CURIOSITY ABOUT THE UNKNOWN

Winners know they don't know everything about anything. They welcome new input and perspectives on what seem familiar situations. Losers find it threatening to be shown their areas of ignorance. Not knowing makes them feel insecure. Their resistance to admitting or learning what they don't know makes them inflexible, slow to acknowledge need for change, and slow to adapt to change.

No one is absolutely the master of his fate, able to surmount every problem and emerge unscathed from each setback. But look around you. You'll see that there are clear winners and losers in the game of life. There are those who live life as a stimulating growth experience and those who live out their existence as victims of forces always beyond their control. Your approach on this level intimately affects your chances of success as a negotiator. Winner or loser? Which you are is ultimately your choice.

The Situational Level

In the act of negotiation, there are attitudes related to the situation itself that are extremely influential. Failure to bring these into play creates problems in managing the situation to your satisfaction.

Some of the points that follow will seem self-evident. You may question why it strikes us as particularly helpful or important to list rules of elementary common sense to anyone involved in negotiation. The answer is that we find too many occasions in which elementary common sense is lacking, particularly when the parties come to think of each other as adversaries rather than potential partners. Feelings of urgency, a defensive concern not to be taken advantage of, awareness of inadequate preparation, a sense of discomfort discussing points of vital concern with strangers—all these and more can overshadow what should be common-sense realizations of how to behave most effectively in negotiation.

So here is a brief rundown of important attitudinal constants we think you should keep in mind when going into bargaining sessions.

POSITIVE EXPECTATIONS

Those who go into a negotiation with strongly positive expectations usually come out ahead in achievement of results. It's a matter of mind-set that proves itself in a wide range of circumstances: No one succeeds like the person who expects success and gears up to work for it. Focusing on ingrained doubts or fears tends to make one push less hard and to give in to discouragement or resistance more readily.

The strong conviction that a desired goal is achievable can result in a somewhat higher rate of impasse. The individual convinced that a goal is achievable finds it hard at times to step back even in the face of strong opposition. But the very positive mind-set involved also generally aids one in dealing with deadlocks. Sureness that there is a way out of impasse often leads to the way out.

Positive expectations are an outgrowth of high aspirations, a point often underemphasized among negotiators. Many undercut their own chance of success because they frequently do not start out asking for as much or attempting to get as much as they might. How often do negotiators settle for or make do with less than they might plausibly ask for? We cannot generalize for the negotiating population at large, but our findings suggest a possible overall pattern. In 73 percent of the occasions reviewed in Hank Calero's seminar workshops, the goal levels set at the outset of bargaining appear to have been too low.

The subject of high aspiration sometimes makes people nervous. There are those who assume that stating high goals at the outset of a negotiation is tantamount to obstructionism. By their reasoning, the more you insist on getting, the more extended the negotiation, the more obstacles to overcome before arriving at agreement. There's an element of truth to that, but there's also an acceptance of a premise not actually integral to high aspirations. We're talking about a readiness to *ask* for a particular objective, not advising intransigent insistence on achievement of whatever objective you start out asking for. We're telling you to ask for whatever it is you'd ideally like, not to avoid any compromise that may be required for getting an agreement that still serves your interests.

Unless you ask for what you want, you have virtually no chance of getting it. If you don't try for a goal you'd like to achieve, you are denying yourself the opportunity for its achievement. If you don't push with a positive sense of expectation when you do ask, it'll be easy to refuse you. If you ask, you may still get a "no," or you may find you have to qualify your goal in some fashion because you can't get a "yes" to the exact proposition forwarded. But you won't get even a qualified "yes" if you're too timid to express initial high aspiration and to push ahead expectantly.

ENTHUSIASM

The enthusiastic negotiator loves the challenge posed in any bargaining situation to attack a range of often disparate issues and work some sense of agreement out of all of them. He is a dedicated problem solver. He is aggressive.

Aggressive? Yes, but don't confuse that, as so commonly happens, with *hostile*. Here's how a psychologist at the University of Southern California draws the distinction: "An aggressive individual is goal-oriented and is usually a high achiever. He tends to cause things to happen and get things done. Whereas a hostile person normally is *not* getting things accomplished. That may be the root of his problem." The aggressive negotiator pushes ahead to a solution he visualizes. His push may be resisted on the other side if there is disagreement on the solution, but it is not aimed at injuring the other party. The hostile negotiator, on the other hand, is usually frustrated at an inability to reach goals unimpeded; his reaction is to lash out at the other side in a vindictive manner that is intended to injure.

Enthusiasm can be overdone if it is not balanced with a *sensitivity* to needs and goals on the other side. There are those negotiators who, in their eagerness to get moving, overlook consideration of the priorities that the other side may have. Instead they shove ahead with a one-sided promotion of their own priorities. That kind of pushing doesn't amount to persuasion, and it can arouse genuine resentment on the other side. Fortunately, most conscientious bargainers will catch themselves as soon as reaction from the other side makes it clear that issues must be reviewed from both perspectives. But sometimes damage can result from just those few moments of over-exuberance, particularly if delicate issues arousing strong feelings on either side are involved.

It is sometimes easier to generate the vital enthusiasm needed to maximize chances for success in a team context than when negotiating on a one-to-one basis. Each member reinforces and gets reinforcement from the others. It's a sort of synergy, where the total effect is greater than the mere sum of the individual inputs. Providing your own movitation and keeping yourself in high gear can be more difficult. There's no one to huddle with you when you get discouraged; you have to rally completely on your own. However, if you have that innate enthusiastic, aggressive drive that marks top negotiators, your faith in the negotiating process as the best means of resolving problems will likely carry you through.

A RELAXED FRAME OF MIND

The best negotiators are usually the most relaxed in a bargaining situation, avoiding formality as much as possible. They react with a seeming casual spontaneity to questions that arise in connection with the issues under discussion, thereby minimizing chances that any particular question is seen as one they hadn't thought of or considered when deciding on a desirable course of action.

They do not brush off important points the other party brings up for consideration. They carefully prepare for discussions and take achievement of their objectives seriously. But they do these things with an attitude of friendly ease with those facing them. They are not thin-skinned under criticism and have a well-developed sense of timing for good-natured humor. Their approach is that of friends meeting to share in opportunities for every possible mutual benefit. This approach repeatedly proves the most effective for motivating a second party to be cooperative.

PERSISTENCE

The most successful negotiators are those who stick to opening position or demands tenaciously. They stress the importance of what they seek to achieve and do not concede issues until evidence is overwhelming that they cannot win support for a position taken. They use all their powers of articulation to convince the other party that stated goals can and should be met, and marshal their persuasive abilities to achieve those goals. They do not admit defeat readily. Naturally, even as they stress and adhere to priorities set for themselves, they work hard to tie those in positively with needs on the other side.

Those who make concessions quickly without comprehensive discussion or lengthy efforts to achieve their initially stated objectives tend to defeat themselves in the negotiating process. The other side soon sees that simply playing a waiting game can elicit concessions. When circumstances are governed by constraining factors such as time and competition, readiness to make compromise concessions quickly can be important, but that readiness should then be operative on both sides.

Those who make large concessions all at once are often viewed as negotiating from weakness. Such concessions are seen as evidence that the conceding party is so frantic for agreement that further concessions can probably be achieved. Or they may prompt a doubt that the conceding party will stand behind commitments already formulated at the bargaining table, the concession being interpreted as admission of weakness. A restrained and measured approach to making compromise concessions is generally viewed as reflecting a position of strength and security.

ATTENTION TO DETAIL

Those skilled in marshalling facts and data to support or substantiate their statements of position have a head start when it comes to achieving their goals. But attention to detail doesn't stop there. Irrational and emotional factors are operative in every negotiation, and must be taken into account when motivating an opposite to agreement.

The greatest chance of success awaits those who can integrate details of fact with details of feeling. Even as they respond to emotional factors affecting the opposition, they refer back to aspects of objective reality that both sides must take into account. When their position on an issue is questioned or challenged, they're ready with pertinent supportive facts and/or figures, providing a background against which the other party can more readily understand their position and the importance of the objectives being pursued.

HUMOR

We tend to focus on negotiation as a Serious Matter aimed at the resolution of Serious Issues. Certainly the seriousness of a situation has to be faced up to, but even then a bit of humor can be appropriate and useful. Some experienced negotiators would amend that to "especially then." Humor works like nothing else to help keep or put things in manageable perspective. It can work to your advantage in several different ways.

As a Self-Teaching Device

There's hardly a more serviceable aid to orienting oneself to new patterns of behavior than humor. Here's an example of how humor can be used to help you remember what to do in a specific circumstance.

In preparing for the section in Chapter 6 on responding to threats, Bob Oskam asked a colleague what his reaction was when threatened. "Oh," he said, "I used to get rattled and usually started blustering back immediately without thinking. The net result, of course, was that things got more complicated for me, rather than less; I then had the impact of my own nonsense to deal with as well as the threat. I eventually learned that the best response for me initially is to FART." He laughed at Bob's expression of surprise. "F-A-R-T," he spelled out, "First Ask for a Repeat of the Threat. Once that popped into my head, I had no trouble keeping myself under control, and threats haven't seemed quite so ominous since."

As a Means of Holding Attention

Anytime someone speaks at length on an issue, however serious, there's a tendency for the listener's mind to wander. Winston Pendleton, in his book *How to Win Your Audience with Humor*, illustrates this in an anecdote he tells on himself:

"The other night after I had finished making a speech, I overheard a lady say to her husband, 'That certainly was an inspirational speech, wasn't it?' And her husband said, 'It was all right, but thirty minutes of rain would have done us a lot more good.'"

As a Way of Making a Point

When you want to zero in on something particularly important, try to manage it with an apt humorous comment; the point will usually be made more memorably. The trick, of course, is to use a maxim, quip, or anecdote that really does accomplish getting across what you intend to communicate. Otherwise you can wind up making an impact quite different from that you wanted to make.

Actress Cornelia Otis Skinner received wide acclaim for her performance in George Bernard Shaw's play *Candida*, and the playwright himself sent a congratulatory telegram stating, "Excellent. Greatest." The actress was so honored that she immediately wired back, "Undeserving such praise." Shaw humorously sent another cable reading, "I meant the play." Miss Skinner was annoyed. She retorted by wire, "So did I."

As a Way of Breaking Tension

Negotiating isn't equivalent to officiating at a solemn religious ceremony. The development of the skills and attitudes necessary for conducting a negotiation to best advantage doesn't require suppression of one's natural good humor or sense of spontaneity in relating to people. These, rather, are traits characteristic of the most effective negotiators we've encountered over the years. It gives them a genuine down-to-earth quality that encourages easy, flowing dialogue and fosters movement toward agreement. Much of the point behind Hank Calero's training seminars in negotiating is to get those attending out of the habitual authority roles they so often assume, with all their trappings of seriousness and self-importance, and pull them back to earth in dealing with other people. Good humor is a most valuable tool for accomplishing that.

It is difficult for some people to toss off just the right off-the-cuff remark or witty quip. We don't recommend that you go to great efforts to force yourself to be funny. Forced humor invariably falls flat.

Be alert to the fact that humor is a somewhat subjective phenomenon. Not everyone finds the same things funny. It's not so awful if you venture a remark or joke that others don't get or don't see as particularly rib-tickling even if they do get it. It can be awful if you say something that is in poor taste or denigrating of anyone, whether present at the bargaining table or not. Avoid ethnic slurs, no matter how cute you may think an expression of them. Don't go for off-color commentary in any circumstance where an opposite might be sensitive to or easily embarrassed by that. Don't make a joke at someone else's expense, even if that someone is on your side of the bargaining table. It can still leave an impression of your lack of sensitivity to others, among whom, of course, will be those facing you.

Be natural. Use humor to display your better nature, not your prejudices or lack of consideration. Humor is a powerful tool for positive effect, but like many power tools, using it the wrong way can injure the person attempting to handle it.

4

Mastering the Process

THE PROCESS of negotiation always keeps you jockeying for advantage to some extent. Most negotiators are aware of that. They realize that a great many problems that crop up during a negotiation are caused by either or both sides seeking to gain advantage. They know you can take all the basic considerations into account, polish your negotiator's personality, and still find yourself on the short end of the stick in a given situation. What they have difficulty with is identifying specific aspects of the situation that contribute to problems experienced. They're not fully tuned into the situational elements of psychology that have to be taken into account at every turn. They don't know how to isolate the particular factors influencing the course of affairs in given situations.

Mastering the process of negotiation requires blending fundamental considerations with a clear view of the specifics to be dealt with. You must pay attention to the unique combination of factors in each situation as well as understand the process on a general, more abstract level.

In this chapter and those that follow, we'll approach the process of negotiation from the perspective of what variables may be operative in specific situations. We'll always refer back to fundamentals in advising ways to avoid or work through problems that crop up. But now that we've primed you on the more general conceptual and attitudinal level, let's look at specifics you face in any encounter and consider how you can maximize your advantage in those.

THE INFLUENCE OF LOCATION

If you negotiate with any regularity, you know how broad the variety of bargaining sites can be. You also realize, no doubt, that different locations can affect your ability to concentrate on and achieve your objectives in an encounter with another person or group. But that realization is often a subliminal one with many who negotiate, so we think it useful to review common negotiation locations and their characteristics. Conscious awareness of advantages and disadvantages attached to various locations can aid considerably in planning specific encounters.

Offices and Conference Rooms

We normally associate negotiation with an office or conference room dominated by a large table, usually more or less rectangular, occasionally round or oval. A closed room holds everyone's focus on the process in progress. The four walls limit physical movement, and the table centers everyone's activity and attention. Facing each other, the participants work to agree on an agenda, then move to deal with the issues at hand. Or if it's a simple matter of two individuals meeting across a desk, there may be an immediate discussion of issues.

It all seems very straightforward and simple, assuming that both parties are disposed to negotiate with each other in good faith. But in truth the location and how it's used can have a perceptible influence on how matters develop. Certain considerations tend to provide one or the other side with certain psychological advantages.

Whose office or conference room is going to serve as site for the sessions? The host or home team will invariably have something of an advantage. They will be more at ease by virtue of being on more familiar territory. Then, too, the host party will have much readier access to support information and support personnel should either become necessary or prove useful. The opposite party will be just the slightest bit disoriented, not quite so at ease in that unfamiliar environment. And the distance from support services may prove quite disadvantageous should it happen that information not at hand is wanted to help carry a point. The host party also tends to control the schedule to some extent by deciding when to take breaks or adjourn sessions.

But there are other influential factors. The structure of the conference area can affect the tenor of the proceedings. The more formal the arrangement, the more the tendency to emphasize formalities. Rectangular tables separate sides and split groups more than round tables do. Where it's important to minimize real or seeming hierarchical distinctions, as when management negotiators conduct a grievance procedure, it's advisable to choose an informal seating arrangement. The parties' sense of ego, authority, and pride flourishes more readily in a more structured setting. And that gets in the way of promptly undertaking the resolution of points at issue. The free expression of creative ideas can be impeded if the setting suggests some kind of pecking order between or among the parties to the meeting.

Hotels and Motels

Wanting to avoid some of the difficulties noted above leads many who arrange group encounters to settle on hotel or motel sites so as to be in a neutral location. Or the choice may be only a question of escaping the interruption of telephone calls or other business matters. Some believe that being away from the office promotes concentration on the immediate details at hand because less intrusion is likely. In certain sales situations, the choice of a hotel meeting may be because one of the parties is temporarily using hotel space to display or demonstrate products or to make some other formal presentation requiring hotel services.

We've found hotels or motels particularly suitable when a multi-faceted formal presentation is important. When the presentation segment is concluded, the parties can either continue the meeting in the same location or move to another, depending on preference. Hotels are also well suited for preliminary discussions determining what the terms and conditions of later negotiating sessions will be, again providing a neutral ground where neither party can feel at an advantage in outlining its position.

Hotel sites are particularly suitable when there's need for discretion. There's less chance that uninvited personnel will complicate the proceedings. There's also less likelihood that someone's indiscretion in a home setting will prematurely alert news media or other third parties to an ongoing development.

On the negative side, when a hotel site has been picked for the sake of ensuring secrecy, those participating may feel a vague sense of discomfort. A clandestine atmosphere in which each person feels obliged to maintain silence as to the proceedings sometimes impedes openness within the proceedings themselves. A certain openness within the proceedings is a prerequisite for coming to any agreement that depends on compromise and concessions on either side.

Restaurants

Untold numbers of business deals are worked out while involved parties eat breakfast, lunch, or dinner together. The business lunch has become an American institution, with so noticeable an effect on restaurant income around the country that a howl goes up from restaurateurs whenever government threatens to set limits on how expenses for this kind of "entertainment" may be written off.

Discussing business over a restaurant table has its advantages and its disadvantages. Among the chief advantages is the informal and unstructured nature of the meeting. The mood is generally more convivial, the tempo of discussion less hurried. The sense of competition is muted, and the tendency toward defensiveness reduced on both sides. Look around you in any restaurant heavily patronized by a working business crowd. You will see individuals at other tables in conversations punctuated by a nodding of heads, indicating that some more open sense of agreement seems to prevail in this setting than is often the case in an office or conference room. We know of a businessman so impressed with this difference in moods that he intentionally schedules most of his important business negotiations over lunch or dinner. He reaches the important agreements in principle while eating, then hammers out the final details of the settlement later. He calls restaurants "the launching pad of business deals."

The greatest disadvantage to the use of restaurants is the amount of interruption and distraction that continually intrudes into conversations between the parties present. There are the waiter's questions and comments to deal with; there is the fact of a noise level that may require people at the same table to speak at a volume that is not comfortable for them. Tables may be so crowded together that privacy is compromised. Chance meetings with other people known to either party result in brief conversations that pull attention away from the discussion at hand. And there are the usual things that can adversely affect the enjoyment of eating out: poor service, uncomfortable seating, food that is of a poor or indifferent quality. Any one of these can hinder the development of the relaxed atmosphere you want to establish.

To minimize possible negatives in a restaurant setting, we suggest the following: First of all, select a restaurant where you know service is efficient and friendly, where you know the food to be carefully and well prepared, where you can be reasonably sure of comfortable seating and a general noise level that is easily tolerated. Reserve or ask for a table that is located away from the entranceway and away from the kitchen area. That way you minimize chances of being distracted each time someone enters or leaves, or each time that a waiter brushes by. Avoid looking around to make eye contact with other acquaintances who may chance to be in the same room. That will reduce the likelihood of interruption for unexpected casual conversation. You can also make arrangements to eat where a buffet luncheon is being served, thereby eliminating the need for dealing with the waiter for anything more than ordering cocktails or coffee.

Bars and Lounges

The advantages of conducting part or all of a negotiation in a bar or cocktail lounge are very similar to those cited for meeting in a restaurant. There are similar disadvantages—and then some.

The obvious difficulty one encounters in this setting is the unpredictability attached to mixing alcohol and business. For that reason alone we advise choice of some other site when undertaking important business meetings. (If you're engaged in an important personal negotiation, the same holds true.) But there may be occasions when you find yourself socializing over a drink with someone that you've been bargaining with earlier in the day. You may see this as an occasion to bring up points of interest informally, as you would over lunch or seated together in an automobile, away from the pressures and strictures of a formal conference environment.

If you can do this over *a drink,* you may find that the setting does work to your advantage; however, avoid the temptation to discuss issues over *drinks.* The possibility of an embarrassing slip of the tongue becomes too substantial. Even should you not commit any indiscretion in your conversation, you may arouse suspicion that you are covertly hoping to prompt your opponent into an indiscretion. That, of course, is a tactic employed by some, but it is one that falls into the category of dirty tricks. And a negotiator who comes to be known for or suspected of employing dirty tricks is one who loses credibility in future dealings.

Automobile or Aircraft

Sometimes parties to a negotiation travel together, often to where business meetings are scheduled to take place, or to a location ostensibly intended to provide some respite from the pressures of business. Some kind of conversation is inevitable, most likely discussion of either side's view of the situation in which they're involved together or in which they hope to be involved.

Although it isn't likely you will find yourself conducting entire negotiations while in transit from one place to another, it is wise to be alert to any opportunity that presents itself for developing a positive relationship with someone you hope to come to agreement with. Sharing travel facilities can provide the same kind of informality that makes restaurants so congenial to this process. You find yourself seated next to your opposite, rather than across from him or her. You do not feel the pressure of an agenda set to govern the pace of your meeting. You can sound each other out on points of mutual interest or difference without the inhibition of a feeling that some commitment is being demanded of either of you right now. And yet you are perfectly free to make a commitment where both of you are in clear agreement.

When the opposing parties consist of groups of people, each with some voice of influence in the structured negotiating sessions, travel sometimes presents a good opportunity for a sort of "divide and conquer" tactic. If one of your opposites has a decision-making capacity very much influenced by the advice or comments of a hard-liner on his side, the opportunity may arise to divide the groups as they travel to or from a meeting place. It may even be possible to shunt out the hard-liner temporarily.

A European businessman whose firm maintains extensive contacts with Eastern European and Soviet enterprises once confided that this was a common ploy used by his company. Visiting negotiating teams from the Communist countries commonly include a government security agent. Formal bargaining sessions are characterized by a sense of reserve and caution that impedes both the flow of information between the parties and movement to any mutual compromise. The Western European company has learned to make lunch or dinner arrangements at some distance from the formal negotiating site. When it is time to adjourn for lunch or dinner, the groups are splintered into mixed subgroups that can be accommodated in an automobile. Then en route to the restaurant, it is possible to exchange information and work out certain deals or agreements in principle between members of the two negotiating parties without the government agent able to observe or immediately influence the discussions.

Because of the privacy it affords, an automobile is more suited to furthering negotiations than are commercial vehicles or conveyances. When using the latter, distraction is created by others sharing the passenger space. There is also the chance that a third party who is not totally disinterested may overhear a conversation that is meant to be confidential. *Always be circumspect when discussing important business details in a public environment.*

Golf Links, Tennis Courts, Etc.

Many deals are concluded in the course of engaging in what looks like a wholly recreational activity. The shared enjoyment of a golf game or tennis match can facilitate an easy communication that leads to acknowledgment of shared interests along other lines. And the sense of pressure so common to a formal setting is relieved.

One of the major disadvantages is that both parties may become so involved in the competition of the game that other considerations are put aside altogether. On occasion, the players' competitive natures may be such that tensions build out of the game, rather than the game serving to moderate any that may have existed.

How Do You Choose Location?

There are probably as many different sites for negotiation as there are locations on earth where two people can meet to talk to each other.

Sometimes it's not so much a matter of planning a discussion of issues in a particular location as it is of discovering an unexpected opportunity for that wherever you happen to be. Keep a broad view of the possibilities in any setting you find yourself sharing with someone you have dealings with. Don't limit your view of the negotiating process to formally arranged encounters convened in preannounced locations and following some kind of preset schedule.

Of course, when it comes to arranging formal encounters, you do want to choose a setting that works to your advantage as much as possible. Making that choice amounts to weighing the practical and psychological advantages you want to maximize to the extent possible in that location. The easiest way to go about that is to draw up a checklist of considerations.

How Many People Will Be Involved in the Meetings? If it's a matter of a group of more than four or five, there are immediate limitations on what's practical.

What Is the Range of Suitable Meeting Places Available? Consider factors of convenience and expense from the perspective of both sides.

What Kind of Support Facilities Will Be Required? Consider access to telephones, availability of audiovisual aids, information resources, and the need to have support personnel close at hand, whether secretaries or experts.

What Is the Time Frame Within Which Discussions Must Be Concluded?

What Do You Know of the Other Side's Needs or Preferences in Respect of Location? It can be as simple as recognizing that someone else doesn't care for Chinese food, which rules out meeting for lunch at a Chinese restaurant. It can be as complicated as taking into account a whole range of factors, including taste preferences, expense, comfort, convenience, and requirements related to the presentation planned. As a rule, it's advisable to check all these out before making final any arrangement to meet.

Where Will *You* Feel Most Comfortable? Once you've taken the practicalities into consideration from the perspective of both sides, you may find that several alternatives are open to you. There's almost always some latitude for the host party in reaching a decision on location. As long as there is, and provided you don't overtly set up things to put the opposite party at immediate disadvantage (which can lead to resentment or annoyance you'd rather not have to deal with), you might as well pick the site that you feel most at ease in.

What Need For Discretion Is There? Would it be better to meet unobtrusively as far as any uninvolved personnel or third party goes?

Build in any other relevant consideration that affects your situation, and afford the other side some input if retaining their good will is at all important.

Whatever choice you make, the essential qualification is that the line of communication you want to establish or maintain be clear and unimpeded. Review what preconditions bring you together with the other side, so that any element of favor it's important for you to build or retain is taken into account. The location you arrange can affect the impression you make on others you hope to do business with or win favor from. Don't start off on the wrong foot with a poor choice of settings for your encounter.

When it's the other side that's charged with responsibility for making arrangements, review considerations that apply to you. Then use your influence with the other side to see that those are taken into account. Don't take it for granted that your needs or preferences will be evident or considered without a word from you.

WHO'S GOT THE POWER?

Negotiation inevitably involves calculating relative power positions. Depending on how things add up, we conclude we have more or less power than our opposite, or that things are balanced in this area. Then again, we may see power shifting kaleidoscopically, now appearing to be here in this form, now evident over there in another form.

Power affects how you pursue your objectives, but it can also play a part in your objectives themselves. Your aim may be to demonstrate that you have it, to win more of it for yourself, and to thwart or diminish the power you see existing on the other side. Thus the end of the negotiation isn't measured just by specifics relating to issues raised, it's also affected by where you feel you've ended up on the relative power index.

What Is It?

Power is a strange combination of the tangible with the intangible. In some ways you feel you can see it clearly, that you can measure it fairly accurately. Yet in other respects it remains a vague, shifting force. Who has it depends as much on who is *thought* to have it as it does on any calculable preponderance of assets or influence. Power is not a static quality. It builds, sometimes gradually, sometimes with amazing rapidity; it dissipates the same way. It shifts from one side to the other and back again, or it remains firmly in one camp, frustrating all efforts by the other side to prevail.

Power is an evaluation of relative position. The party that holds the upper hand is the party that has greater power. It has the ability to push its priorities over those of the other side, objections or resistance not withstanding. But power exists across a wide range of circumstances. It can be fragmented and usually is to at least some degree. In most negotiations each party holds something of an ascendant position in one area or other, with the power in one cancelling out or forced to give way to power exerted in another.

Where Does It Come From?

What are the common sources of power that negotiators draw on?

SUPERIOR MATERIAL RESOURCES

In our society this frequently translates into more money or greater assets expressed in terms of money value. We generally consider that the party with superior resources is the more powerful, but that's really only a rough rule of thumb. Also relevant is the extent to which resources are immediately available to be drawn on. It can happen that a party with superior material assets has them tied up in such fashion that they can't easily be employed to advantage in a present situation.

A GREATER WEIGHT OF AUTHORITY

In the social context in which two parties operate, one may be able to influence or prompt the imposition of legal or social sanctions more readily than the other. This is clearly the case where one party is an agency of government with a clear regulatory or other executive mandate. But even where two parties ostensibly play the same role and function as equals, one may be able to invoke authority more readily than the other. An example would be a computer software producer able to prevail against IBM through invocation of antitrust regulations designed to encourage competition in the marketplace. In that case, it can even happen that a much less powerful organization in terms of material resources still prevails because the advantage in this area more than offsets inequality on the material level.

A GREATER DEGREE OF SELF-SUFFICIENCY

It's simply a matter of being less dependent on, and hence vulnerable to, outside forces to maintain whatever position has been established.

INFLUENTIAL FRIENDS

In a very meaningful and real sense, one party may be able to wrap itself in a borrowed cloak of power. It is common practice everywhere for influential people to promote the interest of parties they favor. If you have friends in high places, that can provide you real advantage.

SUPERIOR KNOWLEDGE

"Who is forewarned is forearmed" is an old familiar maxim. The party who more fully understands the reality of a situation will be able to formulate more appropriate, directed response, thereby retaining control of the situation.

GREATER ADAPTABILITY

When things are in a state of flux, as they more often than not are, the party that can adapt most quickly to changes affecting vital interests has the power edge. In business this is generally a function of organizational flexibility, but it is also dependent on the availability of talent to handle change and transition smoothly. Look at the American automobile industry during the early eighties. It's pretty clear that failure to adapt to market changes has considerably weakened their power to meet challenges posed by competitors.

A LESSER SUSCEPTIBILITY TO TIME PRESSURES

On occasion the situation facing one party requires that a line of action be instituted and implemented within a limited time period, or priority interests will suffer. Factors that would cause any suffering may well exist completely apart from any influence the opposing party can muster. Just the same, if the opposition has the capacity to wait things out without suffering comparable loss, it has a power edge.

GREATER DETERMINATION TO PREVAIL

This is one of those intangibles that nevertheless has a demonstrable effect on power balance. A party with superior material resources, greater weight of authority, and superior knowledge may gain no power advantage if not prepared to work them to good effect. A party with more limited resources in these or other areas may, by virtue of greater determination, prove more powerful.

GREATER READINESS TO TAKE RISKS

Depending on the element of prudence and on a certain amount of good fortune, this can provide a power edge. In some negotiations it becomes evident that one side is much more cautious and tentative in its moves than the other. For all the superiority it may enjoy in what seem important power areas, it's afraid to risk losses there. And that can effectively diminish any ascendancy it holds over the other side.

Because power exists across such a broad spectrum of circumstances, the question of who's got the power often has no definitive answer. If it's clear that your situation depends on just one deciding factor, then you can probably establish who's got the power there. However, a creative negotiator works to balance power factors to the extent possible. Faced with an opponent with more substantial financial resources, for example, he'll make an effort to develop superior information resources, to prove more adaptable, to call in influential allies, to play time to his advantage, etc.

Power! Power! Who's got the power? If you can keep yourself from being cornered by the other side's ascendancy in any obvious area of superiority, you may very well discover *you've* got the power. The first step to achieving it is to recognize that other power sources exist than those that are most obvious.

COMMON MISCONCEPTIONS ABOUT NEGOTIATING STRENGTH

Closely related to a perception of who holds a power advantage in the circumstances leading up to negotiation is a recognition of what constitutes a strength as far as behavior in a negotiation is concerned. Who isn't convinced that being strong in dealing with an opposite party will lead to obtaining maximum advantage in a final agreement?

There are always those who find it difficult to be strong and are acutely aware of shortcomings in this respect. They realize that in a given encounter they have not been able to represent their side as well as they had hoped to. Chastened by this awareness, they resolve to learn from their mistakes and approach subsequent negotiations with a greater sense of alertness to pitfalls that previously tripped them up. They're determined that in subsequent bargaining sessions they will be strong. (Of course, some, fearing repetition of the same experience of failure, will actually avoid future involvement in negotiation to the extent possible.)

Others go into a negotiation with an initial conviction of strength that they manage to retain through the entire process, but somehow agreement still eludes them or proves problematic. These individuals are frequently less successful in the long run than those who become aware of weaknesses that handicap them. This is because their sense of strength is based on misperception. Although they think themselves in masterful control of the situation, they really stand in their own way when it comes to getting results. They mistakenly interpret a particular attitude or tactic as reflecting strength. In their case the admonition "Be strong" reinforces what are actually poor negotiating practices.

There are four basic misconceptions relative to being strong that trip people up in specific negotiating encounters.

Misconception No. 1

The strong negotiator is hard-nosed and uncompromising in pursuit of his goals.

This is an out-and-out fallacy. Negotiators who adopt this attitude are in reality likely to hinder their chances for success. They will be rigid, inflexible in their lack of readiness to explore alternatives that may appear to require concession or compromise. That increases the likelihood of impasse developing on any issue on which there are substantial differences; it also increases the difficulty in working through an impasse. Since their attention is so overwhelmingly focused on winning their own objectives, they are apt to be inattentive to needs that exist on the other side. Lacking sensitivity to the other side's needs, they prove limited in persuasive abilities. They can articulate what they want from you, but they are not sufficiently tuned into your wants to win your enthusiasm for giving it to them. Rather than motivating opposites by stressing the potential that exists for both sides to advance their priorities and self-interest through agreement, hard-nosers doggedly push ahead articulating and insisting only on their demands. Inevitably the other side comes to feel itself forced into an adversary position, as opposed to being enlisted as an ally in pursuit of common goals.

Always keep in mind that the genuinely strong negotiator, while firm in expression of his needs and committed to achievement of his objectives, is rarely inflexible or uncompromising. Some confusion is at times engendered by characterizing someone seen to be successful as hard-nosed. That is really a misreading of persistence. We advise persistence—that is, pushing with purpose and determination for what you want out of a negotiation. We do not advise stubborn resistance to change or an unyielding refusal to move to *any* compromise or consideration of alternatives whatsoever. Resisting intimidation and pushing hard for a *quid pro quo* in any area where concession or compromise is requested are signs of genuine strength. But a hard-nosed digging in of one's heels in a blanket refusal to consider the other side's priorities or proposals slams the door on opportunities that could be explored through dialogue. It's no sign of skill to bring the process of discussion to a dead halt.

Sometimes even the best bargainers will find further discussion futile. The demands from the other side at times allow no chance for meeting needs that exist on their side. In that event, they will balk at making concessions the other side is pushing for. After a certain point they may well move to discontinue the negotiation. How do you distinguish this situation from that of the hard-nosed, unyielding, poor negotiator? After all, here too we have people digging in their heels and refusing to compromise.

The distinction isn't one to be drawn only on the basis of how a negotiation is terminated, it's drawn on how the negotiation is conducted from beginning to end. When the behavior of the genuinely strong negotiator is viewed throughout the entire process, the distinction becomes clear even when circumstances are such that in the end demands from the other side cannot be accepted and contact is broken off. Before that point, a readiness to address serious attention to the needs and priorities on the other side will have been evident. The strong negotiator will have been accommodating and prepared to work out—or at least consider—possible compromise proposals. The strong negotiator will speak of "our needs" and "what we're aiming for" in a context clearly including the other party, not just in a one-sided fashion. When it actually comes to the point of breaking off a negotiation, the skillful bargainer will strive to do so in a manner that leaves the door open to a possible later resumption of dialogue. And in all this the negotiator will demonstrate an openness and flexibility resulting in the fullest possible discussion of the issues.

Uncompromisingly hard-nosed negotiators rarely get to a full discussion of issues because it is characteristic of them to want to consider issues from one viewpoint only. They often terminate bargaining sessions without leaving an opening for later resumption of discussions. They isolate themselves from the other side during the negotiation process and in the way they break off the process. They may do this with grand illusions of forcefulness and strength, but a look at the net result in terms of the relationship that continues with the other side will generally reveal them to be the poor negotiators they are.

Misconception No. 2

The strong negotiator is secretive and divulges an absolute minimum of information to the other side during bargaining sessions.

Negotiating workshop/seminar attendees reveal themselves somewhat schizophrenic on this point. In the questionnaires circulated among them over the years, Hank Calero has found 78 percent indicating disagreement with this statement. They say they don't view disclosure of information as a weakness, or secretiveness as a strength. But when observed during simulated negotiating situations, practice reveals that less than half this number—37 percent— disclose information they feel might prove at all useful to the other side. We've taken our cue from actual practice rather than from expressed opinion in coming to the conclusion that here is another common misconception when assessing negotiating strength.

Managing information effectively is where the real strength lies. Usually that involves a readiness to disclose some fact or policy decision that the other side may not be aware of but that can influence them in their deliberations relative to the negotiation. Hoarding information, like hoarding money, really contributes little to one's ultimate welfare. If its potential worth is in its utility as a medium of exchange, then its true value is not realized until it is put to use.

Those who manage information best generally follow a policy of incremental disclosure. They recognize the value of information as a medium of exchange and trade off pieces of it for information or concessions that have value to them. They may be thrifty with their information, but they don't practice a policy of secretiveness. They do recognize that information is negotiable only once, so they carefully avoid gut-spilling, where every bit of information that might be useful in trade-off is disclosed in one blurt.

In Hank's seminar workshops he uses the case study of a building contractor who can save $900,000 if the buyer for whom he is working will extend the scheduled completion date by three months. The three-month delay will enable the contractor to purchase foreign steel and substitute less expensive control and monitoring devices in the chemical plant that has been contracted for.

In fully 50 percent of the simulated negotiations on this issue, the individual playing the part of the contractor tries to get the completion date extended without passing any savings along to the buyer. Those who follow this strategy are on the whole much less successful than those who disclose that there is a saving to be achieved—even if they may not reveal the full amount of saving—and tie that saving to the delay. Most buyers are willing to consider delay when they're advised that potential savings they can share in are possible.

In this example, the best response comes when the contractor starts off with a remark to the effect that "There might be a possible saving we can realize." Then, as would any negotiator, the buyer asks, "How much?" or "Where?" The contractor explains, "Well, we think there might be a saving if we purchase foreign steel, but there would have to be a schedule extension to allow us time to take delivery." Further questions from the buyer lead to added particulars about the savings potential. In posing these questions, the buyer reveals elements of his basic position: whether a scheduled extension is likely to be granted if savings are deemed sufficient. The contractor may be able to stipulate a saving of "at least a couple of hundred thousand dollars" to be passed on to the buyer, or he may find a more complete accounting is demanded.

As you can see, in the hands of an experienced, skilled negotiator, incremental disclosure is a tactic of strength. Negotiators who opt for a policy of secretiveness are actually in a position of weakness by comparison. They deprive themselves of a tool that can be very effective for moving an opposite in a direction that could be to their advantage.

Misconception No. 3

In a negotiation, the person doing the talking is the person who is in control.

We observed the fallacy in this when we considered the importance of listening. Often the person doing most of the talking is *not* in control. Consider the various reasons that may impel someone to keep talking and talking in an effort to sway or impress an opponent.

MAKING EXPLANATIONS

A negotiator talks because he is in the process of explaining something to the other party. The explanation sometimes grows out of a question that's been asked, or it may be an attempt to clarify a position taken on a particular issue. However, often the explanation is defensive in nature, a torrent of verbiage that doesn't contribute much, if anything, to a better understanding of the perspective being defended. The listener is likely to lose interest rather than be swayed or impressed in any direction. He may get bored or just plain angry because his valuable time is being wasted by someone who has little to say but talks on and on anyway. The speaker keeps throwing out more words, hoping that the sheer weight of them will have some effect, that the impression of an explanation will emerge even if there's not much by way of genuine explanation contained in all that's said. An occasional, inexperienced negotiator on the other side may fall for this, but most will grow impatient and/or annoyed.

SALES EFFORTS

Another reason why a negotiator talks is to persuade or sell the other side. But too many negotiators are poor salesmen. They fail any proficiency test because of a tendency to overkill—to sell their idea/concept too hard, without giving the other party a chance to express and define interest. They are often not good closers and pass up golden opportunities to nail down a deal. By the time they've finally allowed themselves to listen for a response from the other side, much of the enthusiasm that may initially have existed will have dissipated.

Overselling impresses many as another kind of defensive maneuver. While you rant on and on and on, your potential buyer begins to suspect that maybe all the emphasis on positives is being projected to cover up a negative.

Also characteristic of the overselling negotiator is the tendency to be counter-oriented rather than opening-conscious. By this we mean they've psychologically prepared themselves to meet possible objections to their spiel to such extent that they stop listening for responses that indicate an opening presented for moving to conclusion of the deal. And in so doing they again demonstrate lack of control over the situation. Those who believe that the proper focus in negotiation is on countering obstacles posed by the other side implicitly establish a separation of interests as natural. Better to shut up before the other side starts to share that focus. Give your opposite a chance to explore the positives; listen so that you can tie your remarks in to those.

DEFENSIVE MANEUVERS

In many negotiations you may be challenged to defend a position you're taking, needs you're citing, or some practice you have put into effect. If previously you've appeared to be putting yourself on the defensive, your credibility will have diminished by the time you find you must offer a *genuine* defense of your perspective or position.

Negotiators who talk too much in explaining positions taken or in selling others on a perspective are likely to carry the same fault into responding to real challenges posed by the other side. They quote chapter and verse of every conceivable argument on why they should get, have, or be granted whatever it is they are asking for. In many instances, the flood of reasons, facts, and logic that pours forth contains a myriad of inconsistencies. The more they speak in their own defense, the less convincing they are. They often wind up sinking under a mass of contradictory statements that come back to haunt them later.

The strong negotiator, on the other hand, provides the most direct and succinct response to any challenge posed by the other side. There's no compulsion to overwhelm the opposition with a flood of self-justification.

VOICING CRITICISM

A great deal of talk also emanates from negotiators who take a critical stance at the bargaining table. They have swallowed the myth that critics are in control. Somehow a sense of superiority develops as they lay their garbage on the other party. Apparently they anticipate that the other side, squirming under the impact of comments calling into question their motives, conduct, or objectives, will "sue for peace" by moving to concede issues all the more readily.

But it doesn't often work out that way. In reality, critics often accomplish nothing more than irritating the other side. They undermine themselves by evoking resentment and resistance, which rarely motivates anyone into making compromises or concessions. Experience demonstrates that the tougher the tactics, the tougher the resistance. It's no demonstration of strength to prompt others into resisting consideration of your perspective and priorities.

ASKING QUESTIONS

Some negotiators show themselves out of control when they ask questions that have not been carefully thought out or prepared. Response to the questionnaires Hank submits routinely to his seminar attendees reveals that only about 30 percent ever take time to work on what questions to ask and how to ask them. Consequently, questions are frequently so poorly worded that they do not elicit clear answers suitable to the circumstances at hand.

Too often there's no thought to how questions can complement an overall bargaining strategy. For example, in a team context it can very often be useful to assign one individual primary responsibility for raising whatever questions need to be answered. This allows others on the team to develop alternate roles, as in the classic tough guy–nice guy combination that proves serviceable in many encounters. Where no consideration is given to constructive use of questions, they can work at cross purposes. At times essentially the same question is asked on separate occasions by two or more spokesmen on the same side. Weakness is then painfully evident to all involved.

Misconception No. 4

When a proposal or statement of position is followed by a period of silence, the person who breaks the silence loses. The strong negotiator, according to this view, has the last word, not the first.

Ridiculous! More often the person who knows how to break a silence first is the one able to hold the initiative. A prolonged period of silence, extended because of some fear that whoever speaks first will be revealed as less strong, is nonsense. Hank found this out through personal experience years ago. At one point in a negotiation, he found himself locked in a long period of silence. Finally his opposite took the initiative, and control, by saying, "I take your silence to mean you've just agreed with everything I've said." The man made the silence appear as an indication of acquiescence or agreement and showed no fear that in being the first to break the silence he would lose anything.

Unfortunately each of the misconceptions we've identified here continues to be operative. But it isn't a cold, hard-nosed attitude, secretiveness, outtalking the opposition, or an ability to wait anyone out that make a strong negotiator. It's the ability to get results. And that ability usually hinges on characteristics that hidebound, determinedly rigid bargainers find it difficult or even impossible to adopt as their own. They're afraid they'll lose their sense of control, and that very fear shows them up for the weak negotiators they really are.

MANEUVERING FOR ADVANTAGE: BLUFFING

Because in a negotiation you're always in some way angling or probing for advantage—as is whoever faces you—you'll resort to tactics you hope will provide an advantage. Of all these tactics, bluffing is probably the most difficult to master. It is a form of pretense, and its successful use depends on it not being recognized for what it is.

Bluffing takes two forms: In the first, you work to mislead an opposite by maintaining a false bold front in the face of a situation that potentially poses some difficulty for you. In the second, you attempt to move your opposite in a desired direction through implicit or explicit threat of some action that you are actually not in position to take.

Poker Bluffing

Bluffing in the first instance works very much like bluffing in poker, where players try to mislead other players by betting or raising the bet while holding relatively weak cards. It's a standard game tactic, and everyone indulges in it from time to time. There's no stigma attached to it *per se*. But there is always a risk of discovery, and the poor negotiator, like the bad poker player, is apt to lose more than he can really afford to.

The risk is actually greater for negotiators; they don't get the chance to recoup on the next deal of the game. Each side comes to the bargaining table with its hand dealt for playing the game, and that's the only hand it plays. Each side generally expects the other to engage in a certain amount of bravado, to maintain a facade composed of some pretense. Only if one side really has few or no genuine negotiating counters and gets caught pretending that it does, and depending on the attitude with which that pretense has been projected, is there likely to be an angry reaction and the danger of a complete break in the negotiations. Then again, if the exposed hand offers the other party *nothing* of interest, then that will probably cause a break-off, not outrage at the pretense. Otherwise the second party is likely just to play its own hand to clearer advantage.

Poker bluffing, as we'll call this first type, requires skill and judgment to carry off successfully, particularly if the bluffing negotiator is really in a bad bargaining position. Beware of getting caught too often in an attitude of pretense—that compromises your overall credibility seriously. Avoid appearing too obnoxious in trying to sustain a false bold front; if you get caught, things may backfire very unpleasantly.

Of course, the main thing is not to be caught at all. To be successful in carrying it off, your poker bluffing behavior must be believable. You must be sure that your verbal message is consistent and supported by appropriate body language. If you don't maintain a consistent stance, your evident wavering between bold self-assurance and any degree of hesitancy will give you away.

Threat Bluffing

Threat bluffing is a different matter altogether. Usually when we think of problems arising as result of bluffing, this is the type we have in mind. Poker bluffing is more or less routine, expected and accepted up to a point. It's not construed as malicious misrepresentation of the truth.

Threat bluffing is by its nature disturbing because it *does* involve articulation of a threat. It is an offensive maneuver, at its worst an open attempt to intimidate, always at least an attempt to play off the other party's fears that an opportunity for hoped-for gain is about to be lost. And because you're explicitly trying to play off the opposite party's areas of greatest sensitivity, you risk a much more volatile reaction.

Your Achilles heel is that you can't carry out the threat. If after issuing a threat to hit your opponent where it hurts it becomes evident that you really can't, the temptation to take a swipe back at you will be strong. No one likes being threatened.

But threat bluffing can sometimes provide a negotiator a tremendous psychological advantage at the bargaining table, so it will always remain a tactic negotiators consider when seeking that kind of advantage. When it works, it provides one of the quickest shortcuts available to getting one's way on an issue. When it fails, however, it may result in one's own position being seriously weakened or compromised, because a threat that backfires thrusts a wedge between the parties.

DECIDING WHEN TO RISK A THREAT BLUFF

If you decide to retain the tactic of threat bluffing as a weapon in your negotiating arsenal, you will do well to consider it in light of the following:

Is Your Objective Worth It? That's the first consideration. Is achieving it of such import that a bluff or two, with the risks entailed thereby, is worthwhile? If not, you're foolish to attempt the tactic. Then it's probably not your objective that motivates you, it's your pride or vanity.

What Will You Lose if Your Bluff Doesn't Work? Is the risk of loss here acceptable? With threat bluffing you stand to lose credibility, good will, trust, respect, etc., if your gambit is seen for what it is.

Is Your Timing Appropriate? Bluffing isn't something that works well on a spur-of-the-moment basis. You need to plan the timing in advance and work out execution in careful detail.

Is Your Behavior in Bluffing Consistent with Your General Behavior? Good bluffers aren't friendly one moment, then hostile the next. Issuance of a threat under any circumstances implies a previous build-up of strong feelings evident to the other side. If you decide to risk a threat bluff, be sure you've laid the appropriate groundwork: explicit expressions of strong disappointment, discouragement, disapproval, outrage, etc.

Is Your Bluff Maneuver Apt to be Recognized as a Standard Tactic? Some negotiators bluff so regularly that it's possible for the opposite side to recognize the *modus operandi* and anticipate issuance of a phony threat. Then the tactic has no effect whatever other than to make you look pompous and foolish. Threat bluffing is more effective for those who hold it in reserve for rare occasions, for those who are ordinarily seen as calm and reasoned in their approach to bargaining. The habitually blustery person will find the tactic doesn't work very well for him.

Will Your Bluff Assertions Stand Up to Scrutiny? Often enough the negotiator issuing a bluff threat backs it up with statistics or other facts that "prove" his hard-line contentions. If those facts and figures are obviously erroneous or in disarray, they won't serve the back-up function well if at all. And then the bluff itself is apt to be seen for what it is.

Is Your Body Language Consistent with Your Bluff Language? Your opponent will inevitably catch nonverbal clues to your behavior, so suppress the ones that might undermine you—nervous blinking of the eyes, clearing your throat before you utter the threat, swallowing hard, licking your lips before speaking, flushing, nervous perspiration, darting eyes instead of "gunfighter's concentration." Your gestures and posture have to indicate determination and an aggressive forcefulness if your threat is to be believable. You'd better be a good actor if you want to be credible.

Are You Prepared to Have Someone Call Your Bluff? If they do, don't back off right away. Probably the other side is just testing you to see if you are bluffing. Novice bluffers usually withdraw at once like kids caught with their hands in the cookie jar. Stick it out for at least a while if you're going to use the tactic. If you've chosen your threat with good forethought, your opponent should be very reluctant to risk the chance that you might not be bluffing.

We don't recommend threat bluffing for everyone—it's not a natural tactic for every negotiator. If you decide that you can use the tactic to good advantage at times, we strongly recommend you review your situation in light of the questions we've posed for you here.

RESPONDING TO OFFERS—ALTERNATIVES AVAILABLE

Because negotiation inherently implies a jockeying for position, you regularly find yourself faced with how to respond to an offer made to you. You don't have to opt for a tactic like bluffing when it comes to pursuing a route to advantage; you can't avoid making decisions on what to do when someone names a price, proposes a compromise, suggests a possible area of concession. You have to react.

What do you do when presented an offer along any of these lines? Do you take it or leave it? Will the answer that works most to your advantage be "yes" or "no"? If that's how you think in terms of responding to offers, you probably have considerable difficulty dealing with them, because you've limited your choices. The key to resolving difficulties in this area lies substantially in recognizing that you have a much wider range of options.

The ability to recognize and exercise these alternatives can make a positive difference in the chances you have to achieve your goals.

Conversely, failure to distinguish that there are many alternatives available can result in your missing an opportunity to carry an issue important to you.

What follows is a review of possible responses, some more obvious than others. Note that we recommend developing a habit of response that always includes taking the first two options in order. Even when it is a fairly simple matter of responding "yes" or "no," give yourself the opportunity to understand and possibly expand the offer made that these two steps provide.

The Two First Essentials

Listen to It. We've observed that a person making an offer or proposal often gets interrupted before completing what he intended to say. Instead of listening to find out what the complete offer is, the receiver has a tendency to jump in with what he has to say.

Hear the other party out. That is the essential first step in formulating the most appropriate response to any offer made. Before you do anything else, listen for all the details contained in the offer—the action proposed, the conditions set, the time frame that may be involved.

Repeat What Has Been Offered. Many people fail to take this second step. Instead of repeating the offer to be sure of a clear understanding of what it actually is, the average negotiator proceeds somewhat blindly, acting on what he or she *thinks* the offer is.

Take a moment to verify that what has been offered is actually what at first sound it seemed to be. You may find you haven't really understood it for what it is. There's also the possibility that you may elicit a restatement from the other side that clarifies or opens the offer up somewhat, giving you wider latitude for your answering response.

The Further Options Available

Accept What Is Offered. If you find the offer is precisely what you hoped for, then say "yes" to it. Let the other side know in no uncertain terms that whatever has been offered is acceptable and you feel no further discussion or negotiation is required on this point.

Reject What Is Offered. You find the offer is not acceptable and say so outright. Two things can happen here: (1) The negotiation on the issue at hand continues; (2) Things grind to a halt. Because of the danger of the latter you would do well to consider other possibilities before you give a precipitate "no" answer (assuming you want the negotiation to continue). You always have the freedom to say "no" in the event other alternatives do not result in the offer being made more palatable.

Question It. Ask questions about the offer made: "How did you arrive at that figure?" "Does that include the 10 percent discount?" "Is your offer subject to . . .?" You get the idea. Pull out as much detail as you can relating to terms of the offer. There may be something you've missed that's important for being secure in your gut reaction on a yes or no level, or the other side may introduce an element of modification that affects your perception of the situation.

Ignore It. In this case you simply do not respond to the offer, and make no subsequent reference to it. This is the "in one ear and out the other" gambit, and we've found many negotiators skillful in applying it to their advantage. An insincere or otherwise contrived offer may well be hastily withdrawn with no further mention. To the other side, your silence will indicate you've seen through the contrived nature of the offer made.

Postpone Consideration of It. Respond that you wish to delay discussing it until some later time, date, place, etc. The risk is that if you find any part of the offer appealing, the party making it may in the meantime reconsider and withdraw it. Then you've missed the opportunity to get something you want because you failed to take immediate advantage of it.

Make the Other Person Justify It. With this approach you're essentially expressing a desire for more information. This response is closely related to the questioning response noted above. It differs, however, in that here your primary purpose is to get the party facing you to *sell* you more on the relative merits of the proposal offered. The difference is subtle but important.

Modify It. In following this alternative you take as your objective the introduction of an element of change to approach your objectives more closely. For example, someone makes an offer of $100,000 on a piece of real estate. You say, "I might consider that offer if you also include . . ." (which could add up to perhaps another $10,000 in value to you).

Substitute Another Offer for the One That Has Been Made You. This ploy can work particularly well when both parties are clearly very interested in making a deal and time is a factor. For example, one party has just said, "I'll agree to do all the maintenance in your office building for a one-year contract of fifteen thousand dollars." You respond "How about a three-year contract for thirty-nine thousand?", thereby attempting to economize by $6,000 over the original offer when projected across a three-year term. In this kind of situation, your opposite might well respond with an attempt to modify your counter-offer: "I'll consider that if you'll agree to an inflation index."

Appear to Refuse to Discuss the Offer. This differs from rejecting or postponing discussion of it, because in this case your refusal to discuss is intended to force the other side into convincing you that the offer is worthwhile. You don't really mean to postpone consideration of it nor to reject it outright. You merely hope to get the other person on the defensive and then to pull advantage out of that.

Praise It. Sometimes an offer is made after great conflict has erupted, and the proposal is clearly a compromise that requires courage either to make or to live up to. Acknowledging appreciatively the amount of concession the other party is willing to make can go far to facilitate the successful conclusion of an agreement. You can still indicate elements of difficulty—you don't have to accept immediately after offering a strong word of praise. But you will have provided encouragement for continuing efforts to hit on the right formula for agreement, which even the politest "No, thank you" commonly fails to do.

Compare the Offer with Another. This response generally reflects an attempt to discredit the offer being made through comparison with a previous one tendered by another party or with an offer made by the same party in the past. Those who negotiate labor contracts know this option well—it is frequently used by those who are working to hammer out wage and benefit agreements.

Laugh at It. This is a humorous variation on rejection of the offer. But here, instead of sternly saying "no," you lightheartedly laugh it off with a "You've got to be kidding!" Again, if an offer that has been made was at all contrived, the other side experiences the embarassment of being found out. But recognize that this response to an offer that is genuine and involves a difficult concession for the other side may introduce an unwanted note of tension.

You will find that there are occasions in almost every negotiation when any one of these alternatives can be brought into play. You should always follow through at least with the first two essential responses when replying to any offer. Then consider what choice to make from the other possible responses available. You increase your own ability to move toward the goals you seek to achieve through negotiation by keeping in mind that there is this wide range of responses available when an offer is made. You aren't limited to just accepting or rejecting; you can respond in different ways to open up the offer as much as possible or to encourage substitution of another offer more along lines you hope to follow. The choices are fairly broad, and they are available in any negotiation, whether highly formal or conducted totally on an interpersonal level. Learn to employ them to your advantage.

WHEN IS AN OFFER FINAL?

Everybody at one time or other comes up against a situation in which a "final" offer or proposal submitted for consideration turns out not to be final after all. We know of a negotiation in which one participant actually made seven "final" offers. After each one he adamantly insisted that this was now his "last and final" offer. In a similar fashion, some salesmen are continually adjusting a "last best" price quote.

Obviously, in circumstances like these it's in a bargainer's best interests not to fall for a "final" or "last best" offer/price if another more "final" or better "best" offer is still possible. The problem is how to know when what's indicated as "final" or "best" really is that.

The problem is not actually so serious. The "final"/"best" ploy is used so regularly among negotiators that it makes sense to adopt a patient skepticism about any offer or price put in these terms. Question it. Probe for more information. Press for something better. You'll be surprised at how negotiable most "final" offers and "best" prices are.

It usually pays to discount the sense of pressure an opposite tries to apply by throwing out a "last offer" ultimatum. It's used too often as a scare tactic. Wait out the other party; let him see that you expect another offer. Often you'll get one. On those occasions when it's finally evident that no other offer is to be expected, you can generally go for the last one made. Not many negotiators face the "one-hour manager's special" featured in some department stores. Once an offer's made, usually you can expect to achieve at least that. (Of course, your attitude and behavior during the waiting game does have some effect. Don't be too smug or condescending in waving off an offer that doesn't quite suit you. Stay cheerfully matter-of-fact.)

False Finals

There are a variety of circumstances in which you are likely to find yourself responding to a "final" offer that isn't necessarily final.

TRIAL BALLOON

In this case, your opposite uses the term to test your reaction to what is really an initial statement of position. At the earliest plausible moment, he'll identify a proposal as final, then wait to see whether you'll accept it or question it. As a general rule, he doesn't expect you to believe you're already at a point where this is your only option. He's really just gauging your reaction to ascertain how tough an opponent you are. On occasion the test provides an immediate payoff—the person presented with this "final" offer actually goes for it. When that happens, negotiation on that issue winds up quickly. The person who's made that "final" offer has pulled off a great coup, winning a deal that he probably hadn't counted on.

BEST OFFER OF THE DAY

There are other negotiators who speak of "final" offers and "best" deals to refer to a bottom-line position they're holding to for that particular day or session. What they're really stating is a refusal to concede more at this time. It's not a test of your resolve that's involved; it's their unwillingness to give up any further hope for advantage until they've taken the opportunity to review the situation. Some will need to discuss an aspect of the issue with a superior, other principal, or an interested third party before any other concession can be contemplated. But once they've had the time to consult with others, it may yet prove possible to elicit a new offer. However, that won't be forthcoming until consultations have been held. No amount of pressure, criticism, or intimidation will prompt a revised offer before then. The best one can do is recap the relative positions and reach an agreement in principle concerning the state of discussions to that point, with a reaffirmation of mutual goals being worked toward. Pressing insistently for immediate additional concessions in this situation can prove to be an annoying irritant.

A variation on this situation, where one's opposite feels it requisite to confer with others before agreeing to consider further concessions, is that in which one's opposite simply insists on being allowed time to "sleep" on the position reached. It presents you with basically the same need to exercise patience. The difference is that your opposite does have authority to agree to a revised offer—he doesn't have to check in with someone else. Here you need to proceed cautiously. It may still be politic to allow him the time he needs to weigh further options. However, on occasion exerting additional pressure for an immediate decision or change of position can be worthwhile. Your opposite may be wavering sufficiently within himself to respond to a slight push from you.

Wait or Push?

How do you know when to wait and when to push? The key to sorting out the circumstances facing you lies in developing your awareness of cues given in what is said and how something is said.

META-TALK CLUES

In the next chapter we'll elaborate on the concept of meta-talk. Meta-talk is a style of speech in which the meaning isn't so much *in* the words used as *behind* the words used. The truth is often other than the words alone would indicate.

In a "final" offer situation, you may hear your counterpart come out with a statement that starts with a phrase like "Although I have been given full authority to settle . . ." or "My mandate allows me to conclude an agreement; however . . ." Behind these words you'll sense that any further concession first has to be cleared with the organization or party represented by your opponent. Otherwise why even make the point? Someone with authority rarely goes out of his way to emphasize that he has it; he simply has it and exercises it. An alert negotiator listens for telltale comments that betray a hidden truth. When it appears probable that an offer has to be cleared through other channels, comments to the contrary notwithstanding, he holds off applying insistent pressure for immediate response.

BODY LANGUAGE CLUES

Be alert to body language. If someone throws out a "final" offer while sitting back in his chair with ankles crossed, he's probably just fishing for a reaction. The languor of the body position is at odds with the kind of tension you can expect a genuinely final offer to generate. Note also that certain habitual gestures frequently accompany the articulation of dubious statements. One of the most common is a person covering his or her mouth with a hand while making such a statement. Other related gestures are movements of the hand to the nose, ears, or eyes while speaking. The psychological explanation is that the hands betray a subconscious fear that what is stated—a falsehood of sorts—won't prove acceptable, so there's an instinctive move to cover it or distract from it. A failure to maintain eye contact or a rapid blinking of the eyes also often betrays an innate nervousness about the acceptability of what is being said. (For more insight on the subject of body language, see Nierenberg and Calero's *How to Read a Person Like a Book.*)

The nonverbal cues that are congruent with a genuine final offer are those that suggest both an openness and a certain intensity of commitment. The person making the offer is more likely to be leaning forward, even sitting on the edge of his chair. He'll maintain high eye contact; he'll speak very deliberately, with a minimum of throat-clearing or verbal tics along the lines of "you know" or "well . . . uh."

We don't mean to dissuade you from utilizing the "final best offer" ploy yourself as a tactic for winning advantage in a bargaining situation. It's a fairly common ploy, and it can be used to good advantage.

It's also a pretty old tactic. In Genesis 18 the story is given of Abraham's intercession with the Lord on behalf of that portion of the population of Sodom that could be deemed righteous. The Lord agreed to spare Sodom if but fifty righteous people could be identified there. Abraham managed to work that figure down to a mere ten individuals, although he could very well have accepted as final a figure above that. Unfortunately for Sodom, there weren't even ten worthy people resident there, so the city was destroyed anyway. (This is one of Hank Calero's favorite negotiating stories. It does provide pretty substantial precedent for allowing a variety of figures to be presented as possible final offers.)

COMMON SENSE ABOUT MAKING PROMISES

Politician Sam Bluster was elected to serve in the United States Congress. During his campaign he time and again stressed his intention to speak out in opposition to any policy or program that raised the cost of decent government for the people. Three months into his term a bill passed Congress raising the salaries of senators and representatives by a hefty amount. Congressman Bluster voted with the majority in approving the raises. As he prepared some time thereafter to visit his home district, one of his aides ventured to ask if he wasn't concerned about being called out for going against his campaign promise.

"Good heavens, my boy," the congressman expostulated, "what does a raise for Congress have to do with the cost of decent government?"

Promises. Everybody makes them, but it's unlikely anyone can boast a 100 percent record of keeping them.

Since promises are part of the stock in trade for negotiators, it seems appropriate to comment on how they are commonly used and abused in negotiations. That requires us first to review what a promise actually is.

What Is a Promise?

The dictionary identifies a promise as "a declaration that one will do or refrain from doing something specified." Does that seem clear?

Well, does it matter what kind of declaration one comes out with? If you pay attention to small children, you'll note that the word *promise* figures very prominently in their vocabulary. They also learn early on that not every declaration to do or refrain from doing constitutes a promise.

The truth of how the world often operates comes out in a remark made by a six-year-old child to her playmate of about the same age. The playmate was distressed and angry because her friend had welshed on some previously made bargain to share. These feelings were vociferously expressed with repeated cries of "You promised!", with such emphasis on the "promised" as to make it clear that some sacred precept had just been violated. The friend, a supremely self-assured budding semanticist if ever there was one, finally retorted, "I did not promise I was going to give you any—I just said I would."

As adults we presumably move beyond the belief that a promise, to be fully valid, must be labeled as such. Nevertheless, we don't really ever accept that every declaration to do or refrain from doing amounts to a promise. For one thing, most of us would probably tack on the adjective *serious* to indicate a quality required in order to render the declaration a promise. Of course, in introducing that modifier, we also introduce an element of possible confusion. Not everyone takes the same things seriously. But although that problem does arise, the bulk of the problems in this area result from overlooking a further element in the meaning of *promise* as it's conventionally understood.

Implicit Promises

Subsequent dictionary definitions introduce the matter of expectation. Make a statement that provides someone grounds for expecting that you will perform along certain lines and you can also be said to be making a promise. One can obviously attach qualifiers to that, too, but one inescapable fact remains. Not only can you be seen to be making a promise without explicitly labeling it as such, you can create the impression of promising something without necessarily articulating a clear declaration that you will do or refrain from doing something in a specific circumstance.

You can see something of what's involved by referring back to the anecdote at the head of this discussion. The public there can probably legitimately feel a promise was made and broken. To take it out of the context of a joke, what is your reaction when a government official responds to an allegation of wrongdoing with "Well, that's certainly something that we will have to look into"? Not unreasonably, you're likely to feel you've been promised an investigation. If later you learn that no investigation was ever conducted, you will probably feel a promise was broken. How forbearing would you be with an official who protested "I never promised a thing"? Not very, we expect.

This same kind of situation can arise in a negotiation. If you say that you will check something out, discuss an issue with someone, or feel a review of circumstances of one sort or other ought to be initiated from your side, your opposite will probably hear that as a promise. Try using the six-year-old girl's line we cited and see how far that gets you.

Promises are as much a matter of the way something is stated as they are a matter of the exact words used. You will save yourself a lot of potential embarrassment and resentment from the other side by keeping that in mind when it comes to making any kind of declaration. Avoid creating expectations in those you're dealing with when you do not intend that anything of a prescribed nature should be expected.

Broken Promises

Getting people to understand what a promise is or is seen to be would provide enough room for major improvement. But the difficulties go far beyond that when it comes to promises. Often the problem isn't misunderstanding whether some declaration amounted to a promise, it's that a promise actually was made, but injudiciously or in bad faith.

You will probably make the distinction in your mind that a promise made in bad faith is worse than a promise that is made injudiciously. But that distinction often proves irrelevant. The other side will react to the fact that the promise hasn't been kept. The bad feeling that gives rise to isn't likely to be moderated by an excuse that the promise was made carelessly or imprudently. The damage to the other side remains the same, even if it's no more than shattered expectations.

There's a variety of promises that get negotiators into trouble and a variety of situations that prompt them.

PROMISES YOU CAN'T KEEP

Some people will make a promise they know they won't be able to keep even if they wanted to. They give in to the temptation to make the promise anyway because, in the short run, just the promise wins them the cooperation they want. Delivery on the promise comes after the cooperation. By the time the other party realizes it's been had, the promiser has been able to take the advantage desired. If the wronged party has taken the promise entirely on good faith, without incorporating it somehow into a formal contract or other record of agreement, it can prove a bitter, possibly costly lesson.

The lesson learned can be just as bitter and costly if a negotiator unintentionally makes a promise he can't keep. This can come about in a number of ways.

Lack of Authority. Sometimes a negotiator makes a promise that he has no authority to make. The people or company he speaks for won't back him up. This sort of humiliation can be avoided by taking the time to be sure you understand how far your limits of discretion extend when speaking for someone else. When in doubt, don't. Clear all statements that might be read as promises *before* making them, if you have any uncertainty about their acceptability to those you represent.

Lack of Resources. In other cases, a promise that is made can't be kept because the resources required to fulfill it simply aren't there. If the other party bases any substantial investment in time, energy, or material resources on the promise made, it will give them little comfort to learn that the miscalculation on the negotiator's part was unintentional. You are expected to have a pretty accurate sense of what you can or cannot accomplish with the resources you have *before* you start making promises. This is especially true in business. Saying that you "would have if you could have" counts for little, if anything.

The same holds true for promises that can't be kept because an unrealistic time frame has been established.

PROMISES YOU DON'T KEEP

A promise made in bad faith is by definition one that won't be kept. Besides those, however, there are other promises that don't get kept for one reason or other. The reason rarely does the promiser credit.

Poor Follow-Up. If there's poor follow-up on stated intentions, the net effect may be no delivery on the promise made. Should the reason for failure to deliver become apparent, the negotiator who made the promise loses doubly as far as credibility goes. First, his side will be faulted for not living up to a commitment clearly made. Second, the ineptitude demonstrated through poor follow-up will reinforce a conviction that this is one person or outfit not to get involved with again. Subsequent proposals for cooperative ventures are likely to be met with an admonition to "get your act together first." Some compelling proof of follow-up capability is going to be required before a party that's been burned once consents to work with that same opposite again.

Changed Priorities. Some promises are not kept because the party that issued them has in the meantime changed its priorities. The change downgrades the importance of the advantage originally seen as likely to result from fulfilling the commitment. Where this happens without immediate effort to advise the opposite party, we'd say this amounts to a breach of faith. However, immediately notifying your opposite that your priorities have changed and so, you're sorry to say, you can no longer adhere to a previously declared intention won't necessarily win you points either. It was good of you to let them know right away, but they'd rather you had fulfilled what you had promised. Besides, what about *their* priorities?

Forgetfulness. Inexcusable as it may appear, some negotiators will at times forget about a promise they've made. Despite intending to live up to it, they nevertheless don't.

Put yourself in the position of facing an opposite who's that careless about something you understood to be a serious commitment. How ready will you be to rely on subsequent promises from someone that thoughtless? It may turn out that the fault doesn't lie directly with the negotiator himself. Someone in the organization behind him was supposed to be taking care of it, but that will still not help the negotiator's credibility with the other side. Because a promise was not kept, subsequent promises are going to be received with much more skepticism.

PROMISES THAT AREN'T CLEAR

These get you into trouble if your lack of clarity leads your opposite to expect something you didn't intend. If the failure to come through is later brought to your attention, you can, of course, deny that any commitment was actually made. That won't win you anything, except perhaps a round-robin argument of the sort children get into so frequently: "You promised!" "Did not!" "Did too!" "Didn't!" "Did!" etc.

You can avoid this potential source of bad feeling fairly easily if at the end of your bargaining sessions you review positions established and commitments made. That way both sides explicitly state their understanding of present positions and promises made or heard. If there's been a lack of clarity, that can be established before expectations build up to a point where one side starts counting on them or acting on them. Avoiding the kind of vague generalities that can lead to misunderstanding is a preventative.

PROMISES THAT BOX YOU IN

You can get into trouble when you make a commitment that later limits your ability to adapt to changed circumstances. Keeping the promise may subject you to the possibility of loss or keep you from taking advantage of an opportunity for much-desired benefit. Breaking the promise wins you the censure of the party you made the promise to. One way or the other you lose on this one.

Make a concerted effort to avoid promises that tie you down to specifics in such a way that adjustments can't be made if changes in circumstances affecting those specifics occur later. Or try to incorporate an understanding that anticipates a need for adjustment in the face of some possible change. The cost-of-living adjustment in certain wage contracts grows out of this kind of situation.

FORCE MAJEURE, THE ONE GOOD EXCUSE

Force majeure is a concept in law that refers to the unavoidable impact of powers beyond one's control. Suppose you're a merchandiser who promises to deliver a set number of items by a specified date. Two weeks before delivery is due, your warehouse burns down and there's no way to get replacement inventory in the time allotted. There's no way you can make good on your promise. Or suppose you promise to deliver estimate figures on something at the next day's encounter with your negotiating opposite. There's a computer breakdown that evening which makes it impossible for you to hold to your promise.

Nobody expects you to deliver on a promise if an unexpected accident or other development suddenly makes it impossible to do so. What must be clear, however, is that you *would* have made good on the promise but for the intervention of misfortune. Don't expect to get away pleading *force majeure* if it's apparent that you can't deliver because you miscalculated your ability to deliver in the first place. You're not the victim of *force majeure* there, you're the victim of your own ineptitude. Occasionally circumstances will be such that you can plead *force majeure* when the real fault lies with you rather than with an unpredictable development beyond your control. But don't assume you can get away with that every time. If you do that with an opposite who recognizes that the fault really lay in your miscalculation, you will look all the more foolish, not to mention slightly dishonest.

Minor Promises

Promises, promises. There are all kinds of promises, from little glib ones of relatively minor impact to major commitments that form the basis of contracts drawn up between the parties. Don't assume that the remarks here are aimed only at the major commitments. Glib little promises that you don't think anyone should take seriously can cause trouble. An opposite who sees that you don't take the little promises seriously is going to be cautious about trusting you when it comes to the big ones.

If you are seen to be faithful in performance of minor promises, you will be taken that much more seriously when it comes to a promise with substantial impact. Understand that any declaration you make that you will or will not undertake a particular action—even one that strongly suggests what you will or will not do (whether or not you ever state an intention in narrow specific terms)—can be read as a promise. Beware of allowing expectations to build up in areas where you don't intend that they should. Promises are the currency with which a negotiator obtains cooperation and agreement. Don't devalue that currency through making declarations carelessly, or through subsequent failure to follow through on them.

5
Weighing the Competition

IT TAKES at least two people to negotiate, and it's important that you play your own part with skill and sensitivity. You must be self-aware if you hope to pursue your goals with any chance of success. But you also must be tuned in to the other person or people you're up against, and not just on an abstract level, treating and responding to the other side as a faceless entity with an assigned role in the negotiating process. You have to deal with the people involved on a direct personal level, taking their likes and dislikes into account, adjusting to their style of presentation, exercising patience and tact in efforts to influence them toward decisions you favor.

The entire point of a negotiation is to work through differences in perspective to arrive at an agreement. That's the gist of the process, and those who participate in it have to accept the fact that priorities vary according to which side of the bargaining table you're on. If everyone shared the same priorities, there wouldn't be much need for negotiation.

Even in the friendliest of encounters many negotiators get tripped up by their failure to recognize the full dimension of the differences existing between the two sides. They're prepared to deal with priorities that differ from theirs. But they have a tough time accepting that personality differences also exert tremendous influence on the outcome of negotiation, even though these may have little if anything to do with differences in priorities established. They forget that individual differences can complicate communication as much as any difference in the position taken on the issue at hand.

Our object in this chapter is to help you avoid as well as deal with problems that arise on the level of interpersonal exchange in negotiation. You can't realistically hope for the best cooperative agreement possible if you don't know how to deal with difficulties that personality differences can give rise to.

THE OTHER PERSON ISN'T YOU

We all too readily make assumptions about others' behavior that grow essentially out of the way *we* relate to people or react to events. We have a tendency to view others as individuals pretty much like us. Oh, we know they're not us, but we regularly forget how really *unlike* us they may be. Subconsciously we project our reactions upon them—we assume their response to what is said or done in any given situation will be pretty much what ours is. At the very least we assume that it will be a reaction we can understand in light of our feelings and experiences. That can lead to trouble, because very often it doesn't work out that way.

Here are a number of common assumptions people make that lead to problems in interpersonal communication.

Faulty Assumption No. 1

That as an individual your opposite naturally views the world in the same broad terms you do, with pretty much the same general likes and dislikes.

Here we're talking about perceptions of the way things are and the way things should be. Problems often develop when you begin speaking in terms of your own prejudices—when you state as an absolute value something that is really only a personal preference. You may have sorted out all the differences in perspective that relate to the issues and still fail to take into account how incidental remarks hinder development of the cooperative atmosphere you hope to see established.

Women will be more alert than men to the problem that arises when it comes to attitudes on sex roles. Women, whose position in business and the professions is in the main not established as long as that of men, commonly report discomfiture at remarks or behavior that reveal a male counterpart's innate conviction that "it's really a man's world." Faced with that attitude, a woman negotiator may find it very difficult to feel that the interests on her side can be pulled into alignment with those on the other side. The implication from her opposite that the optimum order is male-dominated is one she will resist, and that resistance may very well carry over to affect her reactions to proposals made regarding the issues at hand.

Let's look at another example. A businessman was exploring opportunities for cooperative endeavor with a major importer-exporter but unwittingly torpedoed his own chances for working out the agreement he sought. The importer-exporter reported the circumstances like this: "We were working on the possibility of a joint venture to import certain types of machine tools from Taiwan and Japan. It seemed there was a way we could both profit, and I found myself very receptive to the prospect. But just about then this guy came out with a couple of remarks that betrayed a most denigrating view of Orientals and Oriental culture. I have a lot of dealings with the Far East, and I have enormous respect for the achievements of both the Japanese and the Chinese of Taiwan. Once I heard this fellow betray his basic insensitivity to those, and then to see him taking for granted that I shared that . . . Well, I just couldn't maintain any enthusiasm for getting into a joint venture with him."

Prejudices in other areas—religious, political, regional, etc.—can have the same effect when dropped on an opposite who doesn't share the same values or likes and dislikes. So be wary of any off-the-cuff remark, quip, or joke that reflects your judgments on the world around you if you're not certain your counterpart shares those judgments. You may find it difficult to imagine that anyone could hold a viewpoint contrary to yours in any given area. Nevertheless, people do.

Faulty Assumption No. 2

That your opposite forms his or her opinions as result of access to the same information available to you, or that he or she shares the same general background of experience.

How often do you find yourself routinely nodding "yes" to someone's interjection "You know what I mean" without being altogether sure you do? The situation described is one you're not familiar with; the role you're being asked to empathize with isn't natural to you; the facts given seem to allow another conclusion than that which has just been drawn. But you understand that as often as not "You know what I mean" is just a rhetorical device. The listener isn't expected to take it seriously, because it's not really a check on his or her understanding. It's more an expression that people use to mean "Of course you agree with me."

Try a little experiment the next time someone uses this phrase on you in this way. When someone says to you "You know what I mean" and in truth you don't, say "No, I don't know what you mean." Occasionally someone will respond with an articulate explanation of how his or her opinion was formed, but at least as often the individual so confronted will demonstrate confusion and even incredulity that the viewpoint expressed doesn't win your automatic understanding and concurrence. They will have assumed that your experience can only have led you to reach the same conclusion as they did.

In Hank Calero's negotiating seminar workshops he's seen this faulty assumption in operation over and over again. At times, when the response to a negotiator's "You know what I mean" is in the negative, he sees great frustration build up in the person originating the remark to which automatic assent was expected. That person evidently finds it almost impossible to believe any right-thinking, intelligent person could draw a different conclusion, and suspects the person on the other side of deliberate obstructiveness. A tension builds from that point onward and further impedes communication thereafter. The first negotiator clearly expected to find a comfortable mirror image of himself in his opposite, and he is completely thrown by finding his expectations torpedoed. He finds it difficult to accept as natural any difference growing out of the other person's own unique combination of experiences.

Faulty Assumption No. 3

That your opponent responds to the same motivating forces you respond to.

Negotiators who have truly mastered the art of persuasion recognize that one of the first tasks facing them is identifying what rewards will motivate an opposite to commit to some policy or activity not previously contemplated or considered desirable. They know the range of possible motivations is wide. They're aware that what motivates them may not be sufficient to impel a counterpart to change or review priorities.

Unfortunately, there are many people who don't explore this area adequately. This is most frequently the case where the primary motivation on one side is financial. The spokesman for that side will often reiterate over and over again the dollar benefits to accrue from a particular move. Since money is a powerful motivator with so many individuals and organizations, that emphasis will frequently have the desired effect. However, there are instances where it might be more effective to invoke the likelihood of benefits other than money to an opposite, to explore whether these might be used as a rationale to motivate a decision in the desired direction.

Here's a list of other major motivating factors that might be invoked:

Enhanced prestige	Avoiding trouble
Increased security	Avoiding criticism
Competitive advantage	Conservation of assets
Protection of reputation	Greater public visibility
Saving time	A chance to show individuality
Avoiding effort	Keeping up with the times
Contributing to the public welfare	Added work satisfaction
Expansion of information resources	Opportunity to exert influence

You can probably think of other motivating factors that you might respond to. These may come into play for others as well, but be aware that when and how they come into play can differ substantially from person to person or organization to organization.

It can at times be useful just to ask bluntly what motivation would impel movement to a desired commitment. You might get a response that alerts you to possibilities you haven't considered. But you won't always get an answer you can work with. Your opposite may be fishing for more than he'd settle for, or he may not consciously have considered an alternate motivation that would be of similar influence to the one he has uppermost in mind. You always have to probe to ascertain where the emphasis in motivation really lies.

Faulty Assumption No. 4

That your opposite wants to listen to everything you have to say.
Identifying this as a faulty assumption may puzzle some. After all,

the reasoning goes, any negotiator who won't pay close attention to whatever the other side has to say risks missing an opportunity that may present itself.

This is at times true. However, those who have negotiated with any regularity will have encountered situations where someone launched into a discussion that clearly went off the issue(s) under consideration. No one likes being part of a captive audience. Personal observations and anecdotes can be valuable for throwing things into perspective, but they can be annoyingly intrusive as well.

When that happens, our readiness to consider other perspectives with some bearing on the issue fades. We don't like someone to take half an hour to make a point that could have been made in two minutes. We don't appreciate someone getting carried away in pursuit of a line of thought that fascinates him but doesn't interest us at all. We cannot maintain enthusiasm then for efforts at exploring further opportunities that might exist. Our only eagerness is to escape the tedium.

Faulty Assumption No. 5

That your opposite's sense of language is the same as yours.

This assumption has two dimensions: first, that the person facing you uses the same vocabulary you use; second, that he or she responds to the same style of speaking that you respond to.

The first is something most negotiators can take in stride. One party uses terminology the other party isn't familiar with; the latter party asks to have that terminology defined or explained. (From time to time you'll run across people who are so insecure about appearing knowledgeable and in control that they will actually let an opposite get away with a use of jargon they can't follow. Don't let your ego trip you up that way.) Most negotiators realize that they should make no commitment dependent on or affected by factors that haven't been satisfactorily explained. A good negotiator is never so timid about revealing ignorance of a terminology he does not understand that he goes through the entire process pretending he does understand it.

The second dimension—style of speech—proves more troublesome for people. There are otherwise skilled negotiators who habitually fall into an informal pattern of speech that is regularly punctuated and amplified by the use of vulgarities or curses. They probably feel this gives them the advantage of the common touch—of being one of the boys. Except sometimes it doesn't. Sometimes they face people whose sense of propriety is highly offended by this free resort to "barnyard talk." Instead of acting as a lubricant to open discussion, the rough language takes on the quality of an abrasive.

Always ascertain whether salty phrases are likely to offend before flinging them freely about.

Men might note an additional caution. Most women, especially in business contexts, do not particularly care for the condescension implicit in such endearments as "honey," "sweetheart," or "beautiful." This goes double when formalities are otherwise being observed in every respect. Address all your colleagues with the respect that befits an equal.

It's inevitable that we make judgments about the people we encounter across the bargaining table. What we look for and see in others is always to some extent what we know and feel in ourselves. Even so, we have to recognize that there's always another set of experiences and viewpoints in every person we meet.

To boil it all down to a single point to keep in mind, always remember that the other person isn't you. He or she will be at least somewhat different from you on everything, and very different on some things. So don't expect that other person to relate to the issues or to you as though he or she were a duplicate of yourself. Recognize and accept that your opposite's individuality requires your broadening your frame of reference beyond the limits of your own perspective and experiences.

CAUTION! NEGOTIATORS SPEAKING

A serio-comic placard on sale in the novelties section of a local card shop reads, "I know you think you understood what I said, but you should know that what you think isn't what I meant." Sometimes it might be useful in a negotiation to flash that card at an opposite.

Because negotiators are always working to merge two separate perspectives into a single, focused agreement that will prove acceptable to both parties, it is essential that a clear understanding of issues and positions be imparted from both sides. That's self-evident. But all too often people speak in a fashion that clouds understanding rather than contributing to it.

Two habits produce this effect. They are so integral to human nature that it is unlikely you can ever put a complete end to them, either in others or in yourself. But being aware of them will put you a far step ahead toward keeping your lines of communication clear.

Thinking Out Loud

Often what seems a clear statement of position or fact is really just someone thinking out loud. What you hear as an affirmation of need or perspective is really an off-the-top-of-the-head reaction to a situation you are describing or proposal you may have made. It will probably reflect some instinctive point of conviction. But it is not necessarily the last word; it may not even be immediately pertinent to the needs of either party in the circumstances at hand.

Take for example this situation: A components supplier is working to conclude an important sales agreement with a potential key customer. The supplier has carefully calculated all the factors influencing his ability to meet the other man's needs. He's demonstrated the quality of his product; he's indicated he is competitive on cost. Now he's talking about delivery.

SUPPLIER: "All right, so we can provide you two thousand units at a unit cost of $17.50. And we'll have those to you . . . let's see . . . the best delivery date I can give you is May 1."

CUSTOMER: "That's too late. I want a commitment for April 15." (If the supplier's best delivery date really is May 1, then his first reaction may well be to write this contract off as lost. But let's have him hang in there a moment.)

SUPPLIER: "April 15? That's absolutely your latest date for taking delivery?"

CUSTOMER: "Look, I've been dealing with two other suppliers in this area for the past five years. I haven't found either of them very reliable on delivery dates. The only way I ever get the components when I need them is to specify their availability at least three to four weeks in advance. I need those units to roll onto an assembly line on May 8."

In this situation the customer's immediate response was to react according to past experienced difficulties. His first statement was, in effect, a thinking out loud that only appeared to be a definitive final statement. At that point, had the supplier assumed he understood, he would have missed eliciting the real statement of fact—and the opportunity to conclude a mutually satisfactory agreement. May 1 can work as a delivery date. The point is that the customer must feel secure about the supplier's reliability in delivering on schedule.

There are times when a first response will prove definitive. Just the same, it's always worthwhile to take a moment to prove your understanding of the situation at that point. Sometimes you can do this simply by maintaining a moment's silence, allowing your opposite to elaborate on or rephrase what he or she has just said. Otherwise, repeating or rephrasing the statement as you've understood it, or just questioning it, can reveal the discrepancy between what you thought was meant and what the other party actually intended to say or was thinking. You'll be surprised at how often a discrepancy exists between a seeming statement of position and what proves to be the actual thought running through your opposite's head.

Meta-Talk

The other blurring activity that so often clouds understanding is the frequent tendency for people to speak in terms that disguise a hidden meaning. This is something we tend to associate with politicians who are not prepared to come clean in admitting a political blunder or responsibility for an actual wrong they have committed. When a principal in a scandal confesses "an error in judgment on my part," we are often with good reason skeptical as to whether the "error" really was no more than an inadvertent mistake.

A similar kind of deliberate muddying is regularly employed in negotiations. And picking up on the message when parties are engaging in this meta-talk requires recognizing right away that the real message is usually *behind* the words used rather than in them.

Proving understanding by paraphrase or question is just as likely to elicit more meta-talk. What is important is recognizing the point behind the statement. You must be aware that certain statements crop up repeatedly with minor variation in numerous situations,

usually disguising the same message. Veteran negotiators will probably have heard at least several of the following on any number of
occasions:

**"Our Position Is Very Firm, and We Are Deeply Committed to Our
Goals and Objectives."** For this you can read, "Whatever concessions
are asked of us won't come easy." This type of statement is usually
made at the outset of bargaining. It's particularly common where the
parties are also speaking for public consumption, as is often the case
with labor-management contract negotiations monitored by the
press.

**"Some of the Issues Involved are Very Emotional, and We Hope Each
Side Will Keep Other, Equally Important Issues in Perspective."** For
this read, "We hope the *other* side will act responsibly." From our
experience of meta-talk, the party that makes this kind of statement
is the more likely to act in an immature, emotional fashion.

**"In Consideration of Our Long Association and Mutual Interests, We
Want To Present This Proposal, Which We Think is Most Fair and
Reasonable."** The meaning behind this is usually, "We know you
well enough to realize you probably won't go for this, but we're going
to float it by you anyway, just in case." With this kind of comment
you also find parties trying to cash in on a previous association,
hoping this will win concessions that might otherwise not come
through easily. Use of the words *fair* and *reasonable* is an obvious
attempt to make refusal more difficult for the other side. But you can
see that for what it is, a cornering maneuver designed to make any
rejection appear unfair and unreasonable. That barbed implication
can backfire by arousing the other side's resentment at the effort to
paint it into a corner. *Acceptable* would be a better choice of terms
than *fair and reasonable.*

"Now We Know You'll Be Pleased At This Proposal . . ." This is
similar to the previous line. Read, "Let's see if they'll bite on this
one." The opposition is gauging your initial response to get a sense of
what should be the next offer to make. That will generally be quickly
forthcoming, assuming you reject the first offer. However, don't

mistake the substitution of a further proposal as a retreat on the other side's part. This is customarily a planned maneuver, so don't develop a sudden overconfidence.

"Although We've Settled the Important Issues, There Are Still Some Minor Areas of Difference." For this you should understand, "The negotiation may seem to be just about over, but we still have some *gets* coming to us." And you can be pretty sure you won't conclude a settlement that's final until those "minor" differences are resolved.

How to Recognize Meta-Talk

Since meta-talk commonly sounds like any other kind of talk, how do you recognize it for what it is?

The important first step is to be aware that it exists. Once you're alert that not everything is meant the way it's said, your instincts will help keep you on track. Often it's just realizing that what's been said really adds nothing or serves no purpose if taken literally. It's an effort to plant an idea or cultivate a desired response in your mind—to steer you into more or less automatic agreement with what's just been or about to be proposed.

Probably the best way to recognize meta-talk coming from others is to acknowledge your own use of it. Meta-talk isn't just something other people confront you with; it's something you yourself inevitably employ at times. You use it to probe your opponent's position, to suggest positions on your part that you're not yet prepared to commit to openly, to warn indirectly of a feeling or reaction that you hesitate to be explicit about. Tune into your own use of meta-talk. Listen to the way you express yourself at moments when you're not being direct, and you'll have strong clues on what to listen for in others. Then as you negotiate, listen and watch. You'll hear familiar terms; you'll see body language clues. And you'll find you can even make up a list of statements in common "meta-usage."

Remain clear in your perceptions of what people are or may be doing when speaking and you'll find it easier to chart your way through a negotiation. You will learn to understand the communication even when couched in terms that present the message indirectly. And you will know to ask for clarification when an expression of reaction or fact is not what it seems. With the awareness of common speech habits that blur and/or impede clear communication of feelings or ideas, you'll find yourself much less susceptible to the frustration of confusion in a situation where it's important you know what's going on.

HOW OTHERS HANDLE CONFLICT

Although ideally negotiation is between two parties who calmly and logically pursue the objective of agreement, the truth is that often it isn't. Frequently it's between two people meeting in circumstances that reflect or create a sense of conflict. They aren't wholly comfortable at what they're doing. As a result, they behave in less than an ideal manner.

There are definable traits demonstrated by negotiators confronted with conflict, character patterns related to how they respond to it. Some negotiators follow just one pattern. Others react first one way, then another. What's noticeable is that many negotiators adopt a predictable character pattern. When watching them approach a conflict situation, it's not difficult to predict what the nature of their reaction will be. It's unfortunate that too often their pattern of response to conflict prompts them to adopt a character trait that is inappropriate for getting through the situation at hand in best form.

The Ostrich

This person has so difficult a time dealing with conflict and confrontation that he prefers to act as though nothing's happening. He refuses to face the situation that exists and either seeks to continue on as if no problem has surfaced or subsides into silence, hoping it will disappear by itself. He may betray a certain inner turmoil. You might note a rush of color to his face and a nervous energy in his movements, but he will not give any verbal indication that he's attuned to the situation at hand.

Naturally the result is that the state of tension between the parties continues for an indeterminate period—until someone else figures a way through it. In a team context, initiative may be taken by a fellow team member, but that person won't be able to rely on meaningful support from his ostrich colleague. In a one-to-one negotiation, the opposite party winds up having to push doubly hard for resolution of the difficulty—it's a tedious task trying to solve a problem between two parties when one of them won't acknowledge its existence.

Because of his unwillingness to get directly involved in a conflict situation, the ostrich naturally misses the opportunity to gain any advantage that taking an initiative could provide. The other party holds the initiative by default, although exercising it can be infuriatingly difficult in the face of the ostrich's passivity. First you usually have to pull the ostrich's head out of the sand, to get him to admit the problem exists. Only then can you win his acquiescence to a solution for it.

Sometimes you can deal with the difficulty by concentrating energies on solutions without insisting the other person admit to anything. If you can exert your initiative at this point to develop alternatives that set things up to your advantage relative to the situation you see, then it matters little whether anyone else admits to anything or not. Take the initiative, since your opponent won't. Identify precisely what concerns you, indicate that you see this or that approach as most fitting your needs under these circumstances, and then push for the solution you favor. Don't argue. If your ostrich opponent tries to duck out with an "I don't see any difficulty here we need be so concerned with," bypass his attempt. Your approach should be something like: "I want to take this into account in the event there is some problem here. If there's no problem, so much the better. Then this precaution should prove unobjectionable to you now; it will save us any misunderstanding later."

Press your initiative. Address the problem situation directly, but avoid argument. Develop your alternatives and push in the direction you want to go. Whether he likes it or not, the ostrich will wind up having to respond. You can generally maintain some sense of slow forward movement as long as you avoid argument about what is or isn't a problem.

The Side Stepper

This person characteristically responds to conflict with evasion. He'll immediately change the subject or try to flip the fact of conflict into another area where he won't have to deal with it.

Here your only effective response is firm refusal to be distracted. Put off a distracting side issue with a calm remark that pulls you back to the issue at hand. Keep your cool, lest your evident irritation with the situation become the side issue. At times it can help to wrest the initiative from the other person by pulling attention back to the issue with an immediate proposal for consideration. Once in a while you will find you just have to state flat out that you feel it essential to face the area of difficulty before proceeding to any other discussion. In that case, avoid argument on why you feel that way. You may feel you're risking setting up for impasse, but the truth is, you're as good as there already if you don't work through the problem that's there to be resolved.

The Steam Roller

The steam roller personality habitually attempts to bully his way through any conflict that develops. He uses intimidation and other pressure tactics to push the other side into acceptance of his priorities, without allowing interruption for consideration of their priorities. He tends to sound like a drill sergeant. "I want," "you will," "you'd better," and similar authoritarian phrases rain down on the other side with military imperativeness. He's not interested in a consideration of alternatives, nor does he care about developing an understanding of common needs. What *he* wants is all that matters, and he'll often be irrational and angrily emotional in his insistence on getting what he wants.

The steam roller is noticeably lacking in sensitivity. If you attempt to react with vigorous resistance, that's seen as reason to redouble strong-arm efforts.

Refuse to be steamrollered. Quiet, stubborn persistence is recommended. Don't let yourself be intimidated, and don't let yourself get pulled into a shouting match. You may do well to acknowledge your opponent's emotional state, but don't challenge it. "I realize you're uncomfortable with this situation. We're uncomfortable with it, too. That's why we have to work out some approach that settles the problem for both of us." Make it clear that your priorities are at issue, too, and hang in there without conceding to the effort to run you over.

The Mule

When faced with conflict, this person adopts a stubborn, ornery attitude. Not only does he resist all efforts to budge him from a position that blocks resolution of a conflict, but you'll find he frequently reverts to previous stands and positions, disregarding compromises and agreements in principle he may have made in the interim. The net result is not just impasse at the point at which conflict has developed, it's the undoing of previous progress as well.

Dealing with the mule personality can require an incredible expenditure of energy. A carrot-and-stick approach may work to budge him from his stubbornly maintained position; trying to drag him over to seeing things from a different perspective isn't likely to. Look back to what preconditions put your opposite into negotiation, then push every motivational button while making it clear that achievement of objectives on the other side—which you are open to—nevertheless requires facing up to the conflict circumstance existing now. The trick is to be stubborn in your own insistence on dealing with the problem and yet not to make it an outright contest of wills.

If you are fairly certain that you can develop another area for discussion in such fashion that it provides you another carrot to use, you may want to defer the conflict issue momentarily. Should you decide to do that, make it clear that you are putting off resolution of the issue only temporarily. Explain that evidence of a further benefit will make clear that it's to each side's advantage to settle other differences to mutual satisfaction. Hold the carrot in view, but keep its realization contingent on settling those other differences.

The Chicken

You'll recognize the chicken by his hurry to give in or give up when faced with the reality of conflict. Instead of hanging in there to work diligently for an agreement that's as much in his interest as possible, he bails out. He'll be the first to offer to split the difference, even before he's evaluated what that may mean in terms of consequences affecting him or those behind him. The maneuver isn't a planned compromise. It's a scampering for relief from the pressure of dealing with uncomfortable differences he'd rather not face.

Certainly your opposite's chicken behavior can work to your advantage at times, but there's often a hitch. When the chicken represents others who retain the right of final approval on concessions granted, it can turn out that his side rejects the settlement you thought you'd won. That puts everyone back on Square One, you with egg on your face and the chicken clucking at how things got to this unhappy state.

When you find an opponent reacting with unusual quickness to concede, proceed carefully. Rather than rubbing your hands in glee and jumping for the next concession, take stock. If your opposite is acting as agent for principals who retain final authority on approval, it may be worthwhile to suggest confirmation of support to rule out subsequent confusion. Do that matter-of-factly: "Let's doublecheck that your people will recognize the benefit in this arrangement we've worked out." Perhaps add a line of positives your opposite can employ to do any necessary selling of those he reports to. Where the chicken speaks for himself, nail down how concessions gained will be implemented, indeed that they can be implemented.

The Skillful Negotiator

Here's the individual who doesn't hide or run from conflict. He doesn't try dancing around it. He doesn't complicate the situation with contemptuous arrogance or stubborn intransigence. He acknowledges that differences of position exist and actively seeks to have these aired in discussion. He not only articulates his perspective on things, he asks to have the other side's perspective stated as clearly and completely as possible. Then he works to bridge those perspectives, considering concessions that seem necessary for achievement of agreement, but being careful to elicit cooperation and compromise from the other side as well. He is willing to listen; he is open to weighing alternatives that are suggested and works to develop further alternatives as necessary. He works to keep all options open for himself, and he is supportive of efforts on the other side to evaluate options for acceptability from their perspective.

Clearly we endorse the character pattern displayed by the skillful negotiator. That doesn't mean you don't have to stay on your toes. Even though your priorities are being taken into account, the skillful negotiator's own priorities naturally take precedence. That's not to fault him—he's supposed to be following his own priorities.

Recognize that moments of difficulty occur in the majority of negotiations. Many will be surmountable fairly quickly. Some will be serious enough to prompt you and your opposite into a pattern characteristically followed when in a state of confrontation. Be alert to indications that a particular pattern is coming into play. You may be able to moderate the confrontation somewhat by an adjustment of approach on your part, thereby nipping in the bud any move into a pattern of behavior on the other side that poses greater problems for you. Even if you can't achieve that, you'll have a sense of how to proceed from there.

GAMES NEGOTIATORS PLAY

In negotiations, as in every other human interaction, we often find ourselves facing someone who is less than direct with us, who at times seems to be pursuing some personal objective in addition to—occasionally even besides—the ostensible objective at hand. That's when we can say we are facing a game player.

Our reactions to this can vary. Frequently we respond with suppressed irritation. We may become openly angry, or we may experience bewilderment. At times, even if we don't always want to admit it, we react with a certain excitement. Then it's as though the other person has issued a stimulating challenge that we enjoy rising to. That's because somewhere inside of us, too, lurks a game player who from time to time rather likes having the opportunity for self-expression.

Game playing isn't necessarily an evil, provided the participating parties both play by the same rules. The point of the encounter itself mustn't be subordinated to incompatible ego objectives on the part of either player. The point of negotiation is achievement of agreement. Personal motivations ought not to intrude to disrupt the chance of that. If two game players can maneuver around each other and still keep on track in their interaction, there's no harm done. But often a game player sees you as unequal or pursues goals in such a way as to make agreement difficult to achieve. It's only natural then that you regard the game playing with a sense of distaste.

We see a correlation in game-playing relationships between negotiating parties with relationships that have been drawn in the field of transactional analysis. There, you may recall, psychologist Thomas Harris drew up four basic interactions expressed in terms of "being OK" or "not being OK" vis-à-vis another person. In negotiating we speak of similar interactions in terms of winning or losing.

The interaction that Harris characterizes as typical of well-adjusted adults is indicated by the statement "I'm OK–you're OK." In negotiation we'd say we're speaking of a win-win orientation. An illustrative summary statement would run something like: "I think we can put our heads together and come up with an agreement that satisfies both of us." The "I'm OK–you're *not* OK" dynamic is mirrored in a win-lose orientation toward negotiation. A summary comment here could be: "This is what our goals are, and you're going to have to get it together to meet those."

Transactional analysis also identifies two other dynamics, summarized in the remarks "I'm *not* OK–you're OK" and "I'm *not* OK–you're *not* OK." These have their counterparts in a lose-win orientation and a lose-lose orientation. Because negotiation by its nature focuses on the achievement of set goals, even though some modification of those may be accepted as inevitable, these two orientations are rarely in open evidence. Consider the implicit summary statement for each and you'll immediately see why: "I don't see how I can cope with all your experience in these matters" (the lose-win orientation); "We're both so confused about what we want that I don't see how we can possibly achieve anything in these talks" (the lose-lose orientation). While these attitudes do surface in the bargaining encounters, you'll rarely find them *openly* operative.

The games that provide the most difficulty are almost always those that show the other person holding a win-lose orientation to the negotiating process. Once you recognize them for what they are, you will usually find you can take them in stride. You're thrown off when you know someone is playing a game but you're not quite sure what it is. That's when your reaction is most likely to be frustrated confusion or perplexed irritation; you may actually fall victim to a tactic you sense but don't comprehend. The person who insists on win-lose game playing is obtaining a short-term advantage at the expense of any long-term relationship that may be desirable or possible. But that is small comfort to you at the moment you find yourself victimized by a game that makes you a loser.

Win-Lose Games

As an aid to persevering in a situation where an "I win–you lose" game is being played against you, here's a review of those we've found most common. You may find you can identify one or two others not listed here once you tune into the operative principles behind them.

We've assumed here that it's the other side who's indulging in games, with you the intended unsuspecting victim. There may be occasions when *you're* the one playing games on a win-lose basis. If you're concerned to avoid problems that can grow out of that, realize that your opponent may catch onto your game and adopt a counter strategy. Your game won't get you where you hoped to go, and in the meantime you may have lost valuable trust and good will.

THE BEAR TRAPPER

This is a game in which your opponent successfully works to get you to commit to a stated position on an issue, then puts further consideration of the issue on ice. You feel trapped and helpless, bound by your own expressed commitment, vulnerable because you've demonstrated exactly where you stand while your opponent has committed to nothing and given no indication that your position is influencing him or her positively on the disposition of the point at issue. It's sort of like playing a hand of poker in which you somehow wind up revealing your hand before your opponent decides how to play his hand, which remains concealed.

The poker analogy provides a clue to the defense to employ against this game: avoid committing yourself to a set position on an issue until you have some clear indication of your opponent's position. Keep the taking of a position conditional on a reaction from your opponent that is supportive of you. For example, don't get trapped into a statement like: "We absolutely have to have delivery on these items by August 1, even if we have to pay above the going rate to get them by then." Keep it to: "We're looking for delivery by August 1 and would like to know what terms you would require to assure delivery by that date."

Of course, your own actions can set you up to be trapped, regardless of how you express your needs. In the example above, if you've waited until July 30 to get to this matter, you're already trapped. Be sure you've anticipated your needs so as to retain flexibility or so you can afford to give the appearance of flexibility in your situation. Admitting a sense of urgency or allowing the fact of urgency to be established through poor anticipation of your needs makes you prime quarry for the bear trapper.

LET'S YOU AND HIM FIGHT

Here your opponent plays the role of instigator, getting you to focus on differences that exist between you and a third party of influence or between you and members of your own team. This is one of the easier games to get sucked into, as we're all subject to differences of opinion with even our closest associates, and we usually like having someone else express sympathy for our position. So this is a game you're often well into before you have any sense of what's happened. Your opponent pulls you into it with a feigned concern for your situation that is likely to make you feel quite gratified at first. It will not be until later that you realize he or she is really the only one who profited from the situation.

In team negotiations the correct defense is to maintain unity in the face of the opposition. If differences do crop up, limit discussion of them to a private caucus of team members. Where one member vigorously disagrees with a development at the negotiating table as far as the team effort goes, no signal of that should be flashed to the other side. Rather, flash a signal that indicates a need to sort out differences in a caucus conducted out of sight and out of earshot of the opposition. Under no circumstances should a team member bring up those differences in encounters with the opposition, even if he or she does not feel the caucus has resolved them properly.

Where your opponent tries to capitalize on differences you may have with a third party, the defense is simply to hold to the issue as it exists between the two of you. Don't be misled by "sympathetic concern" expressed over difficulties your opponent knows or suspects you're having with a third party, unless that concern moves you tangibly closer to a solution of any such difficulty. Empty sympathy is the most treacherous kind of diversionary tactic. It feels good for only a moment, and it can fool you into taking a position on an issue that serves your opponent without helping you at all.

UPROAR

Your opponent finds reason to express vociferous indignation or anger at an attitude you've shown, a position you've stated, or an off-the-cuff remark you've made. Whatever the excuse—and that's all it is, an excuse—the point of this game is to disrupt the progress of the negotiation and get you so off balance and on the defensive that you concede an issue by way of appeasement or apology. Or you may respond with anger of your own, so that the negotiation turns into an unproductive shouting match. Then when the discussions break down, your opponent can fault you for the failure.

Because we're so frequently uncomfortable with an expression of outrage directed against us, this game works more often than it should. We may not willingly negotiate with the same individual a second time, but in the meantime we've been intimidated or provoked into a losing position.

The best defense against someone playing Uproar is to remain calm yourself. You can express regret that there seems to be some misunderstanding, but leave it at that. Your opponent may persist in expressing indignation, particularly if this is a game he or she has won before. But if you hold onto your sense of self-confidence and refuse either to make a concession in appeasement or to get drawn into an angry counterattack yourself, the game will fizzle out. Unless your opponent really has nothing to gain by negotiation, in which event you'd have had an impossible time of it anyway, you'll find the talks settling down to business before very long.

CORNERING

This is a more sophisticated game than those just described, but it can lead to results that are just as painful. In this situation a very skillful opponent manages to set up a line of alternatives for you in such fashion that no matter which you select he or she wins something you might prefer not to concede. The test of your opponent's skill is to lead you to agree that the alternatives presented are the only ones available—or, at the very least, the best ones available. In every case, your opponent works to control which ones you will choose from.

One technique followed in Cornering is taking over alternatives that you may indicate you're considering. Your opponent listens to what you propose, responds with a paraphrase or elaboration on it that alters it to his or her advantage, then gets you to accept that version of what began as your proposal. Unless you're closely attentive, you don't realize until much later that you've been maneuvered into a corner.

Beware of over-defending against Cornering. To some extent you will always be subject to the other person or team trying to influence you to act along lines that coincide with their interests. Don't be so resistant to suggestion that you block consideration of alternatives that could prove to your advantage, too.

Keeping a clear view of your interests in light of the realities that exist is your own defense. That's not as easy as it sounds—sometimes you aren't entirely sure that one or other proposal is in your interest; on occasion your perception of reality may be off. Don't close yourself to a consideration of alternatives just because someone else poses them. But don't take it on someone else's word that there are no other alternatives or that benefits will flow to you just because someone said they would. Always review how an alternative will affect you, positively and negatively. Weigh your options. Regardless of what your opponent says about there being no viable alternatives, apply the DO-IT approach described in Chapter 2 to see if you can develop others that fit the situation facing you.

CRY "RAPE!"

If you've ever had the experience of facing someone who leads you to the brink of a good deal in an almost seductive manner and then turns around to accuse you of taking unfair advantage, you've experienced the game of Cry "Rape!" How did you react? With confusion? Were you shamed into a concession you hadn't anticipated? If yes, then you played right into your opponent's hand.

When this happens to you, once again the best defense is staying calm and focused on your own priorities. Don't let yourself get rattled or shamed into a concession that you haven't previously been prepared to make or before you evaluate the effect it will have on you. You may find that a good deal you were almost sure of evaporates and that the hard work of negotiation still lies ahead, but that good deal was an illusion anyway. Keep your head about you. You can often hold your opponent to some of what he or she indicated an initial enthusiasm for. Also use a periodic recapping technique to summarize points of issue and positions established on those, asking your opponent's concurrence with the accuracy of every "how things stand at this point" review when made. That leaves your opponent much less room for evading responsibility for his or her position in any arrangement tentatively agreed to.

BLEMISH

This is a game that's played very simply. Your opponent takes a perfectionist stance on everything, so that no matter what is in the process of being worked out, it just isn't satisfactory. Frequently it's the language of the agreement being worked out that's picked at and picked at.

The object of the game here isn't so much to force you into a concession, although that may be somewhat the case. Blemish is usually played by an opponent who feels the need to demonstrate a personal superiority, to prove power through delaying progress or upsetting the atmosphere of the negotiation.

Blemish is one of the more difficult games to defend against. As with most of these games, remaining calm is the best first line of defense. Also be quietly firm in your resistance to getting sidetracked into trivialities. It also helps to use a recapping technique during the negotiation to define points of agreement as you go along. Note these points down in an explicit manner, winning concurrence from the other side that progress made has been as indicated. Assuming the game doesn't come into play immediately, you may be able to restrict the Blemish player's subsequent maneuvers somewhat.

Perseverance is essential. If you can logically counter your opponent's nitpicking so as to demonstrate the emptiness of his or her claim to superiority, you may be able to nip the game in the bud. But beware of falling into a contest, because Blemish players are usually very persistent and not always susceptible to logic. Avoid getting into round-robin debates on semantic distinctions, or suddenly there will be two people playing Blemish. Stay as methodical and organized as possible in your approach to the issues; you'll find yourself more secure, responding to this game with a clear understanding of issues and perspectives that enables you to see through any claim of fault or blemish in proposals forwarded or agreements in prospect.

NOW I'VE GOT YOU, YOU S.O.B.

This is something of a variation on Cornering. Your opponent in this case works singlemindedly to set you up for a fall. Through her or his maneuvering, you are backed into an inadvertent statement of position or feelings that seems to support a subsequent contention that you are guilty of some inconsistency or other irregularity in the proceedings, and now you must pay. You usually have an advance clue that this game is being used against you: your opponent keeps pushing and pressing you on a particular issue in such fashion as to pin you down to an interpretation that he or she provides you. In this case, the interpretation always reflects badly on you. It's very similar to the technique used by trial lawyers to get defendants or witnesses to implicate themselves in some sort of misdoing.

The defense here is not to let opponents put words into your mouth, to resist their insistence that what you say means what they want to hear. It's also important to be clear in your use of language and your definition of issues and situations. Keep in mind that you are not a defendant in a trial proceeding. You do not have to justify or explain motivation for everything you've done or each position you take. You're there to negotiate, not to plead your case.

Lose-Win Games

As a rule, you won't run into someone who explicitly takes a lose-win approach to negotiation, but there are some circumstances in which that may seem to come into play. Two instances arise fairly regularly, however, where it may serve your opponent's purposes to affect a lose-win attitude—*affect*, because what is really operative here, too, is a type of game playing. The game gives the other person the appearance of incapacity; it seems to indicate that he or she cannot fully cope with the situation at hand. But in truth that seeming inability to cope rarely leads to a winning advantage for you. So while we may to a degree characterize the games involved as lose-win games, beneath the surface these games usually play on another dynamic. The "you lose" element is still there; it's just the language that suggests a "you win" possibility.

WOODEN LEG

In this game your opposite pleads a lack of authority to move to a point of commitment or even to carry through a line of discussion. "My people won't back me up" is the common lament. Should you respond to this maneuver by immediately modifying a proposal by way of concession—to stay within the area of your opponent's alleged range of authority—your loss can be immediate.

The difficulty you're up against in this situation is determining whether what's developing is a game or whether you're facing a true obstacle. It takes a combination of advance research, probing, and intuition to ascertain the truth. The record of previous experience with the other side can be important. A previously prepared profile of the organization your opposite represents can help you come to a conclusion as to what authority has likely been delegated to him or her. In addition, maintain firmness on your position, e.g.: "This is a point of vital interest to us, and we're very limited in our ability to be flexible on this issue." You should be able to elicit some indication that will provide an important clue on whether a genuine obstacle exists or whether you're being subjected to a game tactic. Or you may indicate that you're prepared to modify the terms you propose if your opposite can win authorization for a return concession that meets another of your needs. Whatever proves necessary ultimately, don't be too quick to accept his or her contention of weakness at face value. Where you feel strongly about what's been proposed, respond to the plea of the wooden-legger with an admonition to check it out with whoever does have authority, at the same time reaffirming the importance of the issue to you. Refer to motivating considerations on the other side, then wait to see what reply comes back.

THE HARRIED WORKER

This is usually a fairly obvious game. Your opposite pleads an extremely tight schedule or heavy work load, seeking your sympathy and consequent consideration. The goal is to move you as quickly as possible to a statement of the most favorable terms you can present. The implication is that your opposite's initial statement of position also reflects the most favorable terms he or she can present. Because of the pressures of time and other looming responsibilities on the other side, you are hurried into concluding an agreement without the kind of exploration of issues and potential common interests that you'd prefer. And you don't get the chance to verify that the first deal offered actually was the best you could have gotten.

The best response to this ploy is to get right down to business in the negotiation, thereby demonstrating regard for your opposite's time problem, but to stay focused on your own priorities just the same. Don't get so rattled by his or her plight that you immediately jump to concessions that may not be necessary. Don't fail to question terms proffered if it seems to you that discussion of these is advisable.

Keep Alert!

Chances are that at some point you'll encounter one or other—maybe even all—of the games noted above. You'll find that people use them in interpersonal efforts at influencing your behavior as much as in any formal setting officially designated a negotiation. In either event, your sense of frustration and/or confusion will be kept to a minimum to the degree you stay centered on your own priorities relative to the need to achieve an agreement. Remember that your response to the other side's attempt to indulge in game playing governs to a great extent how much of any encounter will be given over to that game playing.

A repeat note of caution, however. While you should be alert to the possibility that your opposite may indulge in games, also keep in mind that there are instances of bona fide win-win negotiating behavior that at times include elements suggestive of game playing. We've noted that particularly in the cases of Cornering or Wooden Leg, but it's true in many other instances as well.

Use your judgment at all times. You can damage your position as readily by treating an opposite as a game-playing opponent when that isn't the actual situation, as you can by falling into the trap a game-playing opponent sets for you. The review here should sensitize you to games you are likely to encounter. Be aware too that an overly suspicious frame of mind can also work to your disadvantage.

IT'S O.K. TO SOUND OFF

You're in negotiation, concentrating on discussion of the issues at hand when suddenly you hear a remark that gets under your skin. Jones, across the bargaining table from you, has just made a comment that touches on an area of sensitivity for you. You tell yourself he probably didn't realize what he was saying. You decide to ignore what you heard. You're not there to engage in personal exchanges or to get into arguments about the propriety of this or that attitude or behavior. You're there to accomplish a set task. It doesn't seem likely you'll advance your interests by stopping the proceedings to deliver a little lecture on good manners and respect.

So you turn your mind back to the issue under discussion. Where were we? Oh yes, accomplishing the ABC project in cooperation with Foremost Industries, represented by Jones, and trying to do so within cost guidelines you've drawn up. Foremost insists those are unrealistically restrictive. Jones has just introduced a cost analysis done by

Foremost that he maintains is more realistic than your guidelines, "assuming you guys have a sense of reality or really care when it comes to maintaining a quality operation." Your company's been maintaining a quality operation for more than twenty-five years!

Keeping your voice even, you suggest to Jones that you go over the cost guidelines and the Foremost cost analysis together to determine where discrepancies exist and where adjustments may be necessary or possible on either side. Jones accedes readily, but in doing so comes out with a second remark about a concern for quality. Again it sounds like he's putting you down. You grit your teeth a moment, then force a smile the instant you realize you might have been caught looking grim. No sense being thin-skinned. Let's just look at the figures and see what they tell us.

You start going over the two sets of figures together. Jones nods as you explain the rationale of the various guidelines drawn up by your side. Your research has shown, demonstratively you feel, that the project can be completed satisfactorily within the guidelines. Jones takes a few notes. When you've fully explained your understanding of what's possible within the guidelines, he starts his explanation of the cost analysis figures prepared by Foremost. He prefaces everything with "The figures that we at Foremost have worked out, of course, are predicated on providing quality at the best possible cost, not simply on doing the job as cheaply as we can get away with it."

Is this guy really determined to make you out to be spokesman for a cheapskate outfit with no commitment to quality? You bite your tongue and force yourself to concentrate on the figures and the explanation given for them. But somewhere inside you're doing a slow burn that makes concentration difficult. You and your company have been pretty rudely insulted, you feel. And that twerp Jones . . .!

The discussions go on all afternoon, but you're uncomfortable. You try to maintain a pleasantly calm demeanor, but inside the urge to retaliate grows ever stronger. Jones keeps harping on quality as though that were a trait distinguishing Foremost from your company. In your irritation at him you find yourself less and less inclined to believe he knows what the word means. By the end of the afternoon, you're really in a foul humor, and there's not much good you can think of to say about or to Jones. What about his presentation, his figures? Truth to tell, you got so distracted by your growing annoyance with him that you didn't catch all his explanations.

If this scenario seems at all familiar to you, let us suggest the one remedy most likely to keep you in balance when confronted with offensive remarks from an opposite: Sound off! Don't just sit there hiding your feelings, pretending you heard nothing or weren't at all bothered. It doesn't work anyway. You might manage to convince the other person that what he said made no significant impression, but where's the advantage in that if meanwhile your concentration on the issues has been broken, interrupted by growing annoyance and feelings of resentment? Besides, your feelings may have the effect of building into a negative judgment that makes it hard for you to deal with the person facing you. That won't help get you to a satisfactory conclusion of the negotiation.

Why Sound Off?

Sounding off gets things off your chest and out into the open where your feelings can be aired and their inevitable influence taken into account. Consider this. Someone who makes a remark you find offensive may not have done so with deliberate offensive intent. If you speak up at the time the remark is made, you immediately alert him to your negative reaction to what's been said. As soon as it's clear you've interpreted something as offensive, any element of misunderstanding can be cleared away immediately. If thoughtlessness lay behind the comment made, your reaction can prompt a more thoughtful pattern of speaking. Let your opposite know that in order to achieve the most satisfactory dialogue with you, which he may well be concerned to do, certain of your sensitivities have to be taken into account. Sounding off gives you an opportunity to clear the channel of communication between you so that dialogue proceeds as smoothly as possible.

On other occasions, someone may be working a tactical maneuver on you. In the situation above, Jones may have decided your company, being sensitive to a need for quality, could be maneuvered into accepting higher cost estimates if these were presented as essential to maintaining quality. Your speaking up the first time the implication came through that you were at all ready to sacrifice quality might very well have eliminated efforts to work that tactic on you in so irritating a fashion. You can often save yourself the aggravation of being subjected to a tactic that works on your nerves if you speak up as soon as it does so.

On the other hand, there are those who come to bargaining sessions with a needle they simply can't or won't let go of. This is most evident in situations where those meeting each other have a history of antagonism or mutual suspicion. It's especially frequent in certain labor negotiations or when politicians with opposing views get together to discuss issues. What often happens in these cases is that the participants play to an audience at the same time they're negotiating. In their zeal to impress members or constituents of their uncompromising fidelity to principle, their comments assume an abrasive quality that does little to facilitate eventual agreement. However, it's likely some sort of compromise will ultimately have to be arrived at. Speaking up to point out that present remarks or behavior make cooperation much more difficult to achieve can at times serve to cut short negative behavior. On other occasions, speaking out in protest won't cut short the negativity you're being subjected to. The audience still remains to be played to. At least you can feel you've worked to hold things on course.

TWO BENEFITS

Sounding off can provide either or both of two benefits.

To begin with, it tells the other side how you're reacting to what you've just heard. If concern on the other side is to have you react positively, sounding off alerts them that they're taking the wrong approach to that end. Recognizing that you are certain to be less favorably disposed toward them unless they make an adjustment in approach, they do so. The result is less irritation for you and a greater chance of winning your cooperation for them.

But it would be naïve to assert that sounding off will always prompt a favorable adjustment in the behavior of those facing you. Many times it doesn't. But even then it provides you an advantage. It gets your feelings out in the open—you don't end up sitting on them, trying to negotiate while you pretend everything is hunky-dory even as the opposition is expressing more or less restrained contempt for you or for values or positions you espouse. You at least have the satisfaction of letting people know where you stand; you make a statement that indicates your sense of self-respect.

How Should You Sound Off?

There's a wrong way as well as a right way to sound off. The wrong way is virtually guaranteed to make the situation worse, regardless of the motive behind the remark that gave offense to begin with. The right way offers you an effective way of speaking up for yourself or your organization, of preserving your sense of integrity, while maximizing opportunity for transforming an uncomfortable circumstance into one that is more congenial to eventual agreement and cooperation.

In the scenario sketched out above, a wrong response to Jones could be any of the following: "Mr. Jones, I'm convinced *you* have very little sense of what quality's all about, all your references to it notwithstanding." "Mr. Jones, your disparagement of our commitment to quality is highly offensive, and I demand an immediate apology." "Mr. Jones, that's the stupidest remark I've heard all day!"

Each of these is wrong if one hopes to have the negotiation continue on course. The whole point of negotiation is to build bridges to cooperative endeavor. Any retort along the lines of the above confronts Jones with direct antagonism. It will more likely lead to defensiveness and argument than accommodation. You can, of course, take the position that Jones started it, so if things get off course it's his fault. But how does that result in progress toward cooperative endeavor? Trying to get in the last word or to force an apology almost never works to that end.

Any response to offensive comment or behavior that has the nature of an attack on the person involved or tries to force him to eat humble pie is likely to be counterproductive. That person's first impulse will be to dig in his heels. Even if he recognizes he's made an error of judgment, he's not going to appreciate your calling him obstructive or stupid. Just think how little you appreciate it when someone critical of an action or comment you've made impugns your intelligence and good faith while making a criticism.

The right approach when sounding off is to protest the remark or action that you find offensive without turning that into a personal attack. That doesn't mean you can't indicate anger or have to appear apologetic for having taken offense. What it does mean is that you direct your response effectively—that is, so that the offense is identified and protested without arousing a defensive counterreaction that only complicates things.

So what would be an example of sounding off in the right way? Here's one possibility:

"Mr. Jones, you seem to be suggesting that our company has no strong commitment to quality. Frankly, when I hear a remark to that effect, it makes me see red. We have an industry-wide reputation for quality, and that dates back twenty-five years. Our commitment to quality has never been stronger. The cost guidelines you're questioning were developed with quality very much in mind. If you can demonstrate how quality is being compromised, we'd appreciate your pointing that out to us. But in view of the considerable efforts expended through the years to establish and maintain a reputation for excellence, it's difficult to appreciate any suggestion that we're lax in our commitment to quality."

Now, there's a terse little speech that makes the point crystal clear: "Mr. Jones, you've offended us, and we're angry." But there's nothing in it that reflects directly on Jones' intelligence or good faith. If he feels inclined to be defensive, his defense is most probably going to be a disclaimer along the line of: "Oh, I didn't mean to suggest that!" Nothing you've said is likely to prompt a defensive reaction aimed at protecting a threatened sense of self-esteem. If he wants to maintain an offensive of sorts, he can point to the figures he has: "I didn't mean to give offense, but my figures indicate a compromise in the quality area unless certain cost allowances are raised."

You don't always have to respond with an admonitory speech. In Jones's case, you might well have nipped his derogatory comments in the bud simply by asking after the first remark: "Mr. Jones, do I understand you to feel that we're lax in our commitment to quality?" That would in all probability suffice to get him to back away from use of innuendo on the subject. The trick is to know when not to push it from your side. After Jones stammers "No," don't throw in an argumentative last word like "Well, you certainly sounded as though that's what you were saying." Stick with a more neutral comment if you feel you must make one: "I'm glad we have no misunderstanding on that."

You may find certain types of behavior offensive that your opposite will not think of as such. You may encounter someone whose language use allows for considerable profanity that is distasteful to you. Or you may be subjected to off-color references you'd rather not hear. In those instances, let your opposite know your feelings, too. A simple statement will do it best: "Mr. Jones, I find it very off-putting to hear you use so many curse words." "Mr. Jones, that kind of remark (or story) makes me uncomfortable." If Jones is at all concerned to interact comfortably with you, he'll get the message. Most negotiators, even if they view you more as an adversary than a potential ally, will make some effort to respect your sensitivities if those are stated with matter-of-fact courtesy.

Should You Ever Grin and Bear It?

We don't think anyone should sit and swallow without protest whatever negative innuendo, abuse, prejudice, or coarse language comes his or her way. Let your opposite know how you feel.

If the reaction from the other side is one of indifference or contempt for your feelings, however, pause to consider your position. What depends on this negotiation? Is it possible you may still be able to achieve important goals through bargaining with this individual? Is it essential, as it often is in labor-management disputes? If so, avoid the temptation to make a major issue of your opposite's boorishness. You've stated your feelings; now move on to continue discussion of the issues you came to deal with without letting yourself get pulled into an angry shouting match. Maintain your own sense of dignity. Some bargaining agents deliberately attempt to make the other side lose self-control. Don't fall into the trap they set for you. State your protest to whatever negative behavior they subject you to, but do so with dignity and self-assurance. Then, unless the behavior demonstrated is integral to the major issue at hand, continue with review of the issues you came together to deal with.

MAKING AN ALLY OUT OF AN ADVERSARY

It often happens that two people meet to negotiate in an atmosphere of initial distrust or even hostility. Some kind of problem exists between them, and each is concerned that his or her interests not be sacrificed in favor of the other side's interests. It almost seems as if each views the other as the enemy. That creates something of a problem, because resolution of any difficulty that exists requires cooperative endeavor. As long as the two sides view each other as adversaries, movement toward cooperation is going to be difficult.

Let's suppose you're in this situation. You recognize that achievement of the goals you've set yourself requires the other person's cooperation. You're even prepared to give a little if it means getting the benefit of eliminating the problem that exists. But how likely is it you'll get the cooperation you need as long as your opposite thinks of you as an adversary to be defended against? Not very. So how do you get your opposite to stop thinking of you as the enemy? Here's a simple seven-step process to follow:

1. Make it Apparent That You View Your Opposite as a Potential Ally. Don't wait for the other person to take the first step. Too many adversary situations drag on because neither side wants to be the first to back down. Right there's the misconception to lick—that making a positive overture amounts to backing down. It doesn't. If you make it clear that you don't automatically see your opposite as an adversary, there will be less incliniation on that person's part to maintain the defensiveness one naturally holds to when facing a possibly hostile opponent. This isn't backing down for you; it's a step forward to more open communication.

2. Identify the Problem to be Solved as the Source of Difficulty, Not Your Opposite. Point to the fact that the situation that exists is what has to be remedied in order for either side to come up a winner. It's the situation that has to be defeated, not one or other of the negotiating parties. Once that's made evident, it'll be easier for both parties to understand that both can emerge winners from the bargaining sessions.

3. Drop Whatever Tendency You May Have Toward Defensiveness. An adversary situation continues longest when either party insists on firing back whenever the other comes out with a statement that is argumentative, accusatory, or offensive. A vicious circle develops, and rather than things settling down to comfortable discussion, they escalate into ever more tense confrontation. Since the best defense is commonly perceived to be a strong offense, it's easy to see how defensiveness readily makes things worse rather than better. In negotiation, nobody gets killed if he stops firing first. The worst thing you can suffer is . . . Well, if you're sufficiently self-assured, what real damage *can* you suffer?

4. Recognize Your Opposite's Ego Needs. Nobody likes being treated as if he or she were spokesperson for some wrong-thinking, wrongdoing organization and hence in need of personal reeducation. If that person is negotiating on his or her own behalf, it doesn't do to characterize viewpoints expressed as "wrong," "bad," "inappropriate," "shortsighted," "foolish," "stupid," etc. Make it clear you're working to resolve a difference in perspectives, not trying to persuade an errant sinner into seeing how wrong he or she is to hold a particular position. Don't assume an attitude of moral or intellectual superiority. Even if you take an indulgent, benign approach, it will be evident that you are acting in a condescending manner. Your opposite naturally feels as worthy as you. At the very least an opposite expects to be treated as an equal—to be taken seriously, with all statements and opinions considered thoughtfully.

What if the other person doesn't appear to take you seriously? Don't get defensive about it. Just make it clear that *you* take yourself seriously. Explain your perspectives and positions as clearly as possible, and you'll usually find you can move an opposite to serious consideration of them. Courteously observe that whatever problem exists between you is certainly in part due to a misunderstanding of the perspectives on either side, and if that problem is to be resolved, it behooves both parties to make a genuine effort to understand each other's perspective.

5. Adopt a Friendly Tone. That should be an obvious point, but there are people who take themselves so seriously that everything they say is delivered in a stiff, officious tone. Relax. If the person facing you sees that you're at ease and hears a congenial tone in what you say, that person is much more likely to relax and adopt a friendly tone in turn.

6. Display an Open Mind. Let your opposite see that you're prepared to listen to whatever he or she has to say and that you're open to being convinced of the merits of his or her position. You can show yourself amenable to change without having to concede points you're not convinced should be conceded. Listen. Ask questions to prove your desire to understand and your readiness to see reason in the other side's position. Once it's clear that you're prepared to see reason in a position you didn't hold initially, your opposite will begin thinking of you as a reasonable person. When that happens, there'll be a greater willingness to view your perspective on the issues as reasonable, also.

That means a move away from defensiveness to efforts on your opposite's part to arrive at a joint understanding on how difficulties should be approached for satisfactory resolution.

7. Avoid Tricks or Pressure Tactics. That doesn't mean you can't try to maneuver the other side into considering issues from your perspective. It does mean you don't engage in manipulative tactics based on pretense of concern for or interest in the other side's point of view. It does mean that you don't attempt to intimidate the other side into going with your view of the situation. Those are adversary-type behaviors and will be seen as such.

Follow these seven steps, and more often than not you'll find that bargaining sessions initially characterized by suspicion or hostility progressively assume a more positive tone. Instead of working against each other, you and the other person wind up working with each other. The atmosphere that was previously heavy with an adversary spirit will be lightened by an air of mutual respect and a readiness to consider common interests.

6
Overcoming Obstacles

AS SHOULD be evident by now, dealing with problems requires attention to a wide range of considerations. It's not just a matter of labeling some easily identifiable situation or action a difficulty solvable by a formula approach. It's also a matter of a clear understanding of the process of negotiation, positive attitude, interpersonal chemistry, and an ability to communicate reasonably well.

COMMON REASONS WHY NEGOTIATIONS FAIL

Negotiations fail for different reasons. Many relate to difficulties in the conduct of the parties involved. On one level or another, they speak *at* each other rather than *with* each other. It's easy to say it's the other side's fault, but that's a cop-out. You're an integral part of the process, and what you do or fail to do—even if the other person tends to be uncooperative—has an effect on outcome.

It takes two to negotiate. Movement depends on the dynamic between the parties involved. You share problems with the other side. Look at them from that perspective. Don't assign blame; there's bound to be some on both sides. Instead, focus on breaking out of the established pattern of difficulty. Identify what you're doing that contributes to your difficulties. A change there can lead to change all along the line.

Negotiations also fail because of reasons related to the issues. Sometimes the parties are too divided to be able to work out any agreement, but that's less often the case than it's stated to be. Our observation is that a substantial proportion of failures grows out of counterproductive conduct along any one or more of a variety of lines.

Confrontation Instead of Negotiation

In many instances, the parties to a negotiation never actually get around to negotiating. They make the necessary preparations, probably even planning some concessions. But they never get around to offering those. Instead, from the moment of first encounter, it's a "meet the enemy" situation. Demands are hurled with either/or finality. It's a confrontation, and from the first remarks each side starts digging in for battle. A trench warfare mentality develops. "Hold the line! Don't give the bastards an inch!"

The difficulty here is that both parties are adopting an adversary mentality. Look to the guidelines set out in the previous chapter for making an ally out of an adversary. If you don't treat your opposite like the enemy, there's a good chance he won't act that way or will stop acting that way gradually. Treat the other person like someone you can talk to, and you are likely to find yourself talking your way to agreement.

Debating Rather Than Negotiating Issues

Negotiators too often forget they're supposed to be discussing issues and how to move from separate views to a shared perspective on the issues. They wind up trying to prove their view of the situation right and their logic superior. They get themselves locked into a conviction that the way to resolve differences on the issues is for the other party to give up its "incorrect" approach.

Of course, it's inevitable that both sides will spend some energy trying to persuade the other side to see things their way. That's part of explaining one's position, of exploring areas of difference and similarity. In the average negotiation, that sort of effort takes up about 50 percent of the time expended. When efforts to convince the other side of the rightness of your position take up more than that amount of time, you can be sure there's trouble. It's not explaining or exploring anymore. It's a contest—someone's trying to win debating points.

The difference between negotiation and debate extends along a range of considerations.

NEGOTIATION	DEBATE
A win-win orientation	A win-lose orientation
Readiness to consider compromise	Resistance to compromise
Looking for a common ground/position	Defending ground/position

Listening for needs and feelings	Listening for rebuttal points
A spontaneous back-and-forth exchange	A structured back-and-forth exchange
Equal emphasis on questions and statements	Emphasis on statements
Effort to convince the facing party of common interests	Effort to convince third parties of greater comparative merit
Strategic use of disclosure	Unwillingness to make disclosures

If you're spending more than 50 percent of your time following a debate pattern, you're radically increasing chances of getting deadlocked in disagreements.

What if the other party keeps insisting on debating you? The best tack to follow is not to follow. Approach the issues with a persistent openness. Ultimately you'll move the other person into considering issues with you. Don't let yourself be sucked into attaching some kind of abstract value to the holding of a position. Evaluate your position according to what direction you want to move in; forget about evaluations expressed in terms of right or wrong, good or bad, better or worse, or similar judgmental terms predicated on comparison to some imagined ideal.

Don't be afraid to use debate as a tactic to make a point. The key is not to let the tactic take over to become the purpose of the exchange.

Issues Not Clearly Defined

In a problem-solving situation, your chances for success increase considerably if you're clear on what the problem is you're supposed to be solving. Without that, you're searching blind for any solution and can have real trouble finding one.

When you sit down to resolve an issue, first make sure you're in agreement with the other side on what the issue is. You don't want a misunderstanding to develop that only serves to complicate the issue further.

In Australia a couple years ago, a strike of fuel truck drivers tied up transportation all around. Even the airports couldn't function. Drivers and contracting dealers were at each other's throats over the issue of job security. When finally someone got behind the facts of what had actually set off the strike, it all boiled down to disagreement and ill feeling between one driver and one dealer. Each had enlisted the support of colleagues in an effort to prevail, and within days transportation nationwide was crippled for lack of fuel. Once it was clear that what was really at issue was a personal difference, the dispute was resolved with a few "I'm sorry" statements on either side. The job security issue negotiators had started trying to deal with turned out to be largely a matter of conflict-inspired rhetoric.

Ego (Vanity and Pride)

A lot of people are extremely status conscious. They feel maintaining appearances is an absolute priority in all situations. In negotiation they're usually most sensitive to appearances related to power—who's got it over whom.

The ego-centered person is characteristically determined to show no sign of weakness. Rather he'll resolutely demonstrate at every opportunity that he's operating from a position of strength. The first concession has to be yours. You have to ask humbly if he'll consent to consider this or that possible compromise. But all this has nothing to do with what the concession or compromise is; it's all about who bows to whom.

Most people up against that attitude feel the temptation to resist vigorously. "I'll be damned if I'll crawl for that arrogant S.O.B.!" is pretty much how they feel. When that happens in a negotiation, you never get anywhere. You're so hung up by the struggle over appearances and power that the issues get lost in the shuffle.

It's the action-reaction sequence here that leads to impasse. A cool-headed negotiator, secure in his own self-esteem and confident of his own abilities, doesn't permit himself to be drawn into a contest. "The guy wants to think he's superior, let him. I'm here to deal with the issues, not to wear him out on who makes the first move to concession or compromise. If a timely concession or compromise offer can get him to move somewhat in my direction, I'll make the first move." That's the healthy and productive train of thought. Where's the disgrace in demonstrating cooperative good will? If letting the other person go through the door ahead of you results in both of you getting where you want to be, let that person go first. Once your opposite realizes that you don't particularly feel any connection between power or prestige and the willingness to take a first step, he or she won't continue making a contest out of it.

Similarity of Conduct

There's that old saying that likes repel and opposites attract, and to some extent that seems to hold in negotiations as well. Two individuals who speak the same lines, act the same way, and generally share behavioral traits, will often have a hard time getting things moving.

Part of the reason for this lies in everyone's conviction of uniqueness, that no one else is really quite like you. When someone behaves in a way as to suggest he is, you find yourself wary. It has to be an act to some extent. Then again, if someone behaves just as you would, you tend to tune into those aspects of your own behavior that you know serve as cover for negative feelings or motivations. Reflected in someone else, you're easily convinced that they cover the same negativity there. You tend to project your own doubts and reservations onto the other side. Since these rarely come into open discussion through a voluntary disclosure of feelings on your part, you expect them to operate covertly in your opponent. And that affects your capability for developing the kind of trust that makes it possible to bring differences out in the open. You're reluctant to open up on any controversial point because you're afraid in doing so you'll give away your own negative perspective on some aspect of it.

To the extent that this pattern is operative, reflect on what reservations *you* have relative to a commitment to work wholeheartedly toward agreement. Your insecurity about what the other person is up to may mask the fact that you haven't thrown off reservations about what *you're* up to. Dealing with your own hesitation in this area will make it easier to tolerate behavior in others that seems to mirror similar doubts.

Consider also whether you've developed some kind of personal formula approach to negotiation. Sometimes it's hard not to. But a formula approach that's too narrow sacrifices flexibility, which is necessary to a search for creative alternatives in bargaining. When someone else follows a similar narrow-formula approach, you're locked in together. Neither side gets a different enough stimulus from the opposition to change habitual patterns of response that lead only to conclusions you must go beyond.

If this sounds like part of your problem, keep in mind that you can initiate change here by daring to act in a spontaneous manner that is unlike you. Don't be afraid to step out of character, to drop an old pattern of communication. Be the one to introduce a difference. You'll find out soon enough whether the other side in turn develops its own more open approach to the issues. The simple fact of your change will require some adjustment in response, which widens latitude for progress. The only caveat is that you not introduce change so as to narrow the path to agreement.

Emotional/Irrational Outbursts

In negotiation, failure often grows out of sessions deteriorating into shouting matches. One side's response to a point of presentation or the manner of its presentation becomes an emotionally charged release of negative, even hostile feelings.

Psychologists say it's healthy to vent strong feelings. And we don't mean to contradict our own suggestion to sound off in a negotiation. But what we're speaking of here goes beyond sounding off. There's a point where emotion takes over completely. Emotional outbursts don't clear things up so much as disrupt them. What's brought out into the open isn't a "setting the record straight"; it's a lot of irrelevant remarks that have at best only incidental connection with what you're trying to accomplish. As far as you're concerned, these outbursts are an unwelcome self-indulgence on the part of the person from whom they issue.

Don't let them throw you. They usually pass. Keep this bit of Kentucky common sense in mind: A runaway horse eventually tires, and when it does it's fairly easy getting it back to join the rest.

Unwillingness to Compromise

Two people sit across from each other engaged in a staring contest. The first one to blink loses. The negotiator's version is that the first to compromise loses. However, in the negotiator's scenario, unless somebody starts blinking, both sides are going to lose.

To the question "Who should make the first concession?" we reply, "Whoever feels comfortable making it." Forget about that supposedly handing the initiative to the other side. It doesn't have to. You can indicate your readiness to give on a point of issue in such a fashion that it remains clear you anticipate getting something in return, either immediately or later on. Build in a condition you want taken into account. That's how you hold the initiative for getting what you want by starting with a "give." That keeps the focus where you want it—the other side now has to deal with ensuring you remain motivated to follow through on the offer of concession if that is attractive to them. They at least have to respond to the consideration you've presented.

Previous Bad Experience Between the Parties

Think of the difficulty whenever Americans and Russians sit down to negotiate differences. Your instinctive response may well be, "You can't trust those Russians. They never live up to an agreement when it's convenient or expeditious to ignore it."

Trust is critical for a successful conclusion of negotiations. The process doesn't work when there's no faith the other party will honor commitments made. Once burned, twice shy holds as true in this context as any other. And yet there are times when you have to try to work out differences with someone who's welshed on an agreement previously.

In this kind of situation, there's only so much you can do. You can't disregard what happened before. If you've been stabbed in the back once or twice before, you're wise to be very cautious the next time the other person pulls out a knife. He may say he's just going to peel an apple, but you're not going to turn your back while he's doing it.

The one thing you can do is work to tie elements of agreement tightly to what you see as important motivational factors affecting the other party. Make it clear that a breach of agreement will result in loss of an advantage or benefit to the other side. Then maybe simple self-interest on the other side's part will work to keep the agreement in force. Since you can't always count on an unreliable opponent to view his own self-interest consistently, you've got to nail the agreement to whatever element of self-interest seems most likely to remain operative through a variety of possible changes in circumstance later on.

Totally Unacceptable Opening Demands

People sometimes go into a bargaining situation with such a determination to be strong and forceful that they begin with demands that immediately place the other side in a position of having to say no. And everything's in stalemate from that point on. There will be no movement until there's some moderation in initial demands. But because of a concern that moderation will be taken as a sign of weakness, no movement develops.

The situation is much the same as when parties are unwilling to take the first step to compromise. The difference is that there's such a gap between positions that a greater adjustment in position is required to get meaningful discussions going. The distance between demand and reality will be such that backing down to a more real position will expose the bravado with which the initial position was asserted.

Almost always, either or both sides will fail to moderate *wants* in favor of concentrating on *needs.* Those involved have developed a conviction that they can get what they want—they don't have to settle for what they need. The only thing necessary is to hold out for it. The trap, of course, is that holding out is at the cost of any movement to closer agreement. Again, it becomes a contest. With two equally stubborn contestants, neither winds up getting what it wants or needs. Where genuinely pressing needs are involved, obdurate insistence on speaking just in terms of wants will prove particularly counterproductive.

If you're stuck in this kind of impasse, review your situation. Isn't there a way you can re-present your case to move the focus off insistence on getting what you want onto a consideration of how to get what you need? Stop trying so hard to shoot for the moon, and you may be able to get off the ground. Don't insist on a package that gives you everything you'd ideally like before you assume any obligation to consider what the other side wants and needs. As for the other party, when faced with their barrage of wants and needs, work to separate one from the other. Then start addressing yourself to areas you're relatively certain comprise areas of need. Hold out some hope of achievement there. You may well find your opponent coming to a realization of his own best interests: "Let's at least get what we need, then see if we can also get some of what we want beyond that."

Strong Personality Clash

Will Rogers may never have met a man he didn't like, but most of us have. The chemistry just doesn't seem to work between some people. You can argue with, shout at, and otherwise knock heads with someone you essentially respect and find it creates no block in movement toward agreement. But with others you find after a while that you just can't talk with them anymore.

Well, that's how it seems, but you can usually talk with anyone you keep yourself open to. The secret is to overcome your personal negative reactions to them. Think of your exchanges as part of a ritual rather than as personal exchange—they are, you know. It's a process for reaching agreement, not for making friends, even if it is easier to conclude agreement with someone who's disposed to be friendly toward you. Follow through as a good negotiator, putting aside as much as possible your desire to be liked or otherwise favored. Maintain this attitude and you stand a good chance of getting past obstacles posed by personal animosity. Stick to your understanding of the issues and address yourself to them. Don't concentrate your energy on how much you dislike the way your opponent speaks to or looks at you.

You can't avert failure every time it threatens. Sometimes parties are just too far apart to work through to agreement. But so many failures occur when the people involved do not keep themselves open to the challenges of the situation facing them, perhaps more than result from irreconcilable differences on the issues. The individuals who are supposed to be negotiating have gotten sidetracked into some faulty approach to the process.

Whenever failure threatens, consider what *you're* doing that may contribute to that danger. You may be following a faulty approach yourself somewhere. You may not be dealing effectively with the other person involved, thus accentuating the difficulty rather than moderating it. In either case, the adjustment you make to the situation may well be the way to get talks on course again.

MANAGING STRESS*

Whenever people discuss issues from different perspectives, each will experience some sense of strain or pressure. Tension may arise as a result of holding feelings in check—whether excitement, fear, or hostility. Or it may be that anxiety develops, with roots in a tendency to judge oneself incapable or inadequate in the face of a challenge to perform or prevail in an encounter with another person or party. Whatever the stimulus, each negotiator necessarily confronts the fact of stress individually, because stress is inherently an individual experience.

We can probably best define stress as the experience of an inability to cope with or satisfy demands made on us. Thus negotiation, where we are charged with representing interests on our side while contending with demands from someone else, virtually by definition constitutes a situation of stress. There's no avoiding it. A negotiator who seeks to eliminate stress from negotiation has about the same chance of success as a chemist working to produce dehydrated water. The point should not be to seek elimination of stress, but to learn to manage it.

Part of managing stress is simply a reorientation to it on a conceptual level. It is a term we traditionally load with negative connotations. But it need not be viewed only in negative terms. It can prompt creative effort as readily as constitute an impediment to that. We would even go so far as to call it an essential prerequisite to the exercise of creative ability. Without stress there is no impetus for change, whether by redirection or innovation.

Consider the analogy of a violin string. Left slack, there is no sound when the bow is drawn across it. Drawn too tight, it snaps. Under optimum tension, however, it can produce the most beautiful music. Similarly, in a negotiation, the trick is generating and managing an optimal degree of stress, building on it as a positive force rather than suffering it only as a negative influence.

*This section has been contributed by Kaye Raymond of Kaye Raymond Associates, Sydney, Australia.

Where Stress Manifests Itself

Stress always manifests itself within the individual. You can observe this for yourself by noting the varying reactions different people demonstrate toward the same situation. Say you're in a negotiation that's at an impasse. You can expect virtually any response to that fact of impasse, depending on the degree of stress that builds up within each of the participants. One person may betray acute anxiety and frustration; another may remain calm and at ease. One may become abusive and hostile; the other may respond with a new series of proposals or work toward a reevaluation of previous proposals. In a team situation, members of the same team can be observed reacting differently to stress, and the range of reactions, even though all team members are ostensibly operating from the same perspective, can be remarkable. You may see as much disparity within the team as between opposing parties.

Factors Prompting Stress

There are two categories of factors prompting stress: internal and external. The actual experience of stress is always a combination of the two, because it's the person (internal) reacting to the situation at hand (external).

INTERNAL FACTORS

Internal stress factors grow out of your perception of yourself and of goals you set yourself. The most fundamental of these factors are:

Value Judgments. The evaluation of the morality or propriety of your own behavior in terms of whatever ethic you've adopted as your own.

Expectations. Your sense that circumstances are evolving or will evolve in a predictable fashion to an envisioned end, whether ideal or not.

Self-Image. The perception of your place between the optimally integrated individual, whose sense of identity is strong and self-sustaining, and the fragmented individual, whose sense of identity is vulnerable to actual or imagined threats posed by others.

Realism. The degree to which you see the world as it is and work to adapt or otherwise effect change while accepting limitations imposed by the reality of the situation.

Idealism. The degree to which you envision a nonexistent but desired order to things and labor to influence or change reality to conform more nearly with this vision of what is or ought to be possible.

Emotional Needs. The inner experience of a desire to be loved, respected, admired, feared, etc.

While it may seem that these are all distinct from each other, be aware that all of them are continuously operative within everyone, with each exerting an influence on the others.

EXTERNAL FACTORS

External stress factors arise as a result of the individual's interaction with both other individuals and the surrounding environment. We could probably draw up an extended list of possible external stress factors. However, most fit into the following categories:

Externally Originated Norms and Expectations. These can range from general cultural norms to expectations that develop within the context of a particular personal or business relationship. In either case, you experience an evaluation of your abilities and/or performance by an "authority" outside yourself on which you are to some extent dependent and/or to which you are to some degree subject. In negotiation, the immediate source of stress here is twofold. On the one hand, there are norms and expectations on your side, particularly if you're acting as agent for someone. On the other hand, there are those of the person or party you're negotiating with.

Conflict Growing Out of Pursuit of Variant Goals. In negotiation stress develops not only as result of pursuing a different goal from that of your opposite. It also develops to the extent you are assigned a goal by an organization or individual employing you that takes precedence over personal goals.

Communication Problems. The difficulty experienced in getting your ideas or perception of the issues clearly across to others with whom you are interacting. This can include members of your own team as well as the opposite party.

Interpersonal Relations. Having to deal with others who may display personality traits or habitual behaviors that are unfamiliar or even disagreeable at times. Again, this can include people on both sides of the bargaining table.

Resource Limitations. Contending with an insufficiency of resources; dealing with the reality that resources available can be utilized or manipulated in only a limited number of ways.

Time. The degree to which you are either subjected to extended delays or hurried through any phase of the negotiating process, as when working with deadlines. However, this also includes any experience that generates a feeling of impatience or bewilderment related to time expended. An example of the former would be when a dull speaker drones on seemingly interminably; of the latter, when a presentation moves so rapidly that you can't note or absorb cogent points of information.

In all of these categories, stress can arise through interaction with people on your side of the negotiation as well as on the other side. This very elementary point should be kept in mind by those who employ people to represent their interests and by those who select the people who are to work together in a team effort.

How Stress Manifests Itself

There are two basic manifestations of stress: anxiety and adaptation. Accustomed as most of us are to viewing stress from a negative perspective, we usually focus on anxiety as the primary accompaniment or product of stress. We tend to be most conscious of stress when it results in a generalized feeling of unease or disorientation within us, in a fear that something bad or unpleasant is about to happen. We readily recognize it in others when we see them uncomfortable and restless under the pressure of tension that has built up within them.

We're not so quick to recognize that stress is an essential prerequisite to the exercise of creative abilities. It isn't the only prerequisite—simple curiosity also plays a great role in discovery and innovation. Curiosity, however, more generally comes into play in a person's efforts to understand the nature and limitations of the world around him. In working with and relating to others—and thus in negotiation—stress is what more commonly prompts adaptive reaction. No such reaction is likely without stress—it's just not necessary then. So when you see someone working to adapt to the demands of a situation, you can be sure that he is responding to the experience of stress—external factors inherent in the situation and internal factors accentuated by circumstances attending the situation. You can observe this in yourself just as readily.

Note that these manifestations of stress are not mutually exclusive. It's not a matter of being either anxious or adaptive. Some individuals react to stress with a sense of anxiety that can be absolutely paralyzing; others react with immediate adaptive endeavor. But many react in a sequential fashion, experiencing first a strong sense of anxiety and then working to relieve that by putting their adaptive abilities to work. Occasionally initial adaptive efforts compound rather than relieve stress. An experience of acute anxiety follows, to some extent grows out of, the initial effort to respond to the challenge posed by stress.

Some business managers, recognizing that creativity is frequently prompted by stress and the threat of anxiety it poses, deliberately create a stressful environment so as to promote creativity in their employees. Such a policy can backfire. Rather than adapting with on-site creativity, employees may choose to leave to take a position in a more comfortable environment. That's their way of adapting. The other danger of a deliberate policy of heightened stress is generating counterproductive anxiety that does not lead to creative response. Those who use stress tactics in negotiation may experience the same backfire results.

Handling Stress in Negotiation

In negotiation, stress, if not managed, can lead to exacerbated tensions and the paralysis of deadlock or walkout. Properly managed, it can lead to creative, adaptive behavior resulting in two parties coming to agreement.

Managing stress successfully requires adjustment in several areas.

SELF-AWARENESS

The stress factors most susceptible to management are always internal. So the first step to management is developing self-awareness. Many negotiators focus energies on the problems that arise in bargaining, but demonstrate minimal awareness of how stress created in dealing with these affects their own ability to cope. To the extent they are aware of stress working on them, they seem unable to distinguish between that which is generated internally and that generated externally. At times they react with exaggerated sensitivity to a manner of presentation, a point of issue, or some other external stimulus that others routinely take in stride. Chances are the reaction is largely to internal stresses they have not identified but which nevertheless have been building and contributing to a general state of tension. The external stimulus—perhaps just a straw, figuratively speaking—touches off a release of internal tensions experienced.

Learn to recognize signs of tension within yourself. Learn when these are the outgrowth of stress that is internally generated. The list of internal factors given above will help throw into perspective the areas where you are the major contributor to whatever feelings of tension and anxiety build up in you during negotiation. Work to stay in touch with your feelings. Reflect on what it is in you that contributes to your feeling defensive, offensive, resigned, frustrated, anxious, tired, or hopeless. Then review what you can do to change that mood or feeling. Ask yourself: "How can I redirect or reorganize myself to influence this situation constructively?"

YOUR SENSE OF ABILITY

Ask yourself "Do I trust my own ability?" and answer honestly. Qualifying remarks are likely to come out as part of the answer. Recognize that you can't expect to win every time. But is your response generally an optimistic one? Do you feel sufficiently balanced internally to roll with the punches, to work collaboratively with others to achieve goals that satisfy needs on both sides, not just your own? If you are not a solid optimist in terms of your ability to cope with the demands of negotiation, delve into what internal factors contribute to stress here.

SELF-EXPECTATIONS

What are the "shoulds" that permeate your life, either those you adhere to consciously or that operate at a subconscious level? Very often family background, education, social environment, etc., contribute to the adoption of values that you apply habitually but that, upon closer examination, you may find are not in accord with what you actually believe. An example might be the commonly implanted enjoinder to "be nice" in every encounter with every person, regardless of any feeling of anger, disappointment, or indifference that might come into play. Read through some of the literature available (such books as *Creative Aggression* by George Bach and Herb Goldberg or *When I Say No, I Feel Guilty* by Manual J. Smith) to help you develop greater awareness of the values you apply habitually rather than through a consciously made ethical commitment. Likewise, develop a clearer understanding of what such judgmental terms as *good* or *bad* really mean for you. What do you mean when you label yourself or your actions "good" or "bad"? When you apply those labels to others?

Under no circumstances do we mean to imply that a good negotiator follows a sense of values only when it is convenient to do so. What we mean to point out is that the stress generated by adherence to a value system is more manageable when that value system is one you've genuinely accepted as your own, when you know why you judge things good or bad or right or wrong. When judgment grows out of conscious value choices rather than being the result of some vague, inculcated moralism, you are much less likely to doubt your ability to make ethical decisions. You are less likely to be overwhelmed by the stress generated in having to do so.

STRESS-REDUCING TECHNIQUES

A technique that many find useful for coping with stress is a preliminary period of meditation before any negotiating encounter. This reduces or relieves tension that would otherwise interrupt the concentration and openness necessary for optimum performance in a meeting with others. Relaxation is the obvious first step, but the goal is to put the mind at ease as well as the body.

You can apply any of a number of techniques. Which you apply is not important as long as it works for you.

The Internal Emphasis

You will note that this brief review of how to manage stress concentrates primarily on internal factors. That grows to a considerable degree out of the oft-noted truth that "You cannot change the ways of the world; you can only change yourself." In fact, we've repeatedly observed that the ability to manage internal stress invariably results in an enhanced ability to cope with external stress.

The best negotiators are those with a powerful personal style. This is something that grows out of self-awareness and self-confidence, joined with one other element that affects the external situation positively: *recognition that those one faces in any negotiation are feeling stress, too, and must make their own adjustment in handling that.* The same recognition comes into play in dealing with people on your side of the issues.

There are further steps you can take to manage stress that originates externally. The key is always understanding where external factors create conflict within you. If, for example, externally originated norms or expectations build up tension in you, the first step to management is identifying how these conflict with values and expectations you have of yourself. Likewise, if you encounter communication difficulties with others, first analyze where the other person's "wave length" is relative to yours; consider what you can do to express yourself more clearly. By making a change in your behavior, you encourage an adaptive reaction in the person across from you.

Certain practical steps, too, can sometimes be useful. You can study verbal techniques that enhance your communication ability; you can learn ways of managing time more efficiently; etc. But note the focus is still on you. You make yourself more flexible in response to whatever situation exists.

The bottom line in learning to manage stress is to see its positive potential as well as being alert to possible problems that may arise. Stress is a natural, always operative impetus to creative adaptation. The worst problems related to stress grow out of resistance to change—out of the effort to continue following old patterns that don't meet the needs of the situation adequately, that don't provide the flexibility necessary for coping. Stress can be the source of great difficulty, but the experience of stress is also what often puts the wheels of opportunity into motion. Look at it from that angle, and you'll find that you are able to handle the challenges in most interpersonal or business encounters. You won't find yourself tripped up by unrealistic efforts to avoid the unavoidable.

DEALING WITH CONFLICT

When you put any two people together for whatever reason, at one point or other you're very likely to find them in conflict. They may be adopting opposing positions on how to get to a commonly envisioned goal. They may be in disagreement on what goals they should be working together to achieve. Or they may be at odds as a result of some personal antagonism that's developed.

In negotiation, too, conflict is inevitable. You expect that it will frequently be at the root of issues presented for resolution. Often, however, what happens is that conflict arises during negotiation. An example of this might be two people in discussion on how to manage a joint venture finding themselves in disagreement on how any resultant profit should be shared.

It can easily get complicated. While parties may find themselves at odds on the division of material assets ("This is/should be ours"; "No, it is/should be ours!"), they may also be at odds for emotive reasons ("Our name should come first"; "No, our name should come first!"). Sad to say, we regularly see conflict situations where one side's intransigence seems to have but limited relationship to any of its vital interests of organizational priorities, however expressed. It's as common to see people at odds for what appear minor considerations as because of major differences existing between them. In terms of the potential for disruption, conflict over seemingly unimportant distinctions can be as serious as conflict on any other score. It's just as important to deal with if you hope to gain anything out of your encounter with the other person or party.

The Stages of Conflict Resolution

Dealing with any conflict that arises in negotiation is a four-stage process.

ONSET/RECOGNITION

The ground for conflict is laid when one party intrudes itself between the other and the fulfillment of the latter's needs or goals. That intrusion doesn't of itself constitute conflict, it only sets the stage for it. There is no conflict until the second party reacts, pushing against the barrier laid by the other to its achieving what it wants. It is the two parties pushing against each other that constitutes conflict. On occasion it happens that one party will seek to block another by setting up an obstacle to achievement of a desired goal, but the other has sufficient alternatives or resources to ignore that attempt. When that happens, there is no conflict. Conflict is a dynamic between parties in active opposition to each other. It arises out of the actions of both, not just out of the actions of one, although these may have set the stage for it.

Let's suppose you're in a negotiation right now, resolutely aiming for a goal the other side knows you want. For some reason your opposite throws a block. The stage is set for conflict. It's your move. What are the options available, especially if it's true that conflict won't actually materialize until you respond to the provocation?

You Can Pretend That No Threat of Conflict Exists and attempt to proceed as if you don't recognize that your opposite has tried to block you. If you have enough resources or alternatives available to you to make an end run around the obstacle posed, you can simply make that end run and look expectantly to achievement of your next goal. However, an opponent who sincerely intends to block you isn't likely just to sit back and let you proceed nonchalantly toward your objective via some other route while his or her efforts to prevail are ignored.

You Can Accept the Limitation Your Opponent Sets on You. In that event there's no conflict either. But you're not apt to be pleased with the resultant situation. You wind up having to forgo an objective you genuinely want to achieve.

You Can Withdraw from the Negotiation. But then the opportunities you've postulated as existing for you in any agreement with the other party will all fall through, too. You don't concede the issue, and you don't wind up in a fight, but you don't win anything either. Only if the other party needs you as much as or more than you need them is there a strong possibility that the original provocation will be dropped in an effort to retain your involvement.

Although withdrawal ostensibly avoids conflict, fairly frequently it ends up being an actual conflict maneuver. That's because it's generally preceded by threats to withdraw—withdrawal is rarely automatic or immediately total. Where it is, no conflict develops. But where the response to the provocation of a blocking move is to threaten withdrawal, the interaction that ensues is conflict. You're using the threat as a weapon to counter the obstruction posed by your opponent.

You Can Respond with Moves to Counter the Block. In that event you've actualized the situation of conflict. Does that mean the burden of responsibility for the situation falls on you? Consider this example: If you're sitting peaceably on your beach blanket and some bully comes along and deliberately kicks sand in your face, whether or not there's a fight does depend on your reaction. If you ignore the provocation, smile and accept that that's the way things are, or fold up your blanket and leave the beach, there's no fight. However, if you take countermeasures, there will definitely be some kind of conflict, although not necessarily a knock-down brawl. You will certainly share responsibility for whatever happens, but from this example you can see that this isn't necessarily something to feel guilty about.

Do you need to worry about responsibility at all? Actually, once you're in a conflict situation, the matter of responsibility or blame is somewhat beside the point. The energy you expend trying to fasten blame here or there is largely wasted. What you wind up with is two parties throwing accusations back and forth much on the order of two children alternately shouting at each other: "You did . . .!" "I did not!" "You did too!" or "You did . . .!" "So? You want to make something of it?" The attempt to fasten blame only heats up the conflict without contributing to the resolution. To the extent that responsibility is relevant, it's not in the context of blame, it's in the context of identifying the effect of an act of provocation and working to overcome that effect.

That takes us to the second stage of dealing with conflict.

ANALYSIS OF THE SITUATION

You've decided that your interests are best served by stepping up to the challenge presented by your opponent's blocking move. If you've more or less anticipated the development of conflict at this point, you should have some sense of which way to go now. If you haven't anticipated it, then before responding, analyze the situation. Review what is at stake. How important is it to you really? Go over what circumstances triggered the move by your opponent that now presents you with the threat of conflict. Consider whether that move is related to any organizational priorities your opponent is charged with representing, or whether it has its roots in a personal motive. Weigh all your findings in light of how essential the goal is that's now been blocked. Is there an alternative means of achieving it?

Too many people bypass the analysis stage when faced with the threat of conflict. They allow the realization that conflict lies ahead to overcome their self-control. They get carried away emotionally. All at once they're responding—joining the conflict—in immediate reaction to surprise or outrage that preempts judicious consideration of the issues at hand. Before they know it, their outrage has prompted a defensive countermeasure that exacerbates the situation. Even if that countermeasure proves effective in warding off the threat to achievement of a desired goal, it may in addition have the effect of complicating subsequent exchanges. The emotional impact it carries may make further discussions even more tense. And if part of the reflex reaction is to respond with accusation and invective, the redoubling of hard feelings may put a strain on relations between the two parties that threatens realization of any opportunity to move toward cooperative agreement.

If you find you're faced with a sudden development that spells possible imminent conflict, keep your wits about you. Don't feel that your response has to be immediate and in kind. Analyze your situation for a moment first. If that means you will need some time to marshall your thoughts, ask for a brief recess. All you need say is that the situation poses some unexpected developments and you want a few minutes to consider your reply.

WORKING FOR COMPROMISE

In responding to an offensive move from your opponent, you can, of course, take an attitude that permits no thought of compromise.

However, if you do that, you in effect derail the negotiation. You're then in a position of hard-line confrontation that sees you thinking only in terms of your priorities, without a consideration of those the other side may be following at the same time. Your attitude may be "So what?" After all, "they started it" with their move to cut you off from achievement of your goals. Well, that attitude can cut you off from any chance to salvage those goals. Assuming you're in the negotiation to begin with because you see an advantage to be gained in working out an agreement with your opponent, you can wipe out the possibility of gaining that advantage.

To move toward compromise, you have to depend on the conclusions you've reached in your analysis of the situation. You also must maintain as cooperative an attitude as possible toward your opponent. You'll need to explore together the possibility of alternatives that may allow mutual achievement of goals. Poor communicators often have difficulty in this phase of dealing with conflict because they fail to be clear on what their view of the situation is. They are also usually those whose response include emotional reactions that cloud rather than resolve issues.

The cooperative attitude we recommend does not imply a meek acceptance of the circumstances facing you. In fact, that would be self-defeating. Your response should be direct and to-the-point. Maintain a self-assured, assertive demeanor. Speak frankly about the way this conflict situation affects your position. Be firm in your insistence that obstruction of your goals makes it difficult for you to sustain an enthusiasm for meeting those on the other side. But don't make a "federal case" of it. Always make it clear at the same time that you are leaving the door open to consideration of other avenues of action. You're concerned that both of you achieve as many of your respective goals as possible without prejudicing the potential for joint endeavor toward mutual benefit.

Note that compromise doesn't invariably mean that both of you have to settle for less than you really want to settle for. At times you will have to make a concession in terms of a goal you had hoped to achieve. But there are also times when the process of compromise works out to identification of an alternate course that still gets you what you want. In those cases, what generally happens is that your opponent is tuned into a means of getting his goals, too. Rather than conceding something of what you want so as to give him something of what he wants, it may come to your conceding something he wants that you hadn't recognized was a vital issue for him. It's not a prime point of concern for you, so you can still get virtually all of what you want. Compromise often works that way. The chance that it will is maximized if you remain as open and flexible as possible, keeping your emotions under control when responding to a threat of conflict.

OUTCOME

If at the close of negotiations the outcome is satisfactory to both parties, then the agreement is likely to be more secure than if one side settles for a result that doesn't go far enough to meeting its needs. In the latter event, the danger of conflict has only temporarily receded. It's quite probable that the same issue that gave rise to conflict in the first place will resurface as a problem. Maybe not right away, but when it does, you can be sure that it will do so with accented intensity. Consider outcome as a separate stage and resist resting on your laurels until you've reviewed the agreement reached and the course of its implementation.

If you fail to give this phase of dealing with conflict its full consideration, you risk being taken by surprise by an old issue you thought you'd dealt with conclusively. By taking the time to review your achievement of agreement and its implementation, you can anticipate a possible subsequent problem and work to forestall future conflict.

Behavioral Guidelines

Here are some suggestions on how to conduct yourself in a conflict situation. These are useful guidelines to follow in each stage, but particularly in the moments immediately following development of tensions between the parties and during efforts to work out compromise.

BE COOL

Stay calm and even-tempered. Naturally you can't entirely control how angry the other side becomes, but staying calm will serve to encourage serious discussion of issues once your opponent has vented his or her feelings. If you react with loud outrage to assertions or allegations from your opponent, you're just pouring fuel on the fire.

DON'T ARGUE

Don't feel that you have to get in the last word. An outburst from your opponent may surprise you. You may feel it's entirely unwarranted. You have good reasons for acting as you did, but when it comes to a question of reasons, your opponent has his or her own. Unless you want to get into a round robin of "yes buts," it's better to forgo the temptation to explain why your position has greater merit. Start dealing with the effect of the conflict rather than extending it with debate. You may need to trace its origins in order to deal with it in the best possible fashion, but avoid editorial comment on those origins. You won't get to resolution of conflict that way; you'll get into an argument that's really somewhat beside the point.

LOOK FOR A ROOT CAUSE

Try to identify quickly what the triggering issues are. You can't proceed in a positive direction until you know exactly what you're dealing with. If, for example, the conflict has its roots in your opponent's ego needs, you have to make an adjustment taking those into account. Efforts to respond in terms of substantive issues will be off base. (Where conflict is rooted in ego needs, it's sometimes difficult to approach those directly. Your opponent may not realize that his or her ego is interfering with movement to agreement. An effort to point out the problem is as likely to lead to defensive argument as to contribute to solution.)

To the extent you're not entirely sure what the conflict is all about, ask for a clarification of your opponent's position. You're likely to get emotional input as well as a statement of the facts. Don't get defensive in the face of emotional input. See it as an integral element of the other side's relations with you and adjust your behavior as best you can to defuse the situation without sacrificing consideration of the priorities you're there to discuss.

AVOID PERSONALITY CLASHES

Avoid focusing on how much you are annoyed at or dislike the person you are dealing with. Don't start trying to win points in a competition of one-upsmanship to prove your superiority. Focus instead on the relative positions and the specific needs on both sides. Be assertive in pursuit of understanding and resolution of the conflict.

And cultivate patience. The person you're dealing with may be difficult; if so, any difficulty will only be accentuated by your losing your patience.

CHOOSE WORDS CAREFULLY

Avoid using words with a negative emotional/judgmental content. You can indicate that you disagree without telling someone flat out he's "wrong," "foolish," "badly informed," "immature," etc. Using terms like those will inevitably prompt angry replies that sharpen rather than diminish the intensity of conflict. If you have figures or facts that contradict your opponent's assertion, simply state that they indicate a conclusion other than the one your opponent has drawn. Don't add that you've also concluded your opponent is something of a jerk. It won't be appreciated.

STAY OPEN TO CONSIDERATION OF MUTUAL NEEDS

Look for areas of common interest and possible compromise. A defense of your position doesn't deal with the reality that your opponent will not accept that position as a basis for agreement. Not until you consider the situation as objectively as you can from both perspectives do you stand much chance of working around your opponent's obstruction of your goals. Consider the other person's perspective. Make it clear that you are doing so to the best of your ability. You may find that an opening develops permitting you to make or elicit an acceptable concession that meets needs about which your opponent feels frustrated, without eliminating the opportunity for you to get something (maybe all) of what you want. Look for bridge issues between the opposing perspectives. You may very well find an area of commonality that provides a means of crossing over the divide separating the two sides.

AVOID DOGMATIC STATEMENTS

Language that smacks of pedantry and suggests a superior understanding of the way things are only serves to alienate others. Your opponent isn't there as your pupil and has no intention of relying on your wisdom for coming to an understanding of his or her needs. If your opponent has indicated through a provocative act or statement that things are amiss, any academic endeavor on your part to show that things really are as they should be is irrelevant. That's no way to cope with differences. All that amounts to is a sophisticated retreat from dealing with the fact of existent differences.

LISTEN

Always listen to what the other person is saying. And don't just listen to the words; listen to the feelings expressed as well. Ascertain the other person's perspective in relation to your own. Gauge the difference between them. Unless you do this, you'll flounder in any effort made to bridge that difference, since you won't really know what it is. When supporting your position with reasoning and facts to demonstrate your sense of the possibilities, also be alert to the other side's reactions to you. Give the other person an opportunity to express relevant viewpoints. That demonstrates your concern to understand what is at stake for him or her. And it encourages your opponent to seek an understanding of what is at stake for you in return.

There will be conflict situations where even the most artful negotiator has to give in to the fact of irreconcilable differences. Be systematic and judicious in response to conflict. Then, even in the event of failure, you can walk away with a clear conscience, *knowing* that irreconcilable differences make an agreement impossible. You won't lie awake at night wondering if you were at fault because of how you handled the situation. (In the context of negotiation itself the question of blame is often beside the point, but in terms of self-image it's a consideration every negotiator takes into account.)

Conflict in negotiation is as inevitable as conflict in any area of human relations. It happens. You needn't look forward to it, but you needn't fear it either if you've developed constructive responses and self-assurance for dealing with it as it comes along. In fact, to the degree that conflict puts you into an unexpected set of circumstances, it may at the same time provide opportunity for innovative action that serves your interests equally well, maybe even better, than if matters proceeded routinely. Conflict is a specific stress situation. Recognize that it can be the stimulus to creative adaptation even as it poses uncomfortable difficulties. Be organized in your approach to it, and you'll generally find that you can deal with it.

OVERCOMING OBSTACLES · 239

RESPONDING TO THREATS

What is your immediate reaction to being threatened in a bargaining situation? Hank regularly asks that question of his workshop/ seminar attendees, and 95 percent respond immediately along lines of "Call it," "Counter with your own threat," or "Break off the session and leave." Each of these indicates a virtually automatic stiffening of position on the part of the negotiator polled. Indeed this type of reaction is so automatic in so many cases that we term it a "knee-jerk reflex"—a response that comes without even thinking, much as when a doctor taps your knee to test your reflexes.

However, success in negotiation grows out of your remaining aware and in control of what you're doing throughout the process. If you allow others to trigger an automatic behavior response in you— even if that response is to resist a particular kind of pressure—you limit your opportunities for achieving success. It may be that in a given situation the decision to take a hard line in response to a threat is indeed in your best interest. But making a reasoned decision to act in one or other manner is very different from acting that way by reflex.

The making of a decision presupposes an awareness of alternate courses of action. A negotiator who acts with a conditioned response to any stimulus from others is not in control. You may argue whether he is a victim of his own limitations or of the opposite.side's tactics, but he's clearly a victim.

So what do you do? We suggest following a systematic approach that allows for optimum evaluation of the threat and encourages flexibility in response.

Consider the Threat

Are you sure that you are being threatened? If so, have you understood correctly what the threat is?

Threats aren't always made clearly. Sometimes what at first hearing sounds like a threat is really only an expression of frustration and/or exasperation—a significant reaction, but it needn't be responded to as a threat. On other occasions the opposite party may express a threat in so vague a manner that you're not at all sure what the "or else" consequences alluded to are likely to be. The knee-jerk response, of course, would be to the fact that a threat was made at all—there would be immediate indignation or outrage communicated, whether the threat itself was significant or not. Defensive or counteroffensive language would fly across the table in an instant, or the offended victim of verbal aggression might storm out with an air of injured righteousness. That knee-jerk response would turn what might otherwise still be a fluid situation into a confrontation.

When you hear what sounds like a threat, listen carefully so you can note as clearly as possible what is said. Is it really a threat? What exactly is it you're being threatened with? Is it actually something that can detrimentally affect an area of vital interest to you—that is, is it credible? What effect would it have on your opponent's vital interests if the threat were carried out?

At the same time, watch your opponent for telltale indications of the firmness of the threat. Does the way the threat is made suggest that it is serious, or is it blurted out in an unexpected moment of exasperation? Is his body language consistent with his verbalization, or is he nervously downcast, evasive of eye contact? Look back on the course of the discussions up to now. Did you sense earlier that a threat might be forthcoming, or was it a complete surprise and shock to you? An off-the-cuff threat can be as serious as any other, but it is more likely to be the product of momentary irritation.

These considerations can each be weighed in a second. Even so, there will usually be a brief silence between when the threat is made and the thinking negotiator's first response to it. That bit of quiet can be extremely valuable. If you're the party being threatened, realize that these seconds may hold an important opportunity, which you can lose if you jump in head first with a knee-jerk statement as your reply.

Let the Words Sink In

This moment of silence gives you time for considering the content and credibility of the threat. It also serves to focus everyone's attention on what has just been said. If, as occasionally happens, the provocation was wholly unintended or ill-considered, the silence allows the threatening party the chance to reconsider and withdraw the remark. That means a moment of embarrassment for him, perhaps, but you can proceed smoothly past that embarrassment. Your display of restraint at such a moment may be sufficiently appreciated so that the dialogue opens up rather than breaks down.

The brief silence may also spur the threatening party to qualify or explain its threat. The silence works psychologically to your advantage here. Generally the party who precipitated the awkward moment by making the threat will feel the stronger pressure to break the silence first. That can moderate the potential for conflict on the issue at hand. The qualification or explanation may well give you latitude in your response. Even if the threat is restated, it will often be done in somewhat altered phraseology, which can have the result of expanding your room to maneuver when reacting.

Repeat, Rephrase, Recap

Whether or not the other party does break the silence first, you can use one of these techniques to focus on the threat in such a way that some qualification or moderation is introduced. On a rare occasion you might simply by a somewhat bewildered or distressed repetition/rephrasing of the threat, or by a quick recap of how the situation got to the point of a threat, prompt a retraction. If that happens, so much the better, but it's a long shot.

Rephrasing can be important if the threat is vague or veiled in nature. However, you may want to try one particular approach that does at times work on occasions like this: Pretend you haven't recognized the fact of a threat and continue on with your discussion of the issue at hand. If the threat was either unintended or a bluff on the other side's part, you may be able to bypass it in this manner. Naturally, if the threat was intended and meant to be taken seriously, you'll be forced into a response, but again not usually until the other side has restated the threat.

Keep in mind that vagueness can have its advantages. A vague threat may be intended more as a warning than as an indication that a specific course of action will definitely be taken if you do not at once concede or agree to consider the opposition's viewpoint on an issue. If you, on the other hand, insist on treating it in the latter sense, pressing for a definitive statement of what negative sanctions your opponent is thinking of, you will complicate things for yourself instead of simplifying them. Pause a moment to consider what's been said; you may even repeat what's been said. But don't back your opponent into a corner so that he's pushed into articulating a clear and specific threat that he's really not ready to make yet.

Review Your Plan

Although threats are often unpleasant surprises, quite often they can be anticipated. If you've prepared yourself well for your encounter with the other party, you'll very likely have a good sense of where your differences are most acute. You'll have a fair idea of what the other side hopes to achieve; you may well know the exact issue that constitutes the greatest stumbling block between you. To the extent that you are aware of sensitivities and goals vital to your opponent, you can to a degree prepare for the difficult moments that may arise. You can develop tactics to take into account the possibility that threats may be forthcoming at critical moments. You may prepare back-up positions for the eventuality. In a team context, you may orchestrate who responds to what, and how.

Even if you've anticipated a threat, you want to be sure that the course of action prepared is appropriate. So listen and consider just as if you hadn't previously planned a response. For one thing, you want to be sure you've anticipated the situation correctly. You don't want to offer a response that doesn't quite fit in the way you thought it would.

Choose Your Response

The process you've initiated above already constitutes an important part of your general response, but what specific direction will you take in dealing with the threat facing you? A good many alternatives exist.

SILENCE

You can lapse back into silence. But don't make it a sullen, resentful silence: that can serve as provocation to reinforce the threat. An expectant or puzzled silence usually serves best to draw the opposition out further.

ASK FOR A REPEAT OR CLARIFICATION

You may already have questioningly repeated the threat and received an affirmative nod from the other side, but don't be afraid to ask them to repeat it too. Sometimes, particularly if an element of bluff is involved, simply holding the words uttered up for careful scrutiny can lead to their being withdrawn or so qualified that the element of threat somewhat diminishes. There are negotiators who will venture a bluff from time to time but be so uncomfortable doing so that any questioning on your part aimed at "understanding" the threat will prompt a pull-back.

You may also find it useful, even where your opponent is prepared to make good on a threat, to clarify the situation that gave rise to it. Asking for a clarification of a recap of why your opponent feels it imperative to pursue this tactic can at times lead to identification of a particular point of issue or position that you have not been fully sensitive to. Even if you have been, the explanation or recap from the other side may provide you with a clue to pursuing the subject further without risking the head-on confrontation implicit in a threat.

When reacting to a clarification or recap, avoid getting drawn into an argument about who said what or who is acting negatively in the negotiation. Listen without falling into a defensive mind-set. Defensiveness inevitably leads to argument about the relative merits of positions taken or tactics employed, which gets you nowhere, since perception of merit is always relative to one's own perspective. In negotiation you must work to show that alignment is possible between perspectives, not fight to assure one prevailing over the other. And don't argue that the threat you're dealing with constitutes an attempt from the other side to prevail in just that manner. It very well may, but pursuing that point of self-justification moves you no closer to your goals.

LAUGH

Some people possess an uncanny facility for immediately detecting a bluff or recognizing that it is impossible for the other party to follow through on a threat. They see the ridiculousness inherent in such a threat and respond with spontaneous good humor. Naturally this can prove embarrassing or disconcerting to the other side, but as long as the response remains on the level of good humor, it only minimally risks a sense of humilitation on the other side. You do want to avoid that. If your opponent feels humiliated by your response, he'll be likely to develop a grudge against you. That can prove troublesome later, even if you prevail this time. If you do laugh in response to a threat, avoid injecting sarcasm or ridicule into the situation.

EXPRESS DISBELIEF OR BEWILDERMENT

Either of these may be your actual reaction. You've been discussing and evaluating issues with an awareness of and sensitivity to the other party's needs and expressed goals; now it's as if your opposite is completely blind to your good faith in trying to work out a mutually agreeable course of action. "I'm stunned"; "I really don't know quite how to respond to that"; "It's hard for me to believe you want to follow this [threatened] course of action", "I never imagined we'd be unable to work out an amiable arrangement that takes each of our interests into account" are all replies you can use in attempting to moderate the force of the threat hanging in the air. Unless you've all along been taking a determinedly hard-line attitude yourself, there's a chance you will elicit a more open restatement of the position reflected in the threat.

INVOKE GUILT ON THE OTHER SIDE

You can do this by emphasizing your distress and hurt that matters have come to this and the difficulties this sets you up against personally. If your opposite has developed a liking for you, your distress may prompt him or her to find an alternate route to the objective sought via the threat. The motivation to do so grows out of a personal interaction that both sides have experienced as positive, whatever the relation between any organizations represented may be. Of course, this response can't be expected to work where there is a lack of personal rapport between people on either side. Then it may even backfire.

You can invoke guilt at times by referring to interests on either side that will be damaged if agreement is blocked by the kind of intransigence a threat implies. This would seem especially pertinent in labor negotiations, where both sides usually recognize that a breakdown of negotiations results in damage to both sides. However, because the tactic is used fairly regularly in labor negotiations, it is as often ineffective as effective. What happens frequently is that the other party attempts to throw the guilt back: "It's *your* position that's working a hardship on these other people."

If you decide to invoke guilt, it's best to do so subtly. Don't outrightly accuse the person threatening you of a lack of concern for or sympathy with others whose interests are at stake. In today's society, that blatant an attempt to lay a guilt trip on someone too often arouses open anger and/or contempt. Better to indicate your concern that immediate response to the threat—i.e., a hard-line negative response—will cut off a route to agreement protecting the interest of others not directly involved in the bargaining sessions.

REDIRECT THE THREAT

Show how the threatened action directly damages the interests of the party issuing the threat. This damage may lie in the consequences of the action threatened or in your being forced to withdraw (not that you're threatening that at the moment). A condescending attitude of "You're cutting off your nose to spite your face" leads readily to an "I'll show you" reaction, so avoid it. Be patient and forbearing. Be calm and reasoned. But be inexorable. Leave no doubt that actualization of the threat cannot help but lead to unpleasant consequences for your opposite. However, be realistic, too. Don't hypothesize a consequence that is unlikely to materialize.

If you know that the difficulty on an issue is one that your opposite would experience with any party, you may find it useful to point out that inevitability. Remind them that *you're* prepared to continue the search for a mutually agreeable formula. Another party could well be less easy to work with. This tactic often works for sales representatives who find purchasing agents threatening to turn to other sources of supply in order to gain advantage in price or delivery terms.

EXPRESS UNDERSTANDING AND EMPATHY

This works particularly well where the threat grows out of an evident frustration on the other side's part. Your expression of understanding/empathy can provide the encouragement your opposite needs to continue with discussion of the issue that's proving difficult to resolve. In expressing understanding it's not at all necessary for you to concede the issue. Your awareness of the effect the difficulty has on your opposite serves to make him more optimistic that you'll work for a resolution that takes his interests into account.

That can lead to a withdrawal or shelving of the threat, with discussion of the issue resumed on a hopeful note. Acknowledging that you understand why your opposite feels as he does may make him more open in searching for a solution that takes your interest into account as well.

REASON WITH YOUR OPPOSITE

Point out that the threatened action will put a strain on relations between the two sides. Reflect on the realities that make it difficult/ impossible for you to concede the point he's trying to win. Express your confidence that each side's interests are best served by continuation of the discussions in progress.

If you decide to respond with reason, be sure you don't fall into an argument on what is reasonable or who is or isn't being reasonable. Use logic to make your case as strong as possible; recognize that logic requires consideration of the other side's needs. Don't argue about what is logical. Be aware that making a threat is often a tactic that seeks to dispense with logic. The attitude is pretty much "Be reasonable. Do it our way—or else!" Trying to invoke reason in the face of that attitude isn't going to be easy.

DEFER DISCUSSION OF THE ISSUE

Where a threat develops out of an accumulation of frustrations at the lack of progress being made on a particular issue, you may be able to defuse it by postponing further consideration of that issue for a time. It may be sufficient just to request a recess. After a break for coffee or lunch, feelings that prompted an ultimatum may have cooled enough to allow continuation of discussion. On other occasions it will be advisable to move on to another issue altogether and work for agreement there. Naturally it's best to select an alternate issue where prospects for reaching agreement seem more favorable. When agreement is forthcoming, the good will that results on both sides often carries over to ease movement to cooperation in the area that had earlier proved so difficult.

When moving to defer discussion of an issue, it's best to avoid comments that reflect in any way on the position either party is taking. That amounts to an attempt to get in the last word, and as long as either side is determined to get in the last word, there's no defusing of the situation. Keep it to a statement that says you recognize there's a point of difficulty here and you'd like to defer your response—you're not in a position to give an immediate reply. If you'd rather take a break and then come back to the issue, suggest a recess to let you get your thoughts together. If you want to go to another issue, indicate to the other side that you'll need to do some research into the situation before responding, then suggest that in the meantime you'd like to pursue the potential for agreement in another area.

CALL IT

On occasion the most appropriate response to a threat is in fact one of those a knee-jerk negotiator immediately reaches for. When you make such a response, however, be certain it really is the most suitable one for the situation facing you. If you call someone on a threat he's issued, the way you do it should be distinct from the reflex reaction of the knee-jerk negotiator.

First of all, you should be acting on the basis of a decision made upon considering the threat and affirming the other side's actual intent and capability for following through. Weigh the risks involved, something the negotiator acting by reflex tends not to do. Then you'll remain in control of your actions; your demeanor will reflect that control. This is inevitably missing in the knee-jerk response, characterized as it is by an angry emotional quality that heightens tension at a moment when you generally prefer to have it defused. Rather than taking an attitude of "I dare you!" which marks the most typical knee-jerk response, you can reply with quiet regret: "If, under the circumstances, this is what you feel you must do . . . . Naturally we'd prefer to work for another solution."

When calling a threat, make two things clear: 1. You will not give in on the point at issue and are prepared to risk the consequences threatened; 2. You'd rather continue working for a negotiated settlement than see conflict supplant the opportunity for cooperative endeavor.

The knee-jerk negotiator characteristically makes only the first point. That leaves no bridge for the other side to use in backing down from its threat. By voicing the preference for continuing with discussions, you provide your opposite a means of saving face. You will both recognize the fact of backing down on the threat, but the tone and courtesy of your firm reply spare the other side the risk of overt humiliation, which can breed troublesome resentments that may surface later. In addition, should the threat be made good, you're psychologically better situated to play the injured party in subsequent encounters.

Again, this should be on the basis of a decision growing out of consideration of the threat and evaluation of relative positions. Be certain that your threat is credible, especially if you're bluffing to any extent. And here too, give your response in a controlled, low-key fashion that reflects your self-confidence and yet provides your opposite with a route for graceful withdrawal: "If you take this [threatened] course of action, it will be impossible for us to avoid taking countermeasures that serve to protect our interests. Our preference is to continue discussions, as we feel both our interests will be served best by working together rather than through conflict."

BREAK OFF THE SESSION AND LEAVE

This, too, should be a decision rather than a reflex reaction. Rather than storming out in a huff, your withdrawal should be dignified and incorporate the bridge element that allows your opposite the opportunity for reversing himself without feeling obliged to eat humble pie first.

ACQUIESCE

On occasion it can be the best response because it's the only feasible one for you. Let's face it. If you're in a situation where you need the other side more than they need you, or where you're very vulnerable along the line of action threatened, you may be forced to give in. Even so, avoid a panic-inspired reflex. If in giving in to a threat you avoid being stampeded into acquiescence, you may be able to salvage more out of the situation than at first seemed likely. Follow the same decision-making process for evaluating your situation. The very fact that you appear calm and reasoned in your response—especially that you take the time to verify or question the threat before responding definitively—may win you a bit more latitude on the terms under which you acquiesce. The self-control you demonstrate may in some instances serve to expose a bluff before you actually get to the point of acquiescence. (Sometimes you're not in a position to risk treating a threat as a bluff, and yet it may be one.) Even if you know you will ultimately have to give in, recognize that it is usually worthwhile testing with a couple of other responses first.

Stay Flexible

In no case should you regard the responses here as a selection out of which you can pick only one. You would be foolish to limit yourself to a single response; you can obtain a cumulative effect by employing several consecutively. Your first response may be silence, your next to ask for a repeat. You might go on to express disbelief, invoke guilt, and redirect. Following that you could seek to defer discussion of the particular issue. In the end you might be moved to call the threat or be forced to acquiesce. Other combinations of response can also be called into play, depending on the situation at hand. You have to exercise your sense of judgment.

With every response—even when acquiescing—you should work to keep discussion going. Don't burn any bridges that could otherwise lead you back to purposeful bargaining. Maintaining your focus on keeping the negotiation going will often provide you a route to that very end—you'll work around the threat. In those cases where you can't work around a threat, your repertoire of responses (which may include some not listed here) can serve to define, qualify, and/or moderate the circumstances to your advantage. This grows out of your keeping control of your reactions and responding with decisions. The knee-jerk negotiator is not merely at a disadvantage because he reacts within a very limited range of responses, he tends also in those responses to behave so as to crystallize the positions of the two parties in a state of conflict. The other side shares responsibility for that, but the issue here isn't who's responsible, it's how to respond. Don't get caught between a threat and a knee-jerk reflex—you're bound to get kicked.

WHEN AT AN IMPASSE

Few things are as frustrating in negotiation as finding yourself at an impasse. As long as there's any talk on the issues between you and the other party, even if the discussion is marked by angry exchanges or the introduction of only marginally relevant side issues, some sense of movement is retained. You're still apt to feel that both of you are actively working toward agreement; there's at least hope for an ultimate convergence of viewpoints. But the moment either of you announces an intractable position on an issue and that position turns out to be unacceptable to the other side, then discussions can come to a grinding halt. Perhaps not immediately, because it generally takes some probing to determine that the position taken is a final one. But once that's clear, what do you do next? Short of acquiescing to what is unacceptable, how do you get the negotiation on course again?

Simple Tactical Possibilities

Although it's quite possible that a particular impasse will prove incapable of resolution, there is quite a wide range of tactics you can choose from in this situation. A use of one or another of these at a strategic point can get discussions going productively again. A negotiator who can smoothly integrate several tactics into a repertoire of response to impasse stands the best chance of seeing discussions open up again. Several surprisingly simple tactical possibilities can prove useful to that end.

STRESS MUTUAL INTERESTS

In most negotiations, potential common interest is what brings the parties together in the first place. Even if they don't much care for each other, there's some sense of a benefit to come out of the encounter. The moment the negotiation process freezes in impasse, however, that envisioned benefit is endangered. It may never be realized, despite its desirability. So a very useful first tactic to employ in a stall is simply to point to the very real danger that no benefit at all may be realized if the negotiation remains bogged down. Stressing that reality can throw into a somewhat different perspective the relative importance of the particular issue you are hung up on. It's a form of stepping back for the total picture. You don't want a detail that's proven to be a problem to assume a disproportionate priority.

POINT TO NEGATIVE CONSEQUENCES

Beyond pointing to the likelihood that no benefit will be achieved if no agreement is reached, you can often indicate a further possibility: there may actually be a negative consequence resulting from the impasse, and this consequence would be one that the opposite party or both parties prefer to avoid. It's not that you're threatening negative action. The simple fact may be that in the absence of agreement there's an *automatic* negative consequence, e.g., lost income opportunity.

Once you've made the point of no benefit or negative consequence, you have to let it sink in. It's generally best that you avoid harping on the point. That can work to build a resentment that turns counterproductive quickly.

Often it's useful to ask or declare a recess. That provides both sides opportunity for reflection and consultation. If negotiating in a team context, it allows each side time to caucus for a discussion of the situation and its implications. It also allows each side to formulate alternate strategies that may not previously have been contemplated but which would work to break the deadlock. Obviously, neither side is going to want to review strategy in the actual negotiating session.

Sometimes it doesn't even require a formal recess. There are times it helps just to take an informal break for a five-minute stretch, coffee, lunch, dinner, whatever. Simply having some of the accumulated tensions drain away can make it easier for the parties to sit down again later with a more positive attitude toward getting things on course again. In structured bargaining sessions, an informal break also encourages some friendly socializing between the involved parties, and this can have a positive effect as well. It mutes something of the "adversaries at a standoff" feeling that can arise when propounding different points of view on official business. And occasionally a comment or suggestion that surfaces in informal exchange can provide a route out of the dead end that you'd previously thought yourself trapped in.

Techniques for Gauging Differences

Usually further effort is required to get the sessions on course again. While an impasse will now and again develop out of minor points of contention, more often it reflects genuine difficulty in reconciling two distinct points of view. But there is one thing you want to be sure of: that you really are faced with as distinct a set of differences as it seems you are. There are times when two parties think they are in an impasse on the issues when the problem is really that there's a communication gap. In other words, they think their positions are farther apart than they actually are.

There are two techniques you can employ to ascertain the existence of genuinely obstructive differences on the issues.

RECAPPING

Summarize previous points of agreement or disagreement relating to the issue on which you're deadlocked. What this amounts to is a verbal review of the sequence of expressed viewpoints leading to the mutual perception that an impasse has been reached. This review may disclose that you are stuck where you are because you misunderstood either the gist of or the implications of something that was said on the other side, or vice versa. You may have incorporated as centrally relevant something that was intended only as an incidental consideration or that was completely tangential. Or you may uncover a flaw in the logic that led either side to its standoff position.

GRAPHIC ILLUSTRATION OF DIFFERENCES

This serves much the same purpose of clarification. What you do is actually illustrate the relative differences in position on a blackboard or flip chart. Once those are clearly defined and compared visually so that all participants literally see what is at issue, it may turn out that the obstacles to agreement are not as substantial as at first they seemed to be.

But what if they are?

Well, you still have a range of tactics available to you.

A Repertory of Tactical Responses

DEFER THE ISSUE

If you're involved in a negotiation that is covering several points at issue—as is usually the case—it can be useful to defer further efforts on the point at impasse and introduce another issue for discussion instead. Pursue agreement where that is possible. The cumulative effect of an ability to reach agreement on a range of other issues may tip the balance in favor of obtaining agreement on the issue you were stuck on. This is particularly likely if the implementation of agreement on single points resolved is made conditional on a satisfactory settlement of all differences. (We recommend this especially in negotiations on labor contracts.)

Most negotiations, in addition to dealing with major points of concern, have built into them relatively innocuous issues that are of minor importance and can be resolved easily. These we term bridge issues. If you go for a quick settlement of a bridge issue as a means of maintaining some movement in the negotiation, that may well be seen as an indication of amenability to cooperate. You'll have proven that you are essentially oriented toward cooperation without sacrificing a major issue that may be proving difficult to settle.

DISCUSS ALTERNATIVES

If it isn't either feasible or desirable to change to a different issue, it may help to discuss what mutual alternatives are left. It does sometimes happen that the resistance in an impasse has built up only in the context of an immediate struggle to prevail on the point under discussion. Step back from that contest and regard the other choices available for dealing with the problem. Maybe a long, hard look at other possibilities—even if they are not preferable to either of you—will prompt acceptance on one side of what had previously seemed unacceptable. Or else a close look at an alternative or approach that had either been ruled out previously or not seriously considered at all will result in a way out of the impasse.

GO FOR AN AGREEMENT IN PRINCIPLE

Try changing your point of focus from trying to win agreement on the deadlocked issue to establishing an agreement in principle. An agreement in principle has the benefit of reaffirming an awareness of interests held in common and of pointing to difficulties or eventualities that both parties want to overcome or avoid. The result can be that either side's propensity to take an adversary position vis-à-vis the other, which tends to be accentuated in any situation of impasse, is deflated. Pointing up common interests and goals in an agreement in principle can make it easier for an otherwise obdurate negotiator to move to a more specific agreement on how to resolve a troublesome issue.

DISCLOSE ADDITIONAL INFORMATION

If the sessions are in part stymied because you do not want to divulge the full details of how a sensitive issue affects you, or you are hesitant to disclose otherwise confidential information, it can sometimes be useful to make incremental disclosure of information you've been holding back. If it's important that the issue at hand be resolved in a manner that works to your advantage, the cost of such disclosure can be offset by the benefits of the agreement you make possible. Making disclosures in small increments serves to ensure that you divulge only enough to stimulate a positive response from the other side, that you don't tell more than you have to. It can also encourage or entice the other side to be more forthcoming with relevant information from their side. It is *not* advisable to go through with even more disclosure if the other side continues to balk at making any reciprocal gesture.

TAKE A HYPOTHETICAL APPROACH

Suppose for a moment that a particular position held or taken is acceptable, then invite response to a hypothetical situation growing out of that supposition. No one has to commit to anything. But make it clear that the hypothetical situation is within the range of possibility—there's no point going on a complete fantasy trip. Exploration of possibilities along these lines allows both parties to discuss the effect of concessions while leaving it clear that no commitment to any particular concession has yet been made. This kind of discussion can lead to exploring a proposal in sufficient depth to render that proposal either less fearsome or more attractive than it previously was.

THROW OUT A QUICK-CLOSE CONCESSION

Try for a quick close by originating a proposal for immediate settlement of the point on which you are deadlocked. Simply throw out a proposition you can live with and that seems likely to tempt the other side to say yes quickly. For example, "Will you agree to the price we're offering if we agree to pay a five percent bonus for delivery within sixty days?" As you can see, generally—although not always—this involves indicating a specific further concession that you make conditional on the other side's immediately accepting it as providing satisfactory grounds for the agreeement that has up to now eluded you.

You do need to be very calculated in what the concession you offer will be and, if you have to report back to an approving authority on your side, you have to be confident you will be backed up subsequently.

For this reason, it's generally useful to anticipate the possibility of impasse. Devise contingency concessions in advance that will be acceptable to your side. But if you do have a contingency plan worked out, be sure you don't reach for it too soon, or you may fall victim to a common negotiating tactic: waiting out the opposition (in this case, you) so that impatience or frustration builds up to a point where some concession is made just to get through a painfully protracted session that may not yet actually be at a point of impasse. Whatever you do, be explicit that you will only give something on the condition that the other side accepts it as grounds for settlement.

APPEAL TO AN "ALLY"

If in a team negotiation you sense that an individual on the other side is somewhat sympathetic to your position, you can slant your presentation so as to elicit a more open expression of that sympathy. That person may help bring the others round. Be wary, however, of making too blatant an effort to divide the opposition. You could alienate the very person who might have responded positively to a subtle appeal to act as peacemaker or tiebreaker.

PLAY ON FEELINGS

Sometimes just the force of expressing how you feel can strike a responsive chord in those who have been holding you off. Naturally that expression should be diplomatic in its design to elicit sympathy. "I'm honestly disappointed we're hung up on this point, since I've been so optimistic all along on the potential mutual profit in the agreement we're all working for" will get you farther than "I'm really annoyed you guys have no sense of the money we stand to lose if we don't settle this reasonably." Or use empathy: "I can see the difficulty you're having assuring yourselves that this does indeed work to your advantage." The point is to defuse any adversary mentality that may be contributing to or arising from the impasse that's developed. It's remarkable how often a simple gesture of good will or understanding can prompt a breakthrough in a deadlock.

CHANGE THE SETTING

There are times when resistance to agreement is somehow stiffened just through the psychological effect of location, usually when negotiations take place on either party's home ground. The home team may be less open to concessions; the visiting team may be more wary of the other side pressing its home team advantage. (This is equally a consideration when only two people are bargaining with each other.) Then it can be helpful just to move to some neutral ground where no sense of advantage is accorded either party and where the atmosphere is consequently more relaxed all around.

ISSUE A THREAT

When one party is in a demonstrably stronger position than the other relative to issues that divide them, that party can use force or the threat of force to break through the other side's refusal or reluctance to agree on settlement of an issue. There are times when that is unavoidable if a necessary advantage is to be gained out of agreement. But it's a tactic best reserved as a last resort, because you rarely win enthusiastic cooperation that way. And if relative positions later change but you still want or need cooperation, you may then find it elusive.

CALL IT QUITS

This is the final alternative when absolutely nothing can prompt further movement toward agreement. Once in a while it's the only thing that makes sense. You can butt your head up against the wall only so long before you admit defeat. However, guard against succumbing to the temptation to walk out before it's absolutely certain you're in a lost cause. Don't idly use the threat to walk out. The other side may take you up on it, and you'll find bargaining terminates before you've actually given up all hope of achieving some agreement.

An impasse can arise out of many reasons other than that there is no common ground for agreement between the parties. Realize this and consider the repertory of alternatives available to you when it seems neither you nor your opposite is likely to move closer together. You'll find yourself feeling less powerless or frustrated when you first realize you're at an impasse.

More often than not an impasse just indicates a temporary breakdown in communications. Sometimes it doesn't, of course, but you won't come to a premature conclusion that the situation's hopeless if you've first put it to the test by bringing to bear the full range of tactics designed to keep communications open.

NEGOTIATING FROM A WEAK POSITION

It's all very well to present negotiating as a two-sided dynamic, but the situation that prompts a negotiation isn't always evenly two-sided. The needs on one side can't always be balanced against those of the other side. Remarks that suggest a rough equality between the participants won't apply when one side is virtually in a position to dictate to the other. Then what? Are there entirely different ground rules to follow here, as compared to when one is bargaining from a position of relative equality?

Our response to that is an emphatic "No!" As long as the situation, however desperate it may appear from your perspective, is under discussion, you're involved in negotiation. The same ground rules apply. The difference is only in your room to maneuver and in the sense of urgency you feel. The process for resolving your difficulties remains the same. It's just that now you must more than ever exercise skill and sound judgment in the strategy you follow and the tactics you apply.

Even when the other party seems in a position to dictate terms to you, you can frequently influence things somewhat to your advantage. As long as the situation affords occasion for dialogue, you are in a position to negotiate. As long as you're allowed opportunity to express your views, you can use customary negotiating tactics to protect or advance your interests. You may not be able to establish an ideal situation for yourself in the existing circumstances, but that should not lead you automatically to concede defeat. Nor should it drive you to a "cornered rat" response that only increases whatever tension may exist between you and your opponent.

Keep a Broad Focus

The greatest danger that exists for negotiators working from what they see to be a weak position lies in focusing narrowly on that sense of weakness. They risk setting up a condition of self-fulfilling prophecy. They can convince themselves they have no negotiating leverage whatsoever and thus fail to take into account that the other party's participation in bargaining always provides some opportunity to influence the situation positively.

Take the example of a small company absolutely dependent on one supplier for an essential component of its main product line. The supplier has raised its asking price on that component to a level that threatens the manufacturer's market position—an imported substitute may now prove more attractive to cost-conscious consumers. The supplier, aware that the manufacturer has no alternate supply source, seems little disposed to price concessions. Their attitude comes across as "If you want it, you'll have to pay what we're asking for it." The manufacturer's business is but a very small percentage of the supplier's total business, so the supplier will hardly be affected financially if the manufacturer is forced out of business. Clearly the manufacturer is in a weak bargaining position.

One spokesman for this small company very reasonably sees himself in a nearly hopeless situation. It looks as if there's no leverage he can apply to win the necessary price concession. Pointing out that the supplier risks losing the company's business seems unlikely to have much effect. If the company goes out of business, the supplier will hardly notice it as far as any monetary loss is concerned. There's nobody else to turn to. What approach can one take in any discussions on the subject except to point to the bitter reality that the company will be unable to continue in operation if forced to pay the supplier's asking price, and then hope the supplier takes pity?

A second spokesman, however, refuses to limit his focus to the narrow "reality" that no leverage exists. He takes a broader view than one that looks only to the danger or likelihood of being forced out of business. He undertakes a series of calculations projecting likely growth for his company over the next several years. Given present market conditions and evidence of growing consumer demand for the company's product, he estimates that company need for the supplier's component will quadruple in two years' time and could well be ten times greater in four years. From industry reports he knows that the supplier's rate of growth in business volume has been only marginal over the past five years. Now he's ready to go into negotiations with the supplier with evidence that price moderation on the supplier's part now will assure their participation in a rapid-growth industry for several years to come. They can provide themselves a route to much-desired improved business performance over the course of the next few years by taking a more accommodating position on component pricing now. Failure to do so cuts them out of one area that could pull them out of a currently stagnant business pattern.

Weakness, like beauty, is often in the eye of the beholder, at least to some extent. If you look only at those factors that limit you, then you are limited. If you expand your focus to consider potential positives, you will often find you can cite those to your advantage now.

Avoid an Overly Defensive Posture

Some people who negotiate from what they see as a weak position will adopt a sort of last-stand defensive mentality. They concentrate energies on preserving what they have by vociferous resistance, hoping somehow that the volume of their protests and objections will save something.

The problem with this is in part the same as the previous situation: the focus is too much on anticipation of loss; there's a failure to look to or develop positive approaches to the situation. Beyond that, defensiveness usually contributes to increased friction between the parties, which hardly helps if you hope to moderate the effect of what you see as a bad situation. A negotiator whose frustration and sense of weakness prompt him to loud, irrational outbursts is just asking the other side to put him out of his misery that much sooner. The opposition, faced with an increasingly unpleasant situation of argument and protest, is likely to exert its unequal influence to bring an end to discussions more quickly. And then, of course, the opportunity for influencing deliberations toward a more favorable conclusion is terminated as well.

Rather than take a defensive posture, the weaker party is better advised simply to work to keep an open dialogue going. And that dialogue will be most productive if the weaker party takes an attitude of desiring a thorough, dispassionate discussion of all aspects of the situation as it affects *both* sides.

This brings us to a particularly vital point when negotiating from what seems a position of weakness.

Address the Other Side's Needs

Concentrate your energies on influencing the other side's perception of its own needs.

You're faced with a determination by your opposite to take action in pursuit of its interests. The action indicated will prove damaging to your interests, but you haven't the immediate ability to counter it with any action or threat of action of your own. You have no plum you can throw out as an incentive for change here. That's why you're in a much weaker position.

Naturally you can point to and protest the injury you are apt to suffer. Depending on whom you're up against, this may have some effect. But people all too readily turn a cold ear to pleas to consider the interests of others ahead of their own. You are far more likely to prompt moderation in your opposite's actions if you can convince him that those actions ultimately work against his own interests. This sets up something of a paradox. Just when your natural inclination is to press your own interests hardest, your best line of strategy will probably be to address yourself to those on the other side.

In order to pull this off, you frequently have to consider and present your opposite's interests from a perspective he has not yet fully considered himself. Look at the situation just described. There the tack of the more creative negotiator is to point to the supplier's cutting himself out of otherwise achievable and substantial future profits. The supplier up to now has viewed the situation wholly in terms of the present pattern of business.

Note that you can work this tactic of "You're overlooking something that could be important to you" from any number of angles. Since profits are conventionally considered the primary motivation for business activity, it's natural in a business context to see if you can't devise an appeal based on profit considerations. But don't forget that there may be potential interests relating to circumstances other than financial gain. Look back to the list on page 182 for ideas on other motivational possibilities to consider.

While concentrating on influencing the other side's perception of its needs, don't lose sight of your own interests. Advancing those remains your priority. You appear to focus on the other side's interests because your weaker position leaves you only one workable option for prompting change in your opponent's indicated course of action—exercise of the art of persuasion.

Pursue the Issues

Use the time given you to open issues up to further examination. Recognize from the very start that you can't afford to spend time crying. Nor can you afford to spend time on incidentals or trivialities if the situation facing you affects vital interests. You're already at a clear disadvantage as far as holding any bargaining chips goes. Don't compound your disadvantage by failing to make best use of the time you have to exert what influence you can on the important issues.

Using time effectively here means a thorough preparation for the actual negotiating encounter. That's true in any case, of course, but you can often get away with a somewhat more relaxed attitude when the situation facing you isn't weighted so heavily against you. An occasional negotiator facing an opponent from a clearly weaker position makes the mistake of assuming there's not much point to invest-ing a lot of time in preparation. After all, the relative positions won't change: the other side will still hold the upper hand and be in a position to impose terms pretty much at will. Why waste time fight-ing the inevitable?

That attitude is simply defeatist. If you decide in advance to roll over and die, then you forfeit any chance you have to improve your situation. There's no guarantee the best-prepared efforts will save the day for you, but lack of preparation will most surely work to see your worst fears realized. When issues to be discussed come up, articu-lately express your perspective and convincingly address each in light of your opponent's needs and expectations. You may be surprised to find you can influence things substantially to your advantage.

More than one determined spokesman for a weaker position has prevailed against the odds to emerge a winner from negotiations. An opponent who anticipates little more than a helpless squawk of frustration or resigned acquiescence instead encounters someone who initiates a thorough reconsideration of the situation, who mus-ters impressive persuasive abilities to point to uncertainties or dis-advantages implicit in the stronger side's initially preferred course of action. By intelligently drawing out the discussion of issues, the weaker party's spokesman influences a rethinking of positions on the other side. That rethinking leads to gain. What was expected to be a quick *pro forma* look at things already decided as far as the opposition was concerned turns into a series of discussions that can introduce unexpected change.

Project a Sense of Self-Assurance

Don't let yourself be intimidated into silence.

Some who negotiate from a weaker position feel themselves in a position of inferiority as well. At times this is accentuated by an attitude of smug superiority or arrogant condescension from an opposite who likes being in a position of power. Other times just the fact of negotiating from the weaker position is enough to evoke this feeling in them.

Any time you're in this situation, remember this: *Being in the weaker position does not make you inferior.* You have every right to expect to be treated with respect; you do not have to eat humble pie, even if you are obliged to concede defeat in respect of any or all the issues. You need not feel a loss of self-esteem because you are unable to prevail against a stronger position.

Treat yourself and others with dignity and respect. You may be surprised to find that of itself can influence things more to your advantage. Negotiators have the opportunity to demonstrate a positive force of character. That kind of demonstration at times can exert as beneficial an influence in interaction at a negotiation as the most brilliantly thought-out strategic maneuver.

Push for a Win-Win Solution

Always stress the advantages of a win-win solution for both sides.

With one party in position to impose at least some of its priorities on the other, the temptation to set up a win-lose situation can be considerable. Naturally the weaker party is the one slated to lose.

As the weaker party, you will find it can be worthwhile to state explicitly your desire to help work things out so that both parties benefit rather than just one. When the negotiation obviously goes off in a direction that means gains for the other side at your expense, you may still be able to introduce a moderating element. You can acknowledge your opponent's position of power while suggesting it will still prove worthwhile to consider some alternate course of action. "You're clearly in a position where you can insist on settling the issue this way, but let's consider if we can't work out an alternate approach that provides us both a sense of benefit. That'll give us greater incentive to work cooperatively with you in this situation; we'll be that much more ready to work for mutual benefit in a next encounter. You know it never hurts to have a friend lined up." And then you suggest an alternate approach.

When you follow this tack, the alternate approach you suggest should be one that provides the other side tangible benefit where they indicate themselves determined to achieve benefit. You're not likely to make much of an impression if in proposing an alternate approach you don't provide a clear route to benefit on the other side. Then the first course of action contemplated by your opponent is all the more apt to be the course of action that's followed.

Don't Prematurely Assume a Loss

At times you may find yourself in a negotiation where your opponent seems to hold all the point and trump cards and yet be able to play your own hand to eventual advantage. For one thing, your opponent may not realize how much the balance of power weighs in his favor. Sometimes, even if he does, it may not be his intention to press his advantage to its potential limit. He may prefer to work out a win-win solution to the issues facing both parties, or at least be open to possibilities along those lines. Sometimes an opponent who has a clear advantage and knows he has that advantage still proves unable to press that effectively. Whatever the circumstances, it's foolish for you to act as the agent of your own defeat by giving up before you have to.

Don't for a moment think there's any formula that assures your always being able to snatch victory from the jaws of defeat when faced with a substantially stronger opposite. There are times when the drive and determination to prevail on the other side will steamroller right over you. However, on other occasions, when it seems that's what's likely to happen, keeping your head and applying the principles suggested here will be able to save the day—or if not save the day, salvage more out of the situation than you first thought likely or possible. As long as discussions continue, work to preserve, protect, and advance your interests. Be creative. Be calm. Be alert.

RESPONDING TO RUMORS

It's said that rumors are the stuff of small minds. If that's so, then there are certainly a lot of midget minds around. Rumors crop up like

264 • NEGOTIATE THE DEAL YOU WANT

weeds at times, and like weeds, they generally act to divert energy from more productive, priority concerns.

The Design of Rumors

Rumors don't just arise spontaneously. Quite frequently they are deliberately sprung during negotiation with an intent to startle and/or put you on the defensive. The person who springs a rumor wants to put you in the position of convincing him that what he's just mentioned is only a rumor. Too often that's precisely what happens. Discussion of whatever issue is at hand is put aside while the rumor takes center stage. You get into proving that the situation is other than the rumor reports it to be. You're on the defensive and apt in your defense to reveal information that it may not be to your advantage to reveal. Your opponent, of course, is busy taking notes on that information, without bothering about the rumor itself other than as a device to keep you off balance.

Some people who use the tactic of finessing information through invoking the force of rumor will actually preface a remark with "I've been hearing a rumor that . . ." Even that open an announcement of the nature of the allegation that follows fails to stem a defensive response. There's something innately distasteful in hearing that someone might think circumstances surrounding you are other than what they are, particularly if they're made to appear worse than they are. You want your opposite to understand the validity of your perspective. You don't want to seem to be misrepresenting things on your side. So you start quoting chapter and verse to prove how things really are and, in the process, let out information of the sort that an opponent would find difficult to get in a direct manner.

Avoiding the Trap

There's something backwards about the way most people respond to the injection of rumor into negotiations. Their opponent throws out something that has an element of untruth in it, but they feel an obligation to make all the adjustments. But why should they be on the defensive in the face of someone else's allegations? Doesn't it make more sense to have the person who injects the rumor make the explanations?

We recommend that instead of taking it upon yourself to convince your opposite of the falsehood of what he's just related as a rumor, you have him convince *you* of the relevance or import of what he's reported. Don't get hooked into an automatic defensive explanation of how things really are. Let him assume the burden of establishing credibility for what he's just uttered. Ask questions rather than replying with your own counter assertion of fact: "Oh? I haven't heard that. Where did you hear it?" "What makes you feel this has validity?" "Why do you want to get into that?" Keep asking questions to pinpoint as narrowly as possible—and as uncomfortably as possible—what lies behind your opponent's interest every time he refers to some element of hearsay. Of course, if he takes the part of discretion and drops further mention of his interest, have the sense to shut up and let the rumor die.

To the extent you make a responsive statement of your own, keep it short and sweet. Don't start making explanations or giving figures to prove your position. The harder you work to combat a rumor, the more you're caught up in it. Keep your statement to a brief dismissal, matter-of-factly delivered: "There's no truth to that" or "Now, that's one rumor we don't even have to waste any time on." If the other person persists, let him do the talking to convince you why it's so important this red herring issue be dealt with.

Occasionally you will have to work to lay a dangerous misconception to rest. You don't want a particular falsehood to be given any credence, because people's decisions are as much influenced by what they believe to be true as by any objective knowledge of the truth. But you'll know when it's necessary to respond with a statement of enlightenment that dispels a false impression and provides the other side a better understanding of you and your priorities. The misconception will generally be very specific and on a point of essential relevance. It isn't likely to have its source in some vaguely reported rumor that's been heard. Someone who throws out one of those is probably on a fishing expedition, and the fish he hopes to hook and fry is you. Don't be an easy catch.

TUNING IN TO DIVERSIONARY TACTICS

A lot has been written about negotiating tactics, but it's noteworthy that so little attention has been paid to their design. The usual focus is on a trick element to apply in each case: learn this technique and watch the other side fall into its predictable reaction. We prefer to look at diversionary tactics on a more fundamental level. Rather than constructing a list of different diversionary tactics that are more or less in common use at the bargaining table, we want to categorize them according to purpose or design.

You can review the list that follows with an eye toward developing or polishing specific tactics you want to use on others, but we are going to approach them as designs an opponent has on you. Our intention is to enable you to analyze a tactical situation by reflecting on the direction in which you're being pulled or pushed. In each case the effort being made by your opponent is to manipulate you into accepting his priorities in preference to following your own, either on one issue or all of them. The problem that can lead to for you is obvious.

Once you learn to identify the design pattern that any tactic follows, you'll find it easier to react in a manner that safeguards your interests. In some cases you'll be more readily able to turn the tables on an opponent, gaining for yourself the edge he intended to hold over you.

Categories of Purpose

TO INDUCE DEFENSIVENESS

Some tactics aim to put you into a defensive posture from which you feel it necessary to explain, justify, and otherwise go into extensive detail on any or every aspect of your position. Somehow you're intended to feel guilty that you're taking the position you hold. Your opponent will query you on it so as to suggest it isn't logical, isn't well thought out, and/or is counterproductive even when viewed from your perspective.

If during a bargaining encounter you catch yourself working to convince the other side that your position really does have merit, that your objective really is a worthwhile one for you, you're almost certainly being subjected to a tactical maneuver that has as its aim weakening your commitment to your goals. When that happens, stop trying to justify your position. You can easily get yourself back on track with a comment along the lines of "I realize you may not totally comprehend why we're pursuing the objectives we've stated, but they do serve our needs best. Rather than debate that they do, let's see if there isn't some way we can achieve those and at the same time take your interests into consideration."

The net effect in this case is upsetting your game plan. This is usually accomplished by some premeditated behavior or statement that is totally unexpected and/or out of context.

Several business negotiators working as a team designed a tactic to achieve this effect with an opponent who was reportedly somewhat short-tempered. They decided that if they got him angry there was a good chance they'd end up negotiating with his boss instead, who was by reputation inclined to be much more cooperative and compromising. They worked out the timing for their stratagem. At the appointed moment the team member designated to light the opponent's fuse turned and snarled at him, "You're a pompous, unreasonable ass!" To the baiters' chagrin, the response was an amused smile. "Yes, sometimes I am, but I feel open to reason today. Let's see if we can't take advantage of that in working out a good agreement for all of us here." Those "best laid plans" went awry, and the anticipated advantage for the team failed to materialize.

When you're hit with a comment or statement that appears to relate to nothing that's at issue and yet has an implicit or explicit disturbing quality to it, keep your cool. Your opponent wants you to lose it. There's no surer way to get whatever tactic has been designed for this effect to backfire on hin than to remain calm and sweetly reasonable. Suddenly it's the other side that's confused and disoriented. The opposition doesn't quite know what to do next, and the advantage is unexpectedly yours.

TO APPEAR COOPERATIVE

Appear is the operative word here. There's no intention of making any concrete cooperative commitment.

In tactics designed to this end, your opponent in some manner indicates great empathy and understanding for the problems you face or the needs you have. However he regrets he can't accommodate you: company policy makes this course of action impossible; his authority is too limited to allow agreement to that course of action; that aspect of decision-making falls within someone else's area of responsibility, etc., etc. You get nothing but sympathy and encouragement—and a friendly plea to consider his needs positively. Then, because your opponent is such an agreeable, understanding person, because he promises to see what he can do to help you, you're prompted to send him back to his superiors (or home) with some concrete achievement by way of thanks and encouragement on your side.

When this happens to you, there's an easy response. Since the person you're dealing with can't help you, simply refuse to deal with him further. Take your pursuit of objectives to a higher level. Cooperation doesn't consist of sympathetic noises, it consists of a meaningful commitment to action. Don't get conned into a commitment on your part in exchange for empty verbiage from somebody who's playing ineffectual nice guy.

TO PLAY ON YOUR EAGERNESS

The object is to make you think agreement is just around the corner when it isn't.

Your opponent is enthusiastic, ready to go. All the pieces fit into place—almost. "If we can just clear up this little detail . . ." It's the negotiating equivalent of dangling a carrot just out of reach in front of a horse's nose. One step forward will get it, but with that step forward the carrot moves the same distance, still just a tantalizing step out of reach.

In a negotiation, what happens is that you're always about to conclude the much-desired agreement. It's going to be an easy resolution of issues—the other side is virtually pointing to the dotted line and handing you the pen for signature. You reach for it, when . . . "Oh, before I forget" . . . a further "minor" consideration has to be dealt with first. So you figure okay, make a slight concession in the interest of achieving this agreement that's all but concluded, reach for the pen extended you again and . . . "Now let's just clear up this one other thing."

The tactics your opponent uses are all designed to play on your eagerness to conclude an agreement. They make agreement seem certain—all you have to do is help fill in a few empty blanks. Well, as long as there are empty blanks to fill in, don't kid yourself that you're as good as at the point of concluding agreement. If you do, you're doing a negotiator's equivalent of counting your chickens before they're hatched.

TO PLAY ON YOUR SENSE OF DESPERATION

You're led to believe that this is a last opportunity for relief from a worsening situation. Your troubles will multiply, expenses will spiral unless you reach for the solution your opponent now offers you—"But we don't know how much longer we can make this offer." This tactical design is common in high-pressure selling.

Negotiators who fall for tactics of this sort are those who are most easily pulled into a consideration of how bad things are going, how things look worse all the time. What those bad things are can range from the quality of life in general to the predictable availability of some needed product or service. By falling into a shared pessimistic perspective on things, they practically talk themselves into accepting what's presented as a last opportunity to gain or salvage something out of the uncertainty or mess that threatens.

Before you do anything on that order, give yourself an opportunity to verify any alleged indication that the proferred last chance really is that. Consider the remarkable coincidence in your opponent's suggestions that chaos looms in one guise or other unless, of course, you opt for the avenue of relief he indicates. Tell your opponent you're "confirming the situation" with other knowledgeable sources. You may very well find that the alarmist tone in his presentation moderates, that the cost of "relief" may not be as high as at first he thought it would have to be.

TO PLAY ON YOUR GREED

The point here is to convince you of a unique, limited-time opportunity to tie into a venture sure to generate great profit later.

This is the reverse side of the coin from doom-and-gloom tactics. You're not jumping to avoid disaster here, you're jumping to be first in line for that pot of gold at the end of the rainbow. Dollar signs start flashing in front of your eyes, and your own greed does you in.

Enterprise is such that occasionally an unequaled opportunity for profit does arise. When it does, there's often substantial risk involved. At any time that you're promised a chance to get in on the ground floor of a venture that has "unprecedented" potential for generating a lot of income, make sure you go over the risks as thoroughly as you review the income projections. Keep a grip on reality. Take a lesson from all those who years ago jumped at the opportunity to invest in land cleared for development in Arizona and then found they'd bought a piece of desert property far from established population centers, with the nearest water supply half a mile away—straight down.

This is in order to prompt *you* into a more ready concession in other, more critical areas. The premise is that a lot of argument on the part of your opponent, followed by grudgingly giving in on one issue, will prompt you in return to give in on another issue more willingly. With this in mind, your opponent begins by discussing minor areas of disagreement as though they were of major proportion. Impasse seems to threaten. And then just at that point he allows himself to be swayed into a concession. Now the pressure mounts for you to be equally forthcoming, except somehow that pressure is applied in the context of a major issue.

Keep a clear perspective when tactics aim at prompting you to match the other side's conciliatory gestures. It is reasonable for one side in making compromises to expect the other to indicate a similar readiness to sacrifice in the interest of achieving agreement. But you don't want to be bulldozed into major concessions while the other side concedes only minor points that they've made to appear more substantial than they are. Clearly establish in advance what your priority points are and which are secondary. Then make sure any trade-off reflects a genuine balance, not an apparent one based on the amount of noise generated in each case. A concessions checklist can help you here. Keep score on what you give and what you get in return, correlating that with your determination of what the primary and secondary points of issue are. Any disparity in the give-get balance will be quickly evident.

Tactics here commonly aim at holding you off in such a way that you think agreement can still come any moment. They work very similarly to those designed to make you think you're just one slight concession away from agreement. There's an interwoven pattern of seeming cooperation and delay. You start to suspect your opponent is trying to buy time, and just then he behaves in a supportive, cooperative fashion. There comes a period of discussion that appears to be leading to a definite conclusion; it looks as if you'll be able to settle the point at issue after all. But somehow things run into a snag at that precise moment. The awaited resolution evaporates to reappear off in the distance again like some desert mirage. And you, thinking you can still get to it, crawl fruitlessly on, trying over and over again to catch it.

Tactics designed to stall for time can be difficult to counter. You can emphasize time constraints. You can pointedly refer to the repeated delay you've encountered. But those reactions may only elicit an apologetic smile and a vague promise that progress is imminent.

One solution may be to call your opponent on his statement of cooperative intent and then push for a positive commitment. Point out that a promise of cooperation doesn't move things along at all. You require real cooperation in order to be convinced of good intentions. Ask for concrete action and exert pressure for it to emerge promptly. If you've agreed to a concession or other arrangement that works to your opponent's benefit, let him know you can't guarantee holding to your commitment if no definite benefit accrues to you within a reasonable period of time. You can also consider moving to adjourn discussions altogether until the other side proves able to deal with issues in a substantive fashion.

TO IMPRESS YOU

The other side stresses its capabilities and influence to such an extent that you convince yourself you can't lose by going along with their view of the situation. A colleague of Hank's regularly admonishes team members with, "Remember, fellows, our objective is to impress them to such an extent that we don't have to sell them; they'll sell themselves."

Tactics designed to this end can be very effective, particularly in buy-sell situations. Everyone prefers to be associated with a strong reputation for quality and/or achievement. But there's a danger in letting yourself be too impressed—you lose sight of your own priorities in an eagerness to link up with the other guy. That's proven fatal for more than one person or company burning to be part of a winning combination. They got burned because all the win wound up on the other side.

Be wary of others trying to impress you with credentials or past performance. Remind yourself that it's not past performance that benefits you, it's the achievement of your goals in the present situation. Take into account and be pleased at the chance of association with someone or an organization with an impressive record of achievement, but your objective should be to build to a future, not establish a link to the past. Until a pattern of accomplishment demonstrably provides you benefit, treat that as a form of hearsay: "Don't tell me what you've done for yourself or others; tell me—then show me—what you're going to do for me."

TO SOFTEN YOU UP FOR A KILL LATER

You're offered some unasked-for service or benefit with a promise of "no obligation" attached. After you've accepted this gracious offering, your opponent—nay, your friend, as he's now proved himself to be—asks your agreement to a proposition that offers you further opportunity for benefit, but you understand of course that some cost to you is unavoidable. Naturally there's something in it for him, too, but you wouldn't deny a friend opportunity for reasonable gain, would you?

Beware! When somebody offers you a free lunch and comes back to take your order for drinks, you can bet the cost of drinks will more than cover the cost of lunch. Don't get hooked into follow-up commitments out of a sense of guilt because you let yourself be talked into accepting a previous service or favor. Examine any request or proposal your graciously forthcoming opponent presents you as carefully as if it were coming from a stranger. You can indicate your need to do that politely, without any apologies. If your "friend" is as sincere in his concern for your interests as he alleges himself to be, he'll recognize that you have to follow your understanding of your priorities, not his. Don't fall for an illusion of generosity.

In the case of any diversionary tactic, you can discern the design behind it without great difficulty *so long as you keep your fundamental interests firmly in mind.* The aim in each case is to distract you from those. Your opponent wants you to focus on appearances, on fears, on desires for more—more profit, more prestige, more certainty. Then he'll pull additional advantage from you on the basis of reaction to those rather than to reality. Stay grounded in your perception of your priorities as you've established them. Recognize the difference between a genuine commitment that advances your interests and empty promises. Recognize behavior that moves you closer to your goals, and distinguish that from behavior that does not. Keep your own flights of fancy under control.

PROBLEMS OF INDECISION AND REMORSE

Two of the most common afflictions affecting negotiators are indecision and remorse: "I don't know what to do"; "I shouldn't have done what I did." The clearest illustration of how these problems bedevil people in a negotiation probably occurs in the context of sales agreements, where a decision has to be made either to buy or sell and some determination of reasonable cost has to be worked out and accepted. Since the elements involved in the psychology of buying and selling also surface in other negotiating situations, let's focus on them in that framework, where the principles involved tend to be somewhat more obvious. Once understood from that perspective, you will more readily be able to identify parallels in other negotiations.

From the Buyer's Perspective

When it comes to the purchase of an important or expensive item of personal property, any difficulties that arise are usually expressed in terms of buyer's indecision and buyer's remorse.

BUYER'S INDECISION

In making a decision to buy, there are two concerns the buyer inevitably deals with: (1) the determination to get the best price possible; (2) the determination to obtain an item that lives up to expectations. These are common, reasonable concerns, but sometimes they assume a distorted dimension that makes a purchase decision unreasonably difficult.

Getting the Best Price. This is naturally of most concern where a major investment is involved—major as far as the buyer's perception goes. Someone who's wealthy may not be so concerned with whether the Mercedes he's picking up might be available for less through another dealer, or whether a BMW might be more economical. However, the average person doesn't feel he can afford to take chances when it comes to laying out thousands, even hundreds of dollars. That's hard-earned money, and there isn't an unlimited supply to draw on.

The situation is particularly complicated during periods of high inflation, when it's hard to keep tabs on what is or is not a good dollar value. A home buyer, for example, knowing someone purchased a co-op apartment for $65,000 two years ago, may find it hard to reconcile himself to spending $80,000 for that same apartment. So he goes round and round, halfway convinced the higher figure will eventually prove illusory, halfway just hoping against hope that it will. In the meantime, prices keep inching up, or leapfrogging up, as is often the case.

Then there's the nonstop bargain hunter. This person passes up opportunity after opportunity to purchase something at the current going price. He invariably knows someone who lucked out on a deal, paying bargain basement prices for something that shortly thereafter skyrocketed in value. He's after the same kind of deal. It's always only a matter of time before he picks up an item or piece of property that's already worth more than he's paying for it. In the meantime nothing happens except talk.

In both these cases—and in some others—a buyer may repeatedly approach and then back off from a prospective purchase. After a while, it's not just a matter of shopping around. It becomes an unwillingness to make the necessary investment to get the value desired. Once the money is out from under the mattress, the person fears he'll never again sleep comfortably. Once you've spent it it's gone, and with it that wonderful sense of anticipation.

In certain types of purchase arrangements, notably those involving a broker or other intermediary agent, the indecisive buyer is typically suspicious that he's being ripped off. He just knows that the price asked includes an exorbitant sum that goes directly into the agent's pocket, and he balks at that. The commission or service fee is a form of highway robbery to him. There must be some way to avoid paying this kind of ransom. So he shops around and shops around, determined to find a piece of property—and this is especially true in real estate—he can purchase without an intermediary adding to the cost of it. He fails to take into account that the time he spends trying to accomplish everything without the mediation of an expediting agent is an expense factor, too. He overlooks a broker's ability to steer him to what he wants or to help him reevaluate what he wants in light of what's available. The only expense he'll admit to is a direct dollar expense, and he's convinced his own sense of what's possible is as on-target as anyone else's.

Then there are businesses that have something of a clouded reputation to begin with. Automobile dealerships in particular suffer that. An indecisive buyer shopping for a new or used car is prepared to have all his worst suspicions confirmed. He's never convinced a concession offered is really enough, so he rejects that concession and presses for more. If the dealer is willing to drop $250 off the price, that has to mean he's still making a fat profit. So the buyer asks for another $200 off, and goes to the next dealer if he doesn't get it from this one.

The Matter of Expectations. The indecision that develops out of fear that an item purchased may not live up to expectations can also work to preclude almost any purchase. It's sensible up to a point to want good value for your money. It stops being sensible when fantasy takes over, as it all too often does. So many ideal qualifications have to be met before the purchase decision is made that no realistic decision is ever possible. When finally it becomes apparent that the buyer is going to have to settle on something, the focus on pie-in-the-sky has made it unlikely that genuine advantages and disadvantages have been weighed carefully. The decision to settle reflects weariness with the search, not the perception that here is the best available item in its class. Had the buyer concentrated energies all along on evaluating available features, as opposed to searching for ideal qualities that exist only in his mind, the final decision would probably come closer to meeting his needs than is often the case. Ironically, this type of buyer later often finds that an alternate product/property would have served him better, and that reconfirms him in the conviction that he should have stuck to his ideals. And so the pattern is set for a repeat focus on ideal benefits rather than available benefits.

Buyer's indecision in part grows out of convictions and concerns that include a common-sense element. However, common sense also requires taking market realities into account. Indecision growing out of unrealistic expectations too often results in missing the best possible opportunity to get what is needed or wanted. In the long run, the indecisive buyer is apt to make a less judicious purchase than might have been possible with a more realistic approach.

A buyer must deal with the realities of current market conditions, whatever they may be. Bargain-hunting or pursuit of a fancied ideal that "should" be available isn't usually the most practical approach to take. The better approach is to evaluate want or need in light of what is actually available.

Any buyer also has to accept that value has a price. You can't satisfy your purchase needs and have your money to put back under the mattress, too. If you're buying something you very much want or need, satisfaction at obtaining that should reconcile you to the "loss" of the money you spent. Don't compromise that satisfaction by regretting that the money is gone.

BUYER'S REMORSE

This problem hits a purchaser who can't reconcile himself to having spent money for a desired or needed product or service. It's usually expressed in a question or statement along one of the following lines: What have I done? How am I going to pay for this? I paid too much! I really don't need this. How can I get out of the deal?

Sooner or later almost everyone makes a bad purchase decision. Then it's perfectly sensible to review what you've done. Buyer's remorse isn't always a negative to be resisted. The point is to be realistic, to learn from mistakes rather than to allow remorse to give rise to so strong a fear of erring again that future decision-making is impeded. That means examining the realities of the situation in each instance rather than getting hung up in the feeling itself.

What Have I Done? Implicit in this is a sudden deep concern that the buyer has committed to more than he can handle. In this case, the first thing to do is rein in any inclination to panic. Reassess what you've done in terms of the total result of your purchase decision—benefits desired and achieved as well as cost incurred. Too often the narrow focus on cost gets people frantic. Suddenly you're anxious because you feel you've thrown hard-earned money irretrievably down the drain. Look back to the benefit you hoped to gain. If the immediate actual benefit isn't what you imagined it would be, what about the long run? Is there some way you can turn the decision you've acted on to your advantage? Don't focus your attention on your remorse—you'll only feel that much worse for it. Take a creative approach to discovering and exploiting the potential in what you now have.

How Am I Going to Pay for This? This is a common and logical follow-up question to the first. If you can't maneuver your way out of the purchase commitment, or if you can only at great loss, you're going to have to find a way to manage payment.

The first step is naturally to call the seller, tell him what's what, and see if you can negotiate a workable schedule of payments. Depending on his circumstances and disposition, that might work. But money is usually tight, and most people want it sooner rather than later. In that case, you have to figure out a way to budget yourself stringently to meet demands or borrow the necessary funds.

Borrowing is problematic when interest rates are high. However, there may be other than bank sources to tap: family, friends, colleagues who either might be able to lend you money or would be willing to take over the purchase from you, and with it the payment obligations. Or you might work out a co-ownership arrangement, perhaps on a shared-use basis.

I Paid Too Much! This feeling is much easier to deal with than some of the other feelings of remorse. Just go out and do some comparative pricing. If you find you *have* paid too much, count the experience as a lesson learned and the price difference as tuition for that lesson.

Occasionally you can get relief by calling the seller you dealt with and telling him you paid too much. If he's willing to make an adjustment—and that does happen once in a while—so much the better. If not, it was worth a try. You at least get the satisfaction of speaking your mind, and of course a lesson in the value of comparison shopping.

I Really Don't Need This. This reaction frequently follows an impulse purchase. If this is the first variant of buyer's remorse to strike you, you're probably not facing immediate hardship as a result of the expense involved. Were that the case, you'd have panicked about the money first. Once you recognize this is not a life-or-death dilemma, the situation takes on a less vital dimension right away. At worst you're stuck with something you won't be using all that much.

But many people buy something on impulse they can use and will enjoy—it's just that they don't need it. The attitude to take then is that you are entitled to or deserve a bit of self-indulgence. It can be a worthwhile morale builder, and since productivity in general often depends on morale, that makes the purchase worthwhile, regardless of so-called objective need.

How Can I Get Out of This Deal? When you're in over your head, this question follows hard on the heels of "What have I done?"

Get in touch with the seller right away. Try to negotiate yourself out of the deal. That will often work. Few sellers really want to be tied to an arrangement where receipt of money is going to be a problem. Sometimes, however, you will find a seller who is convinced you do have the resources to pay, even if it gets uncomfortable for you. Then there's likely to be a strenuous effort made to get payment. Also, if a product is involved that you've taken delivery on, once it's been in your house and used, it may not properly be resold as new merchandise. Rather than take a loss because of that, the seller is likely to insist on the purchase price due rather than agree to return of the merchandise.

Most people can afford the purchase they've made. It is more often a question of second thought—something that seemed desirable and/or convenient now doesn't. This is frequently the case with people who acted in haste. They failed to take other considerations into account, to explore other opportunities.

From the Seller's Perspective

The buyer isn't necessarily the only one in a buy-sell situation who experiences difficulty making the decision to go ahead with a transaction or who has uncomfortable second thoughts once a transaction's been completed. The same problems routinely affect sellers.

SELLER'S INDECISION

This usually takes one of two forms: (1) an unreadiness to actually part with the property ostensibly for sale; (2) a determination to get the best price.

Outside of everyday commercial transactions, it's not uncommon to find a person offering something for sale that he's not yet reconciled to parting with. He thinks he's made the decision to sell, but a sense of attachment to the item remains and prompts him to back off from an actual sale. This frequently happens with people thinking of selling something that has significant sentimental associations for them, as with an old home or property that's been in the family for years.

In the second circumstances, it never appears possible to obtain a desired price for the item to be sold. This can be the result of patently unrealistic hopes or expectations of gain. Occasionally it's an excuse. The real reason for an unrealistic price demand is that the seller is in

Pattern No. 1 here; he's not psychologically ready to conclude a sale, so for the moment he's priced the item out of the market.

To the extent that the seller's indecision creates a significant problem, there are steps one can take to get past it. To begin with, review what prompted the initial decision to sell. If the reason is more convenience than need, then the fact of indecision isn't so crucial. You don't have to come to a decision until the force of convenience outweighs whatever reservations exist. If it is a question of need, then review your situation from that perspective. Balance need against whatever reason you have for hesitation. If need outweighs other considerations, bow to the force of necessity. Do what you have to do and go on from there. Don't waste energy squirming in a doomed effort to avoid the inevitable.

SELLER'S REMORSE

Sellers, too, frequently experience regret right after a transaction's been completed. Regret is expressed pretty much in the same terms as buyer's remorse, with the exception of worries on financial obligations incurred.

What Have I Done? This doubt often assails someone who's just parted with something to which there's a strong sentimental attachment, such as an old family heirloom. Afterwards he feels guilty about it. Sometimes there's an ethical consideration, as when someone sells a used automobile with undisclosed mechanical problems. At other times there's a conviction that the terms of the sale were greatly to the disadvantage of the seller.

I Sold It Too Cheap! Where prices aren't set through a standard format applied in regular commercial transactions, a seller may very well convince himself that he could have negotiated a deal for more money.

How Can I Get Out of This Deal? This is customarily a follow-up question to either of the expressions of remorse just noted, at least where that remorse is sufficiently strong to prompt a desire to reverse the deal that's been concluded. In this context, remember that the buyer may well be experiencing his own doubts and remorse at the same time. So it may be possible to exercise an option to buy back what you've just sold. A word of warning, however. Evidence of seller's remorse is at times the quickest cure for buyer's remorse. Seeing the seller eager to get an item back, the buyer automatically raises his estimate of the item's worth to him. There's a sudden sense that maybe he got a pretty good deal after all.

Depending on how important it is to the seller, he may be able to get something back even if there's no buyer's remorse on the other side to influence things to his advantage. In that case, though, the seller will probably have to pay a premium to get the item back.

To avoid seller's remorse caused by economic miscalculation, study your market area before you set a price on whatever item or service you're offering. Work for what you know is a good price, rather than for what you guess is. That way, even if it should turn out you could have done better, you'll have the satisfaction of knowing you still came out ahead. Then stop torturing yourself with thoughts of how much more you might have made. Absorb whatever lesson there is in the experience and go on to the next.

Negotiation Parallels

Buying and selling are often negotiated transfers, so buyer's/seller's indecision and remorse do come up regularly among negotiators. But there are parallels that extend the relevance. These relate particularly to the matter of making or responding to offers in a negotiation.

OFFERER'S INDECISION AND REMORSE

In every negotiation there comes a point where some incentive or inducement has to be offered to motivate an opposite party in a desired direction. Indecision arises because one can't make up one's mind whether now is the best time to make an offer. You put off doing that, thinking that when it's absolutely the right moment to do so that fact will telegraph itself to your brain. Sometimes it does, but at least as often it doesn't—or you ignore it when it does, because secretly you don't want to make the offer; you really hope to obtain your objective at reduced or no cost.

Making an offer also proves a problem for some who have a difficult time deciding what to offer. A rare negotiator frets about offering too little and reaping scorn because of that. Most are worried they'll offer too much. They want to hold off until they're positive they can win the most with the very least. Because that's such a speculative consideration, they hold off and hold off, many times to their own eventual disadvantage.

Dealing with offerer's indecision is very similar to dealing with buyer's indecision. Come to a clear conclusion on what your needs are and what you can afford to pay (offer) to have those satisfied to the degree possible. Then make exploratory offers below that "amount" (it's often not a question of money). If you achieve your objective at lower cost than you planned for, that's all to the good. If you have to use up your budget, well, that's what it was for. If the price is set unexpectedly high, review your options while working to get it down. Don't lose sight of your needs at any point. They should take priority over any hopes for a bargain or qualms about a price that's still affordable, even if higher than hoped for.

When it comes to offerer's remorse, adopt the same focus. The most pertinent consideration is whether you've met your needs. If you find you've miscalculated, that you could have gotten the concession/cooperation you wanted at lower cost, file the information away for future use. If you've so miscalculated that you can't reasonably follow through on your offer, then, of course, you have little option but to withdraw it as quickly and gracefully as possible. You won't win points with your opponent for that, but if you're sufficiently tactful you may not lose too much ground.

<h2 style="text-align:center">RECEIVER'S INDECISION AND REMORSE</h2>

At this point you can probably see the pattern for yourself. The party on the receiving end of an offer isn't sure whether to go for an offer made or to hold out for a better one. The complication arises in that offers can be withdrawn. You can be forced to respond "yes" or "no" to a modified, less generous offer subsequently, at which time you belatedly realize you should have said "yes" to the earlier proposal. Again, indecision is best handled by keeping a clear focus on needs. When an offer meets your needs, beware of holding out for one that provides a fancied bonus. Don't substitute a daydream for reality. If you know you can afford to hold out for a better offer because your needs aren't so pressing, go ahead and consider alternatives. You still risk missing out on a good deal, but you'll have a margin of safety with respect to dangerously compromising your interests.

With receiver's remorse, apply the same common sense. When you learn you could have got more but at least your needs have been satisfied, take the experience as a lesson learned and apply it the next time you can. If you've accepted an offer and then find out it's caused you to compromise in an area that can spell trouble, go to your opponent immediately and inform him of your miscalculation. Tell him the offer as accepted puts you in a position of jeopardy. Renegotiate the offer. Unless you've already tied yourself down contractually, you should be able to get out of your awkward commitment. Don't expect to win popularity points in doing so, however.

REJECTOR'S REMORSE

At times a party who's rejected an offer on second thought realizes it might have been wiser to accept it. The complication here is that the price usually goes up—one has to pay or concede more in a second effort to obtain an offered advantage. The offering party, sensing a greater need, takes the opportunity to require more *quid pro quo*.

A tactic frequently used in real estate acquisition can at times be put to good effect here. The receiver, who knows the offering party at one point was ready to provide a particular consideration at a stated "price," goes back to the other side several weeks later and asks for the same consideration, now at a lower price. The unexpectedness of this causes opponents some uncertainty. Now they're wondering whether they can get what they originally asked for. They're thinking you're not especially anxious for the advantage previously offered—otherwise why would you act to discount it? In their concern to hold the line at the previously stated price, they won't think to raise it higher still. You win the second chance without having to pay the premium you'd normally have expected to pay.

Indecision and remorse can probably never be totally eliminated from the negotiation process. Nobody ever knows completely all that is or isn't possible. Because some element of uncertainty is virtually always present, some grounds always exist for delaying a decision or for second-guessing a commitment just made. As long as you keep your attention on your needs, however, you'll find indecision and remorse fairly manageable, even if you can't eliminate them altogether.

7

Managing Team Negotiations

A LOT OF the most important negotiations conducted between organizations are handled by teams speaking for each of the parties rather than by individuals meeting one-on-one. This creates greater potential for complications, but it doesn't change the nature of what each side is there to do. Nor does it introduce that much change in how they should go about it. Team negotiation follows the same general ritual format that you use in negotiations between two people. In terms of understanding how each side should conduct itself for maximum effectiveness, all the same considerations apply. The need to listen, the importance of taking needs on both sides into account, possible lines of strategy and tactics either to develop or guard against—all these and more have the same application in a team situation as between individuals.

The difference that does exist is entirely related to the number of individuals participating and the need to coordinate activities of all individuals working on either side. From an organizational perspective there are still only two parties involved (except where a multiplicity of organizations is involved). Each team is supposed to function as an integrated unit, working with singleness of purpose in pursuit of one line of priorities. The difference is in the extra elements of control and precaution necessary to assure that the group does indeed function as an effective unit.

WHAT MAKES FOR—OR COMPROMISES— EFFECTIVE TEAMWORK?

There isn't much need to go into detail on the traits that either facilitate or compromise teamwork. Most of these will be known to you. Problems that arise in team situations aren't usually the result of

283

participants being ignorant of what teamwork requires. They generally grow out of focusing on ego needs rather than on common purpose, out of communication gaps between team members, or out of inadequate orientation to the task at hand.

Here are two checklists of traits: the first deals with factors to be alert to in terms of teamwork; the second treats factors to beware of.

Effectiveness Traits

- Awareness of each member's abilities and how to bring these into play to complement the abilities of others on the team.
- Keeping all discussion of differences within the team behind closed doors.
- Avoiding any tendency to label differences of opinion between team members in judgmental terms of right or wrong.
- Drawing clear and respected lines of authority.
- Group discussion of decisions reached, with final authority resting with the team leader.
- Avoiding differences that relate to personality issues rather than to the task at hand.
- Knowledge on each member's part of his assigned role and when to contribute to deliberations at the bargaining table.
- Attentive observation and sharing of observations by all team members.
- Determined effort to multiply the options for achieving benefits.
- Understanding group priorities and a united front in bargaining work to advance those.

Traits that Compromise Effectiveness

- Autocratic team leadership, with a leader arbitrarily imposing his views on team members.
- Refusal by team members to respect the team leader's authority.
- Failure to establish a united front on goals and strategy before going into bargaining sessions.
- Open antagonism on the part of any team member to goals the team is pursuing.
- Failure of team members to take on their share of responsibility.

- Loyalty expressed to personalities rather than to the total team effort.
- Overt sympathy expressed for opposition positions by a dissenting team member.
- Oversensitivity to imagined personal affronts on the part of a team member.

Virtually all of the positive traits have to be present for effective teamwork. It may take only one of the negative traits to create problems all around.

COORDINATING TEAM EFFORT

Teamwork calls for coordination, and that has to be maintained throughout the course of bargaining sessions. It's inevitable that from time to time team members will have to call a break in discussions in order to develop a common response to new developments, or perhaps to the lack of any new development. This is done in the context of a caucus, a private conference of team members away from the bargaining table.

Many negotiators experience difficulty in this area. They don't know how to handle calling a caucus. They're uncertain of the impression it gives. They're unclear on timing involved and unsure of who should have primary responsibility for calling a caucus. Negotiators who customarily work on a one-to-one basis are often particularly uncomfortable about caucusing. Those who have some experience working as part of a team necessarily have some sense of importance of this coordinating procedure, but even they display hesitation or confusion in exploiting to best advantage the opportunity a caucus provides.

Why Caucus?

You caucus for purposes of coordination. It's a lot like a football team going into a huddle to discuss progress of the game among themselves and to develop strategies for the next stages of play. In negotiation you do the same thing basically, prompted by any of several considerations.

NEW INFORMATION

Your side needs a few moments to absorb and consider the impact of important new information that has an effect on your position on the issues. With an obvious new slant on things, it won't be practical to continue on without a review and possible adjustment of strategy.

A "RED FLAG" ALERT

One team member recognizes an important change in circumstances surrounding a vital issue that fellow team members are not yet fully alert to. A caucus provides the best means for that team member to warn colleagues of something new to take into account. Since teams are generally comprised of individuals with varying lines of experience and expertise, it's to be expected that new problems or opportunities will be evident to some individuals before others. Naturally this awareness has to be telegraphed to the rest of the team if it's to be of use.

DELIBERATIONS ON AN OFFER THAT'S BEEN MADE

The other side proposes a settlement of an issue that isn't exactly the offer you were angling for. But it's something that merits consideration. That consideration is best accomplished in the privacy a caucus affords. Team members can point out and weigh the pros and cons of the proposal without compromising strategy or team unity in front of the opposition. Differences of opinion can be expressed freely, which isn't possible at the bargaining table if team effectiveness is to be maintained.

REVIEW OF STRATEGY/TACTICS

Sometimes a line of strategy or a particular tactic being followed proves ineffective, and it's clear a new strategy or tactic needs to be developed. In the event of impasse, for example, you may want to discuss a disclosure of additional information. You may want to decide whether now is the time to present an offer, or whether a particular offer may be appropriate for presentation. Obviously you can't change your game plan without first coordinating team members. (It is often possible to implement a *prearranged* contingency plan without the need for a caucus. This is done through reliance on discreet signals developed for use in bargaining sessions. At other times, however, it will prove advisable to break for a group consultation.)

DISCIPLINARY PROBLEM

On occasion a caucus has to be called to pull an out-of-hand team member back into line. Sometimes one team member pursues a personal sense of priorities in preference to supporting group objectives. The result is an undermining of the team effort. At times this isn't so much intentional as it is the outgrowth of the individual's overexuberance or confusion about his proper role in the team effort. At other times there may be an actual clash of egos, with dangerous potential for disruption of what should be a coordinated push toward common goals. In either case, your side's goals are in jeopardy as long as any one team member fails to act in a manner supportive of the group effort.

NEW ORDERS FROM HEADQUARTERS

Now and again new developments behind the scene affect the posture taken on a set of issues. New directives may be issued during bargaining talks, with a shift in priorities to be followed as a result. Then it's necessary for the team to regroup. Where the directive is a fairly simple one, that can be accomplished in a caucus. At other times, a recess in bargaining may be necessary to allow for the greater adjustment in position and perspective required.

When Do You Call a Caucus?

Oddly enough, most negotiators sense when a caucus would be appropriate. A problem arises when they don't trust their instincts enough to signal or call for one.

The time to call a caucus is when the need first becomes apparent. Failure to do so out of any self-conscious fear that it will appear a disruption of the bargaining process is self-defeating. The negotiation will just grind on without beneficial progress because you and your team haven't taken the opportunity to adjust to circumstances requiring coordination of a new line of response.

Certainly you should exercise common sense—you don't want to be calling a caucus every ten minutes. If you feel a need for one that frequently, then you haven't sufficiently coordinated your team effort all along. However, you needn't feel guilty about not having organized to take into account every possible consideration or development. You can't know everything in advance, and the other side realizes that, too. Since the other side will require its own caucus breaks for the same reasons that you might call them, it's highly unlikely calling a caucus will elicit objections from them. (When it's the other side that calls a caucus, take that opportunity to review game plan on your side, too. You may find it useful to discuss members' perception of what's happening on the other side.)

Who Should Ask for a Caucus?

Customarily the team leader/chief negotiator asks for the caucus, rather than any one of the supporting team members.

But what happens if your team leader doesn't recognize the need to caucus as soon as you do (assuming you're a supporting team member)? Should you squelch your desire to call for a caucus until he realizes there's a need?

No, of course not. The solution here is to work out a *discreet* signal beforehand by which team members can make it clear that the situation calls for a huddle.

To give an example, one team might use a notepad signal. When any team member feels it essential to call a caucus, he can tear a page from his notepad and fold it over as if to slip it into a folder. That will let the team leader know it's time to call time out. If the signal isn't picked up right away, the team member can pick up the notepad and "noticeably" slip the folded sheet in behind the others.

Arranging a signal is very simple *and very important.* Surprisingly, the overwhelming majority of teams observed in Hank Calero's seminar workshops forget to make such an arrangement. This suggests that in real-life situations the opportunity a timely caucus can provide is often lost. Fifteen seconds of forethought here can save long, wasted minutes at the bargaining table.

Managing Caucus Time

Once team members are together in a separate room for their huddle, what rules of thumb should be applied?

In the hundreds of caucus sessions Hank has monitored in his seminar programs, more than half of the average time expended is unproductive. There's bickering among team members, unnecessary interruption, poor listening, a failure to ask basic questions, etc. Any of the faults that may be displayed at the bargaining table can crop up in the caucus chamber. Sometimes the faults are even more in evidence in a caucus because the discipline imposed by the opposite side's presence is suspended.

A caucus is not a jury deliberation. It should not become an internal debate on issues, with team members trying to hammer out the right and wrong interpretation of things. A caucus is properly a *brief* conference for review of observations and perspectives. It's a strategy session, not a negotiation within a negotiation.

You can call a caucus for any of the reasons indicated. You may even call one as a tactic to give the impression you're seriously considering an offer you already know you're going to reject—you just don't want to do that in a summarily dismissive manner. Depending on the circumstance, the time involved can vary. However, we set as a general rule of thumb that *no caucus should last more than fifteen minutes.* If it does, team members are probably spending a lot of their time arguing.

Controlling time in a caucus is a matter of sticking to a programmed approach, with an eye kept on the clock if necessary. (Of course, sometimes you're on the other side, waiting for the opposition to emerge from a huddle. Time passes; you're more than ready to get things moving again. In that event, a simple message along the lines of "Ladies/Gentlemen, we're ready any time you are" can be effective for getting them back to the bargaining table without further delay.)

TAKE A PROGRAMMED APPROACH

Get Everyone's Viewpoint. Make sure that each team member provides input on how things appear to stand. If the caucus has been called in response to one member's insistent signal, it's good sense to hear that person out first. But then take the opportunity to learn how everyone else sees things. If the caucus has been called for general review purposes, then it often pays to turn first to team members who have not participated as vocally at the bargaining table as others.

Those who talk the most often hear and see the least. Tuning into someone who's been observing more quietly all along can prove valuable. An important perspective may emerge that hasn't been considered before.

Don't Argue Perspectives. When polling team members on their perception of the situation, avoid getting into arguments on whose view of things is accurate or inaccurate. The objective at this point is not to get everyone to agree that one perception is superior to all others. You're gathering information, not giving grades. You want to develop an awareness of what's happening, and you achieve that by letting others express their views freely. An effort to enforce a "proper" perspective at this stage can suppress valuable insight into circumstances facing you.

Define Your Present Situation. Once you've listened to your team members' views of how things stand, come to a specific assessment of where you now are relative to objectives you're pursuing. What have you learned that you didn't know when this bargaining session started? What is working for you in terms of the tactics used to influence the opposition? What's not working? How satisfied are you with answers given to questions asked? In short, work for an understanding of where you now are in this negotiation and how you got there. Hold off projecting into the future until you've got a clear picture of the present situation.

Plan the Next Step. After a consensus has been established on how things stand at present—and only then—decide what step to take next. What information should be released or held back? What line of questioning should be followed? What concession/incentive should you offer the opposition? Plot out the direction the team will follow once back at the bargaining table.

Explore Alternatives. This is part of planning the next step, but a point worthy of separate emphasis. Don't opt for a course of action without doing what you can to expand your latitude for maneuver in efforts to achieve objectives.

Hypothetical questions ("What if . . .?") are particularly useful here. They encourage the development and exploration of alternative approaches to the issues. Incorporate them into your standard reper-tory of verbal techniques. Hypothetical questions set your focus on possibilities for gain in the next phase and prompt a more thorough examination of pertinent variables than do other kinds of questions. They encourage an imaginative approach to the situation facing you.

Recap Caucus Conclusions. Before returning to negotiate with the opposition, recap both the team assessment of where you stand at present and your decision on what step to take next. Recapping is your insurance against team members emerging from the caucus with varying perceptions of what was accomplished there.

Back at the Bargaining Table

The party that called time out should be the first to reopen discus-sions. Now they should respond to whatever situation occasioned their caucus—it's still their turn to speak. What's up? Do they have further information to disclose? Will they accept the offer that's been made? Are they ready to make an offer or counteroffer?

Watch out for the smart negotiator who calls time out and then speaks first thereafter, but with a question instead of a statement. Don't fall for that! Get the negotiator to tell you something about his position at this point. You're still waiting for a response to what went on before his caucus, and you're entitled to that. Make sure you get some sense of focus on what your opponent has concluded relative to what's at issue.

Don't speak first if the other side called time out. If you do, you work against your own interests. You set up a dynamic that enables the opposition to evade disclosing their new position. Of course, if you called the caucus, you might want to try a ploy that gets your opponent to take up the initiative now. However, in terms of "proper" procedure, you should be the one to speak up first upon resumption of bargaining.

OTHER POINTS OF ETIQUETTE

Who Leaves the Room for a Caucus? When no arrangement has been made in advance for a convenient separate adjournment area, the host party should step out, regardless of who called the caucus. It's a point of basic courtesy.

It's best to have a specified adjournment area/caucus room designated in advance. Both teams should be clear on the arrangements
before discussion of the issues commences. It's advisable for both
parties to assure themselves that conversations held in that area/
room cannot be overheard, whether from outside or through an inter-
com system that's accidentally been left turned on.

Caution On Passing Notes! Some negotiators like to minimize the
need for time out by passing notes to fellow team members during
bargaining sessions. That can serve a positive purpose, but there's a
danger involved, too: Note passing sometimes arouses suspicion or
distrust. It can also easily prompt annoyance, in the same way that
continual whispering between team members does. Those engaged in
private side communication can't possibly give full attention to the
speaker at the same time. Besides, the speaker is also likely to be
distracted.

Keep side communication to a minimum. An occasional note
won't do much damage, but if there is much that needs saying, it's
better to call time out for a caucus.

Alternate Caucus Forms

When discussing caucus procedure, we generally think of either or
both parties adjourning to another room for their huddle. That's
certainly the ideal maneuver when it comes to reviewing a point of
vital interest to your side. But an "exit" caucus isn't always possible
or necessary. Sometimes you can interrupt discussions briefly for a
"table" caucus or a "room" caucus.

TABLE CAUCUS

This is simply a momentary huddle right at the bargaining table.
All you need do is say, "Excuse us a minute. We have something to
discuss briefly among ourselves." Then you just put the heads on
your side together for a very short whispered consultation.

ROOM CAUCUS

This is a huddle conducted away from the table but in the same
room. Again, team members confer among themselves in a whisper.
They should take care to turn away from the opposition to the extent

possible. We know of an instance in which an opposition team was able to eavesdrop on a caucus because of the ability of one person there to read lips.

Note that in any case *there's no need to ask permission* to break for a caucus. You have but to announce that you need time to confer among yourselves and excuse yourselves to do so.

THE SECOND DAY: KEEPING A NEGOTIATION ON TRACK

It's frustrating for negotiators to discover on the second day of bargaining that progress made the first day has somehow come unraveled overnight. Issues that had been developed to a certain point—even some that had apparently been resolved—unexpectedly loom up in their original form to be dealt with all over again. The comfortable feeling of accomplishment that prompted sound sleep and sweet dreams the night before turns out to have been an illusion. Within moments of the beginning of the second day's discussions, it's evident the other side has an entirely different perspective on the previous day's achievements. So the first order of business is a painstaking retracing of steps. It's almost as if the first day's work was just a rehearsal that didn't count.

This rude awakening on the second day of an extended negotiation is a rather common occurrence. But it's fairly easy to avoid.

Close Out the First Day Systematically

Half the trick to starting things off right the second day is to close out the first day's session right. There are three steps to this:

RECAPPING

You can usually avoid hours of unnecessary talk by presenting a complete summary at the end of the first day identifying what has been discussed, what has been agreed upon or settled, what agreements in principle have been established, and anything else you think has a bearing on where you stand at that point. Recap everything before adjourning the first meeting.

The recap should not be just a summary of how *you* see things at

294 • NEGOTIATE THE DEAL YOU WANT

that point. It should be done *with* the other side's participation; it should *explicitly* be accepted as accurate by both sides. Don't interpret silence as an indication of agreement with your view of what's been accomplished so far. Too often it's not. Get a commitment that's clearly expressed. If the other side won't commit to an item as summarized, note that as an issue requiring further discussion. Make that point openly as an amendment to your recap, and be sure the other side then indicates that to be an accurate reflection of the situation as it currently exists.

Taking this one simple precaution has the effect of throwing immediately into clear perspective just where the two parties stand relative to each other. It guards against a false assumption on your part that discussions have been concluded on any one issue when in fact they haven't. It also nails down the areas of agreement more securely. An opposite is not going to feel at ease reopening a discussion already indicated to you as closed. He'll realize that looks indecisive and shows poor control of developments on his side.

Recapping is especially valuable in negotiations where topics discussed are complex. The summary of points discussed and positions taken or arrived at by the end of the day tells you where you left off and where to start the next time. Otherwise, the parties may well succumb to a temptation to start over from the beginning. You wind up wasting time and energy repeating what's already been concluded.

Recapping is also important in negotiations including any agreement that either party (or both) will undertake some direct action. This may be action as a result of agreement on the issues; it can also be action promised in pursuit of agreement. Recapping avoids confusion later on as to who said he would do what. It also creates a psychological stimulus to assure follow-through. The party that explicitly restates a commitment to do something will, as a rule, be committed to living up to expectations it has doubly endorsed.

SCHEDULING

Following a recap of what's gone before, outline the points of concentration for the following day. Set up a preliminary agenda to serve as a map indicating the direction subsequent talks will take. Get both sides to concur on where discussion will be resumed, on which issues will be considered, and in what general sequence. This sets a goal. Both sides' attention is pulled beyond what's been covered to what is to be covered. The focus of activity is set on maintaining forward movement.

Here, too, it's important that concurrence be explicitly stated by both parties.

IDENTIFYING PERSONNEL CHANGES

With teams, it's useful when projecting the next day's activity to identify who the participants will be the next day. Sometimes a person present in the first session will not be required the next day. Or conversely, someone may be added to the team because a particular expert's input is required. Knowing in advance that the other side is bringing in counsel, their accountant, chief inspector, etc., makes planning your strategy and tactics for the next day easier. You can anticipate the type of questions likely to come up from that quarter. You may, if you know or can discover something about the other person involved, anticipate possible conduct as well. Ask whether there'll be any change in the composition of the team facing you.

From your own side, mention of any changes in the composition of your team can provide similar advantages. You'll likely find the other side more prepared and more attentive to details in a relevant area of emphasis.

Following these three points of review, you can adjourn the meeting and unwind a bit. If there is work to be done preparing for the next day's meeting, you will now have a specific sense of what that should take into account.

Starting Off the Second Day

Here, too, three simple, routine steps can save a lot of trouble and confusion.

MAKING INTRODUCTIONS

The first order of business should be introducing any new member who may have joined either team. The introduction should include mention of the person's name and title. Everyone should know who they're up against at all times, whether the person seems to have any authority or not.

RESTATING POSITIVE MOTIVATING FACTORS

It's also worthwhile at the opening of a second day's bargaining encounter to restate briefly what it is that brings the two parties together. This helps to reemphasize common goals, needs, etc., that provide the impetus to agreement.

A note of caution, however: Keep it brief. Don't get into a reprise of all the "background music" at this point. Don't dredge up past difficulties that may have existed, opening up possible sore spots not centrally relevant that can still disturb the atmosphere of cooperation you're working to promote. Similarly, don't stumble into a repetition of any controversy you've worked your way through the first day. The easiest way to fall into that is to drop a justification for a perspective you held that the other side didn't share. As soon as your restatement includes any element of self-justification or seeming deprecation of the other side's point of view, you're headed for argument or a rehash of positions that have already been stated.

SUMMARIZING PROGRESS MADE SO FAR

This is the most important item of business for starting off the second day's session on track.

But you'll already have done this at the close of the first day, you may be thinking. Why engage in this bit of repetition?

The answer is simple. First of all, to reorient everyone to the situation at hand. Secondly, to doublecheck that everyone is indeed in accord as you recall or assume yourselves to be. Sometimes a spokesman on the other side hasn't fully taken in the previous day's summation, despite your care to win his assent to every element of it at the time. Then again, someone may be harboring second thoughts, which are best identified and dealt with right away. You don't want reservations that have sprung up overnight operating beneath the surface to frustrate further movement to agreement.

When it comes to this second recap, observe these precautions for avoiding undesirable complications:

Get Explicit Agreement. Have the other side confirm again any statement of how things stand at that point.

Take It One Item at a Time. Don't try to cover all the bases at once. Negotiating is a step-by-step process that requires taking things into account one at a time, not in big lumps. You're not rattling off a grocery list. Make sure each point accurately reflects the other side's understanding of that element of the situation, getting explicit concurrence on each item as it's noted. Then at the end you can't be shocked by a "No" that appears to cover everything mentioned, as you might be if you had made a hurried, nonstop run-through.

Allowing only for an end-of-run-through response makes what a "No" refers to unclear. A number of items the opposition views favorably may very well have been included in the overall roundup. By allowing only for a single "Yes" or "No" response to the entire recap, you miss the opportunity to pinpoint positive achievements as well as to specifically identify problems. Also, when all the issues are lumped together, the opposing side may disagree with one item and then tune out others on which positive agreement had been reached. Then the tenor of the upcoming session takes on a negative tone that doesn't accurately reflect the potential for agreement.

Don't Be Too Effusive. Don't get carried away in rapturous expressions of how wonderfully everything's moving along. You're as likely to arouse suspicion as to prompt additional favorable reaction. Overstated praise smacks of a possible attempt to sugar-coat the issues. You don't have to stroke the other side's ego to the extent of expressing joy and gratitude at their demonstrated intelligence or constructive attitude. An occasional, spontaneous compliment will be perceived as genuine. Too hearty a series of commendations will more likely be seen as flattery—an effort to soften them up for an unpleasant surprise to come.

Now, if you've carried everything through smoothly in delivery of the introductory summation, you'll naturally find yourself taking first things first without repetition of work already done. You'll be wrapping up loose ends you just discovered and/or moving on to discussion of the next issue. Where there is a loose end to be tied down, you'll know exactly what that is. Within half an hour of sitting down at the bargaining table you'll be engaged in a substantive consideration of issues still facing you, as opposed to spending half or more of Day Two trying to get back to where you saw yourself to be at the end of Day One.

Learn to handle the transition from one day to the next methodically and smoothly. You'll find your negotiating productivity increasing. Your sense of accomplishment will be greater because you'll be able to achieve more in a given time. This doesn't require greater effort on your part—just an easily mastered, organized approach to the task at hand. (Although we've emphasized all this in a team context, which commonly requires greater attention paid to coordination, these techniques prove very useful in one-to-one encounters as well.)

8

Special
Situations/Considerations

NEGOTIATION takes place in a wide variety of situations and in any imaginable setting where two people might get into discussion with each other. Since it always remains negotiation, you must pay attention to the same basic considerations. You have to work through the same ritualized process for persuading another party to share in the achievement of objectives you find necessary or desirable.

In some situations, however, the line of communication is not as direct as in a face-to-face encounter. At other times, a face-to-face encounter occurs in a setting that requires an additional focus of attention if you are to be effective. This chapter contains material to help you avoid or deal with problems that can compromise effectiveness in several particular settings of concern to negotiators.

NEGOTIATING ON THE TELEPHONE

Everybody at one time or other concludes important agreements on the telephone. The process of influencing the other party is the same as in any face-to-face encounter, but a few varying circumstances do have to be taken into account.

Reading People

In dealing with people in direct encounter, we all, whether consciously or unconsciously, rely on messages conveyed by their body language. Their posture, characteristic movements, and facial expressions tell us a great deal about what they are thinking. At times body language can be so inconsistent with what is being communicated verbally that we know we should distrust something we are being told. But our telephone system doesn't yet include a visual component that permits us to see and interpret important body language cues. We have to rely on what few cues we can pick up by the tone of voice and the pace of speech. If we haven't previously dealt with the person to whom we're speaking, we're even more handicapped because we have no sense of that person's normal intonation and pace of speech.

ENGAGE IN SMALL TALK FIRST

Small talk at the beginning of a telephone negotiation helps break initial tension and serves to establish some sense of interpersonal rapport. It also provides an opportunity to hear the other party respond to remarks that require no commitment; to engage in normal conversation. The contrast in style and intonation between these relatively relaxed moments and later serious discussion will help you gauge the other side's mood when it's important you have an accurate feeling for their pleasure or displeasure at how issues are being presented.

ADOPT A POLICY OF EXPLICITNESS

Even though you may not be acquainted with the person on the other end of the line—in fact, *because* you're not acquainted—ask that he be as explicit as possible with respect to positions taken, commitments made, and any feelings about them. Say he agrees to a proposal, but only after a moment's hesitation. It's perfectly acceptable then to say, "I sense a moment's hesitation in your response. Is there an area of difficulty for you here?" Or if a comment is passed off as an aside but you feel it may reflect some deeper feeling related to the issues, probe a moment to be sure no more substantial statement is hidden behind it. Although not every quip or aside indicates a matter that requires discussion, often there's a serious kernel of meaning to what's given as a humorous comment.

Hanging Up

THE ANNOYANCE FACTOR

In a face-to-face encounter, there's always the possibility that one of the parties will decide to walk out if talks are not proceeding on a course agreeable to them. But walking out—a statement of extreme discord—is usually a last-resort maneuver.

In telephone conversations, it's easy to give into annoyance or discouragement by breaking off the discussion and hanging up. Many negotiators admit they've hung up on people during a telephone communication whom they would not have walked out on in a face-to-face encounter. However, it can be just as damaging to break off a bargaining session by hanging up on an opposite as it would be to walk out on him.

Hanging up on someone doesn't solve any problem. It can compromise subsequent communication or your ability to turn to that person for assistance or cooperation at a later date. If you need that now, it's self-defeating to hang up on him in a fit of pique.

THE RECESS ADVANTAGE—AND DISADVANTAGE

When you're in a scheduled conference with someone, it isn't so easy to break off talks for an extended cooling period, or for any purpose other than a brief recess. A breaking off too easily connotes failure of some kind. On the telephone, however, it's routine to break off conversation after a discussion gets bogged down. One or other of you says, "Well, I'll have to get back to you on that," and you're in a period of recess that you can put to good advantage—gathering new information, outlining a new strategy, or maybe just giving yourself time to cool off so you can reapproach a difficult situation with regained equanimity. Few people genuinely enjoy extended telephone discussions, so breaking one off is rarely interpreted negatively (assuming the manner of breaking off is courteous). You don't tend to spend so much time in fruitless repetition of viewpoints.

But the relative ease with which you can recess telephone negotiation has its drawbacks, too. Some people are hard to get hold of on the telephone. Recessing a discussion of issues results in no further progress until the next opportunity for contact, which with some busy professionals or executives may be a week or more into the future. That means other priorities come to the fore in the interim, and the priority you represent gets put into the background for the time being. A week later it may not seem as imperative or opportune to pursue it. So weigh what's involved before deciding to recess. If there's no problem reopening the interrupted connection, feel free to adopt a strategy of a series of calls to conclude the negotiation. Just don't assume that any telephone contact that is broken off is easily resumed. What you might otherwise have resolved in one or two determined, extended telephone sessions may wind up taking weeks to work through.

Time in Discussion

Generally speaking, telephone negotiations do not take up as much time as those that are conducted face-to-face. Few people have the patience or desire to talk into a telephone at great length. Even those who are long-winded on the telephone tend to be less so than when sitting at a conference table, where the environment encourages drawn-out discussion.

SHORT-CUTTING

Occasionally a negotiator who isn't comfortable with a telephone will hurry through or even skip points of issue that should be considered carefully. He short-cuts the process because he feels talking on the telephone is a drag. Many negotiators do this unconsciously.

Guard against any tendency to short-cut. The best precaution is thorough preparation, with all notes as carefully prepared as if you were meeting the other side in direct conference. With notes in front of you on all aspects of the issues, you're not so likely to overlook any to your later disadvantage. Before you hang up from any conversation, ask yourself whether you've posed enough questions or received enough input to dispel any uncertainty you may have concerning what the other person is saying or feeling.

Concentration Difficulties

Countless interruptions and disruptions can interfere with smooth conduct of a telephone negotiation. Someone may try to get your attention while you're in discussion; someone else may slip a note in front of you that you find yourself scanning even as you're speaking or listening; you get a signal that someone else is trying to call, on the same line or on an alternate line. In the meantime, you are trying to concentrate on what the other party is saying or trying to work something carefully, perhaps to reflect your best offer on a deal being worked out. What can you do to avoid falling victim to all the distraction around you?

To begin with, avoid negotiating at any time that you're not prepared for total involvement in the process. If a call comes through from a negotiating opposite any time that you're otherwise involved, explain that you are caught in the middle of something very important and ask if you can call back in a few minutes. Then wrap up what you're doing, clear away distractions on your desk, alert everyone to keep away from your door, and briefly review the subject to be discussed before returning the call. Most people who call are amenable to being put off for a moment if it means they won't have to be competing for your attention when you do speak to them. (But no one appreciates a promise to call back that isn't kept. If you say you'll call back shortly and then find you'll be otherwise engaged longer than you expected to be, call back as promised and explain that the conversation will have to be put off a bit longer. Try to set a specific time frame within which you'll get back to serious discussion.) When you're initiating the call, take the same steps to eliminate distraction and interruption.

Take notes during each conversation. There's no way that can distract your opposite as it sometimes does in face-to-face encounters. Be organized in your note taking. Don't rely on words randomly scribbled across whatever scrap of paper is within reach. Write down the name of the person with whom you're speaking, the date and time, and the general subject of discussion. Indicate the main areas of discussion. Write in points covered relating to these. Expand on your notes as necessary immediately after concluding the conversation. Then file them where you can easily locate them when you want them.

Telephone negotiations are at times a prelude to formal negotiation or part of clean-up work after one. Be organized and well-prepared here, too, or you can run the risk of undermining the thought and preparation that necessarily go into a formal bargaining session. You have to be as painstaking in your approach to telephone negotiation as you would be if meeting directly. That means being alert to all the usual considerations that promote effectiveness in negotiation and recognizing where differences call for adjustments in approach.

THE WRITING END OF NEGOTIATION

Negotiators frequently have to follow up on or fill in details of a negotiation via correspondence. They complement or compromise their overall effectiveness here to the extent they can or fail to marshal their thoughts or present points of issue in a convincing, easy-to-follow manner.

The point of a written communication is to communicate. All too many letter and memo writers appear to forget that obvious point. They don't take the trouble to organize their thoughts well; they don't express themselves clearly. The net result is that their writing doesn't get their ideas across and/or doesn't motivate or prompt others to respond in the desired fashion.

To help overcome difficulties in this area, here are some brief comments to make your writing more effective. We'll go over points in two focus areas: basic mechanics and the psychology of effective communication.

Basic Mechanics

We can't offer a capsule course in remedial writing. If you have difficulties with spelling, punctuation, and grammar, obtain a reference aid specifically addressed to those areas of language. But there are several useful mechanics guidelines that can do a lot to improve your writing style.

KEEP YOUR LANGUAGE SIMPLE

Avoid the temptation to be grandiose or trendy in your use of words. Some writers mistakenly conclude that the written word is something beyond good plain English, so they invent or adopt a more formal tone and language. They think the result sounds more official, but it is often something else altogether. Their message gets garbled in high-sounding, often meaningless circumlocution. The language used in the legal profession and the insurance industry suggests that ordinary English isn't adequate for the conduct of business affairs. It is. Keep things on an everyday level as much as possible. A simple word like "now" is still better than "at this point in time"; "a reply in the affirmative/negative" doesn't tell anyone anything more than an ordinary "Yes/No."

If specialized terminology is used in your business, you may find yourself automatically incorporating that terminology into your correspondence. When you're writing as one specialist to another in the same field, that may not create any difficulty, but when the person you're corresponding with isn't a fellow specialist, what you want to say will be more understandable if you stick to everyday English.

BE CONCISE

Say what you have to say as briefly and clearly as possible. Keep sentences to the point and manageable in length. Don't allow your paragraphs to run too long. Otherwise you lose your reader. The main point of what you have to say should not be buried in incidentals or qualifying commentary.

GIVE MAIN POINTS PROMINENCE

Put the basic ideas or recommendations of your message in an attention-getting place at either the beginning or end of a paragraph or discussion section. Don't sandwich them between a mass of secondary statements. They'll too easily be overlooked or not accorded the attention you want them to have.

Highlight a main point by underscoring or by simply having it stand as a paragraph by itself. Then follow it with additional, related remarks as necessary. Or if the main point comes as a conclusion after a series of remarks, the same treatment following those can give it the prominence you want it to have.

Avoid insertion of extraneous details. You may think you're giving more of the total picture by making reference to everything you think has the slightest bearing on the subject. But you're just as likely fogging things up. Resist the temptation to show off how much you know. Get to the point. Otherwise you'll wind up with a wordy essay containing irrelevancies and incidentals that detract from the important aspect of what you want to communicate.

BE SPECIFIC

There are times, particularly when refusing a request, when it can be advantageous to respond with a vague, general statement of some kind. Giving a specific reason for "No" sometimes leads to argument; citation of a vague principle or company policy may make a refusal more palatable.

However, people who look to you for information or a reaction to a proposal they've made are looking for specifics. Unless you're engaging in deliberate muddying of the issues, that's what you should provide them.

You think you do? Well, do you ever speak of "considerable sums," "certain modifications," "some problems," "over a period of time," and the like without going into details? A lot of people do, and in so doing they leave others guessing, without that being the intention. Alluding in general terms to things that can be quantified or otherwise made specific leaves too much latitude for misinterpretation. What's considerable to one person, may not be that to another. "Soon" for one person may be much too late for another. If you can't narrow it down to a specific sum, quantity, or time, at least suggest a finite range, as in "I'll have an answer for you—at least call you back—by the end of this week."

ORGANIZE YOUR THOUGHTS COHERENTLY

Deal with one thing at a time and, in so doing, follow a logical sequence of discussion. When describing any process, do so in the order of steps involved, from beginning to end. When responding to a list of questions, answer them in the order presented. If you're outlining points of issue, rank them in order of importance. (This ensures getting immediate attention for what should be weighed most heavily.)

Afterthought Injection. One of the most annoying, confusing, and yet frequent faults in correspondence or memos is something we call "afterthought injection." The person writing covers a point, moves on to the next—goes perhaps even a point or two further—then remembers something that should have been touched on earlier, at Point No. 1. However, rather than go back, he drops it in where he graph pertaining to a different subject. Even when the effort is made to state the thought clearly, the fact of its being out of place contributes to confusion.

Missing Ingredients. You can bollix up an important business communication by omitting mention of something that ought to be taken into account. It's so easy. You make the mistake of assuming the other person already knows what you know or recognizes what you feel to be an obvious point. But what's obvious to you isn't necessarily so to anyone else. Or you forget to mention a "minor" step in describing some process to another person—it's one of those simple little things you do by reflex, without even thinking about it. But somebody else, if he wants the same results, has to pay attention to all the little unfamiliar details. If he relies on you to provide those when putting a deal together, that kind of oversight can prove the killer.

FORETHOUGHT—THE BEST ORGANIZATIONAL AID

Before you write a memo or business letter, review what you're going to cover and what you want the communication to accomplish. If it's a long letter discussing a complicated subject or several issues, make some notes for yourself before writing it. List items to be covered, then jot down key words pertaining to each of them. Put down your thoughts in the order they come to you but then arrange them in logical sequence. That done, go over the ordered list once again before starting the letter. You're less apt to miss something this way. (But if you do and think of it after you meant to cover it, don't just insert it as an afterthought.)

Your style and organization should ensure, as much as possible, that the person receiving the message understands what you are asking or telling him. Clarity of communication should be your goal.

It can be invaluable at times to have a friend or colleague read one of your letters/memos to doublecheck its comprehensibility.

Basic Psychological Considerations

You invariably want to go beyond just having someone else understand you. You also want to come across positively. You want to influence the other person to behave in a certain fashion, to provide a desired response. That means taking psychological considerations into account.

Here are some to keep in mind. The first ones will seem surprisingly self-evident to you, but years of experience prove that too often the simplest point of psychology is overlooked.

PAY ATTENTION TO SIMPLE GOOD FORM

Neatness counts! A crisp, ordered letter conveys a sense of professionalism. It says, here's someone who pays attention to detail. A smudged or otherwise sloppy letter gives a contrary impression.

Pay attention to correct spelling and basic good grammar. Your letter will convey an impression of your intelligence, which contributes to your being taken seriously right from the start. Keep in mind that letters often circulate to others besides the individual they're addressed to. They may be passed on to people who have no other way of knowing you, who have nothing else on which to base an assessment of you. You don't want a decision-maker you hope to influence getting a bad impression of you and your abilities and perspectives because of a hastily, sloppily prepared communication.

ADDRESS THE OTHER PERSON CORRECTLY

You won't necessarily destroy an opportunity for a cooperative relationship with someone if you spell his name wrong, but you won't win points either. Check a business card or previously received letter, or ask to have the spelling verified when first you hear it on the telephone, even if the name you hear is Smith. Once in a while you'll run across a Smyth or Smithe. On occasion you'll hear something altogether different than what's actually said.

FOCUS ON THE READER'S NEEDS AND INTERESTS

It's the same basic point we stressed in discussing the art of persuasion. Correspondence that speaks only of what you or your side wants and hopes for will not win as positive a response as that including explicit acknowledgment of the other side's objectives.

Follow the four basic steps to winning cooperation from an opposity party: (1) get the reader's interest with an immediate signal that this is a message that can/will benefit him; (2) elicit an understanding of your needs and a willingness on the reader's part to consider those by expressing your understanding/willingness to consider his needs; (3) provide the reader appropriate motivation to cooperate in efforts to achieve goals jointly; (4) win commitment with a positive reiteration of specific benefits to accrue from concluding agreement with you (or from following through on the letter, should that not be in the context of an agreement as such).

You can structure almost any message to build to a cumulative effect via this four-step sequence. Your first paragraph, in which you identify the purpose of your letter, will hold attention immediately because you've at the same time indicated an achievable benefit to the reader. Your next paragraph indicates your understanding of the other side's perspective and aligns your own perspective with that as much as possible. Following that you reinforce any inclination to cooperate by emphasizing how the other party in helping you along lines indicated also serves its own interests. That provides motivation. And you close with a request for commitment with a positive reinforcing reference to the mutually desirable consequences to flow out of that commitment.

All this can usually be accomplished in a one- or two-page letter. The trick is to focus on the essential positives. Don't introduce extraneous, incidental details, for reasons already noted. Don't introduce negatives. Deal with problematic questions and reservations as they arise, always following a persuasive approach in response to them.

ALWAYS MAINTAIN A FRIENDLY, COURTEOUS TONE

Disagreement and disappointment will be inevitable on occasion. But in reacting to those, keep your communication free of emotional, negative commentary on the other side's attitude or behavior. That's not to say you can't indicate strong feelings about any disagreement or disappointment. You can. Just stick to relating your feelings about the situation without being abusive or derogatory to the people involved. Note the difference between the two examples below, both reactions to a last-minute pulling out of a proposed joint venture.

A. Your precipitate, thoughtless reversal of position on our contemplated joint venture has resulted in a substantial financial loss for us. You've in effect welshed on a deal, with no consideration at all of our interests. You are going to have to pick up at least part of the tab for the damages occasioned by your capriciously unprofessional behavior.

B. We're extremely distressed at your recently announced and unexpected decision not to join with us in this venture. You had previously explicitly assured us of your interest and cooperation, and on that basis we had begun to implement necessary changes in our operation to take advantage of the opportunity offered. Now we find ouselves deprived not only of the projected benefit we had anticipated sharing with you, but absorbing a significant loss in terms of time and funds invested in this project to date. Under the circumstances, we feel it necessary and appropriate to ask that you assume a share of the expenses we've incurred in this context.

It doesn't take judgmental statements or name-calling to get the message across.

Attributing malice, stupidity, or careless thoughtlessness to another party on paper works differently from saying the same thing directly to them. People react with an outrage or resentment to a hostile letter that they often don't demonstrate in response to a harshly spoken word. It has something to do with the immediacy of response. In an angry face-to-face confrontation, the storm often breaks and then blows over once both sides have said their piece. A rash spoken comment will more readily be excused as blurted out in the heat of the moment. A written communication by its nature indicates premeditation—malice aforethought, if you will. And it doesn't fade away—it's always there to reinflame bad feelings when referred to again.

So avoid attributing negativity to behavior or attitude others display. Speak rather in terms of effects you've experienced, then be straightforward in your request for any remedy you feel is appropriate. You won't necessarily get immediate satisfaction, but you will have made it easier to reestablish subsequent dialogue.

Remember you have a double objective in all your written communications: to inform your opposite about your position and perspectives and to influence him to a course of action favorable to you. Attention to mechanics assures you communicate the "what" of your message clearly. Attention to simple psychology assures that the reader considers that "what" in the most positive light.

MAKING FORMAL PRESENTATIONS

Negotiators often have to make formal presentations to an audience that includes decision-makers who will subsequently rule on the issues raised. These issues may or may not be discussed at length in subsequent bargaining sessions. The presentation itself may lead to final decisions.

In a conventional bargaining encounter, the active participation of the second party pretty much guarantees thorough airing of doubts, reservations, and uncertainties on both sides. Those can then be dealt with in depth as they come up. But a formal presentation allows less opportunity for this. Less time is available for actual discussion. There is usually less commitment to resolutely working something through to a shared perspective. Formal presentations serve more to introduce *one* side's perspective on issues for possible further consideration. If it is badly handled, opportunities to win further benefit may be cut off.

Few negotiators have any specialized training in making formal presentations. Some assume that the person who is most effective at the bargaining table is also most effective as spokesman in front of a larger group. Unfortunately, all too often that's not true. We've seen a most capable negotiator in a conventional bargaining situation prove totally inept when facing an audience as a speaker. Negotiating across the bargaining table is not the same as addressing an audience.

We've prepared the following brief remarks to aid you in four general areas where negotiators often encounter problems when making formal presentations. Preparation and attention to detail along the lines indicated will go a long way toward ensuring that you accomplish what you want to in front of an audience.

Mind Set—
Establishing Yours, Influencing Theirs

TAKE TIME TO COMPOSE YOURSELF

Whenever possible, allow yourself a few quiet moments before your presentation begins. Use these to compose yourself and mentally review your first remarks. Take confidence from the fact that you've prepared and organized your material thoroughly. (It goes without saying that you should have.) Recognize that your audience will have an interest in what you have to say or they wouldn't be there. Think of them as potential coworkers and colleagues; don't think of them as a jury about to sit in judgment on you. Realize that any questions raised or doubts expressed will reflect the audience's uncertainties—they are rarely intended as an attack on you.

PUT YOUR AUDIENCE AT EASE

The speaker is not the only person who may be uncomfortable and ill-at-ease when the presentation commences. Many in the audience will be apprehensive, too, about what is to be said and about how they will be expected to react. A presentation like this is something more than a monologue they can passively absorb or ignore if they choose. You are setting out approaches for working with them. They have to evaluate the advantages of maintaining or pursuing a link with you or the organization you represent.

A suitable humorous anecdote or joke puts an audience at ease quicker than almost anything else. Hearing the audience laugh and seeing the initial tension broken will relax you as well. That's important. A relaxed attitude on your part makes you that much easier to listen to. However, be sure your humorous remark is appropriate for the setting you're in, and don't get carried away. You're not there to be a comedian, and a small dose of humor usually goes a long way.

BE SPONTANEOUS IN YOUR DELIVERY

Your remarks should seem spontaneous. Speak to your audience; don't read to them. If you've written your remarks out at length, nevertheless work on a delivery that is natural in its tone and pacing and takes the audience's presence and reactions into consideration. Many speakers prefer to speak from notes rather than follow a written text, even if they have prepared and rehearsed with a written text. Reading a prepared text tends to keep the speaker's eyes focused on the lectern and that means poorly sustained audience contact. Delivery tends to be more monotonous. Asides or other incidental comment to maintain audience involvement will either be absent or come across as artificial and forced.

AVOID GESTURES THAT COMMUNICATE NEGATIVITY

Here are three of the worst gestural offenses:

1. *Crossing your arms,* especially when faced with a question or when fielding comments made by members of the audience. This is generally read as an indication of defensiveness.

2. *Pounding your fist and pointing at the audience.* A preacher or politician might employ these gestures to some advantage; they're not recommended for negotiators making formal presentations. They give you an overbearing, dogmatic image; you appear too authoritarian in the way you convey your message. That isn't usually well received.

3. *Nervous hand-to-head gestures.* These are usually interpreted as an indication of insecurity about what you are saying.

AVOID OVERSELLING YOUR POSITION

Concentrate on being clear in your message. The fact that you believe in what you're saying will make the necessary impression. There's never a guarantee others will accept your perspective, but with a sincere presentation that your audience can follow, any disposition to consider your perspective favorably will be maximized. Overselling arouses suspicion: "Why is this person trying so hard?"

DEMONSTRATE MASTERY OF VISUAL AIDS

It's distracting and an indication of poor preparation for a speaker to fumble with whatever visual aids are being used to supplement his remarks. On the other hand, it adds a strong note of credibility for him to be in complete control of all material at hand. There's a great impact in someone going to a flip chart or blackboard and proceeding to outline in detail, without benefit of notes, a great amount of very specific information that another might find overwhelming at first sight. Obviously this takes preparation. If you do use notes, refer to them naturally and unobtrusively.

Handling Your Material

PAY ATTENTION TO SUBSTANCE

Once you conclude the introductory remarks, *what* you have to say assumes major importance. Empty verbiage will be evident for what it is, especially if people are taking notes on points you introduce for consideration. If after a few minutes it appears to your audience that you're being vague or that your presentation has no coherence, they will start to tune you out. You may not be able to get them fully attentive again, even if later remarks are cogent and well developed.

BALANCE GENERALITIES AND SPECIFICS

Most audiences do not mind general statements if they are supported by specific comments or examples. Unsupported generalities come across as meaningless statements of little substance. Specifics must be to-the-point and work cumulatively to reinforce the impressions you want to get across. Just as infuriating as a presentation that is nothing more than a vague recitation of generalities is one that introduces a wide range of poorly connected or contradictory specific comments or examples. In neither case is your audience given organized hard data that could motivate a decision for positive action along lines you mean to endorse.

PACE YOUR MATERIAL FOR EASY COMPREHENSION

Don't go too fast for those who may be slow listeners. And don't drag so that those who quickly grasp points have time to wander off in their own thoughts. Vary your rate of delivery to avoid monotony.

Levity interjected into your remarks from time to time aids successful pacing of material. The laughter serves to win back those whose attention may have started drifting; it reinforces the attention span of others. The short break it effects between points also allows those taking notes to keep abreast of your substantive remarks without it appearing that you've stopped or interrupted your presentation for that purpose.

BUILD IN FEEDBACK BREAKS

By feedback breaks we mean brief periods where you test for audience awareness and/or receptivity: "Does everyone understand how I've arrived at this conclusion?" "Shall I recap the points involved here?" Be alert to general audience reaction. Occasionally you'll find it helps to provide listeners the opportunity to indicate explicitly whether they're following you or not. You learn of any need to adjust your presentation for greater comprehensibility. With positive feedback, you are also reassured as to your effectiveness.

SIGNAL CHANGES IN TOPIC CLEARLY

This makes it more likely that your audience will arrive at the conclusion you want them to be left with. Recapping each major point is a useful device—it allows the audience to review pertinent elements of information for assured comprehension before moving on to a next point to be considered. (It's the same benefit you can win with feedback breaks.)

Audience Response

MAKE NOTE OF AGREEMENT EXPRESSED WITHIN YOUR AUDIENCE

This makes it possible for you to identify which of your points has most telling effect. It also enables you to identify who among your listeners is most in accord with the viewpoint you are promoting. Later you can look to these "allies" for concurrence on further related points you want to impress upon your audience.

KEEP QUESTIONS UNDER CONTROL

If your presentation is so structured that questions may be asked at any time, be prepared to answer some and to defer others to a later point in your presentation. Don't let questions interfere with the flow of your material.

The questions you will probably be able to answer immediately will be those requesting a definition or clarification of terms or issues as you're presenting them. The questions to defer—*do not ignore or dismiss them*—are those that challenge you on the merits of a position taken or suggested in your presentation. Nothing gets you off track more than allowing argumentative comments from the audience to interrupt the flow of prepared remarks. Before you know it, a debate ensues that captures everyone's attention and makes it difficult for you to continue with the rest of what you have to say.

Ignoring or dismissing challenging questions is ill-advised, because that will be interpreted as evading the issue raised. Defer dealing with them, however, until you've had the opportunity to complete your presentation. It may be that the balance of your presentation will undercut your audience's skepticism about a position you've taken or advocate. In any case, you'll have had the opportunity to make all the points you want your listeners to consider. Then get back to leftover questions, answering them as succinctly as possible to the extent they relate to the issues. If they don't relate, point out to what degree they are not relevant, then leave it at that. Always avoid getting drawn into extended debate.

AVOID A DEFENSIVE RESPONSE TO QUESTIONS

The audience has a right to probe for a clearer understanding of the positions you take. You may feel in certain circumstances that a questioner is trying to win points at your expense. Deal with that person matter-of-factly and dispassionately. If you become defensive and the audience senses it, others are likely to jump in and gang up on you.

When faced with someone who seems to be heckling, resist the temptation to respond in kind. You may find yourself outlipped. And even if you're not, you may alienate others in the audience who resent your putting down one of their colleagues. Better to answer quietly, with a self-assurance unruffled by the other's rudeness. Even those who do not share your perspective will almost always respect your self-assurance and courtesy.

Managing Time

DON'T WORRY ABOUT FINISHING TOO SOON

Don't be nervous about running out of material before you run out of time. It rarely happens. Most presenters prepare more material than they have time to use. Concentrate on developing your presentation with well-organized information illustrated to the best advantage. Should you finish your presentation early, use the time remaining for questions or other feedback.

DON'T PASS UP ANY HAPPY ENDINGS

When it's time for you to stop, do just that. Few things wreck an otherwise good presentation more than talking on and on and on . . . Develop a sense of time in relation to the material you have. If you're concerned you won't be able to fit everything in, do a dry run or two so that you achieve a balance between the time you need and the time available to you.

You've sat through formal presentations. You know which speakers have a positive effect on you, which don't, and why. Think about it. Then, in developing your speaking skills, follow this variant on the Golden Rule: Speak unto others as you would have them speak unto you.

MANAGEMENT-LABOR NEGOTIATIONS: SUGGESTED GROUND RULES

Hank has often been asked "What ground rules would you suggest for negotiations between management and labor?" He's compiled a brief checklist of those he thinks most important for resolving issues in this vital area. The perspective adopted here is that of management (in terms of the "you" referred to), but the guidelines suggested apply equally to both sides.

1. Don't Stress the Adversary Relationship. All too often management and labor enter into negotiation with a sense of meeting the enemy. The truth is, laborers form an integral part of your total organization. Without them your company could not manufacture its products or perform its services. Conversely, labor cannot prosper unless the company does well.

Even though you are necessarily focusing on the differences that exist between you, it's important to stress common interests to create a win-win orientation on both sides. Without that emphasis it's too easy to fall into antagonistic win-lose positions that impede coming to agreement. And that can make subsequent agreement difficult to accept if either side is viewed as having compromised with "the enemy." The managment-labor interrelationship is such that a win-lose orientation is likely to lead to lose-lose results.

2. Keep Statements to Third Parties or the Press as Neutral as Possible. Newspaper reports quoting hostile remarks from either side just tend to promote further conflict. Additionally, fearing a possible loss of face relative to third parties, either side may prove more reluctant to back down from initial hard-line positions. And yet some compromise will have to be reached.

3. Don't Indulge In or Accept Personal Abuse or Intimidation. Be firm in your statement of position and in your reactions to others' statements. That's part of working to achieve goals. Trying to push the opposition into acceding to your priorities through intimidation only accentuates any sense of adversary relationship that may exist.

Giving in to efforts to intimidate you only encourages disregard for your needs and interests. The dynamic you want to develop is one of joint consideration of mutual needs. (Follow suggestions offered in Chapter 5 for sounding off when subjected to abuse.)

4. Be United in Your Approach to the Other Side. You're very apt to be negotiating in a team context. Be sure to avoid peripheral squabbles among fellow team members. When differences arise, don't discuss them at the bargaining table—use a caucus or recess to work through them. (See Chapter 7.) Make sure that roles are effectively coordinated. If, for example, you're employing a "good guy–bad guy" tactic, be sure you're both working toward the same objective; be sure your "bad guy" knows when to take a back seat in the discussions.

5. Don't Disclose the Terms of Your Mandate to Negotiate. If the other side questions you on the extent of your authority to deal with the issues, simply respond that you are there to discuss the issues and have been authorized to do exactly that. Then get on with discussions.

6. Avoid Ultimatums. Ultimatums have the effect of painting you into a corner at the same time you're trying to push the other side into a desired position on an issue. Rather than trying to obtain a concession by taking an "Either you . . . or we'll . . ." approach, keep it to an "If you . . . then we may have to . . ." That can suggest a consequence the other side would prefer to avoid without your seeming to be issuing a threat. It will leave you more room for maneuver in the event the other side balks at accepting your position.

7. Resist the Urge to Walk Out. Walking out constitutes an admission that you can't handle the situation. It doesn't settle issues that have to be settled. It crystallizes whatever hostility and anger have been building up between the parties. As with an ultimatum, it can have the effect of painting you into a corner. Because it's an act that will usually be visible to third parties, it again introduces the problem of losing face. That won't be relevant to the issues in dispute and yet it so easily becomes an issue in itself, preempting consideration of those your negotiation was intended to resolve.

8. Handle Less Sensitive, Non-Economic Issues First. These are the issues that usually admit to resolution the soonest. How you deal with these can provide evidence of good faith that will stand you in good stead when the more difficult economic issues are introduced. The positive feelings that grow between the parties from resolving issues where agreement is more easily achieved will help both sides feel more open when discussing sensitive areas.

9. Go for a Package Deal. Make it explicit that each issue settled or heading to an agreement in principle is contingent on acceptance of the final contract resolving all issues. In this fashion, individual points of agreement create a momentum toward resolution of all issues in dispute. You also facilitate compromise on difficult issues, which might well prove resistant to resolution if considered in isolation from the other issues.

10. Keep All Involved Parties Informed. You may be negotiating contract terms with representatives of a national or international union. Don't overlook discussing the issues thoroughly with representatives of the local. The cooperation of the local is, after all, essential to implementation of any agreement worked out with the parent union. If you've maintained a fairly congenial relationship with the local, you may find some support for a position you're taking in bargaining with the parent union. However, keep your discussion with the local to an exchange of ideas and information; limit actual negotiation of issues to the parties who will be drawing up the actual contract.

Following these ground rules won't ensure resolution of every management-labor contract dispute without difficulty. There's no guarantee that following any set procedure will eliminate all problems that arise in bargaining talks. Each encounter brings into play its own unique combination of personalities and issues. But you will minimize the difficulties if you follow the guidelines set out here. You'll be stressing respect for the other side while systematically pursuing your own priorities. The atmosphere you establish will encourage mutual recognition that interests ultimately align: a strong company means employment benefits and security for labor; a labor force that sees its perspectives taken into account will be motivated to better performance than one that sees its contribution discounted.

THE BUYER-SELLER INTERACTION

In many areas of business, buying and selling isn't a matter of exchange on preset terms. Prices, terms of delivery, and other pertinent considerations are all subject to negotiation. Again, every point we've made so far about conduct of negotiations applies here, but it can help to review what's characteristic of the buyer-seller relationship.

The Traditional Relationship

In the traditional buy-sell situation, it's the seller who initiates negotiations. He contacts a buyer or purchasing agent he considers a likely prospect, and approaches that person with a certain professional deference. The buyer is seen to hold the advantage. In fact, it's not unusual for a buyer from "the old school" to be downright hostile at the outset of the exchange. He may well project an attitude of "I'm only seeing you because it's company policy to extend that minimum courtesy."

The seller is commonly faced with having to satisfy another's needs before his own will be taken into account. He consequently has to work from a give-get orientation. The buyer reserves making a commitment to anything until fully assured first of getting something he wants. That puts the seller in the position of having to extrapolate from research and on-the-spot observation what will motivate the buyer to buy. This requires development of analytical and intuitive abilities beyond what are necessary in negotiations where demands/expectations are articulated by both parties at the outset of the process.

Furthermore, even when a seller accurately pinpoints a buyer's needs, he still has to present a convincing case that the goods or services he has to offer will fill those needs best. The buyer, who first takes an attitude of "Why should I spend my time talking to you?" (i.e., "What need of mine do you think you're going to fill?") almost always next takes the attitude of "What makes you think you're in the best position to service me?" The seller inevitably defers mentioning his own needs until he's demonstrated that he understands the buyer's needs and can fill them.

Depending on whether one looks at the process from the buyer's or the seller's perspective, the factors influencing the course of negotiation here vary.

THE SELLER'S PERSPECTIVE

From the seller's point of view, working for and getting a sales contract depend on these factors:

- How much he wants or needs the contract, an element of motivation the other side will usually not feel any sense of urgency about;
- How sure he is that he can get the contract;
- The cost-support data for his price or proposal and whether that makes him competitive with other sellers of the same or similar goods or services;
- How much time is available for working out an agreement;
- The good will or receptivity with which the buyer views him;
- The technical preeminence or superior quality of the product or service he is offering;
- The degree to which he knows there is support within the buyer's organization for his product or service.

THE BUYER'S PERSPECTIVE

From the buyer's point of view the factors to consider are

- Whether there is a need that can be filled or an advantage to be gained from the seller's product/service;
- Whether there are reliable alternate sources of supply;
- Assurance that the seller is eager or anxious to come to agreement, so that concessions on price, delivery, etc., may very well be possible;
- The knowledge of being in control of issuing or not issuing the contract that is being worked for;
- An ability to specify quality and price criteria, although within realistic limits;

- The good will or reputation that the seller has built up previously for reliable goods/service;
- The amount of time available for exploring opportunities across a wide range for purchase of necessary or desired goods/services.

Look at the factors on both sides, and you'll see that buyer-seller relationships are not serendipitous encounters. Each side has to be prepared to explore opportunities in advance of any meeting; both have to be primed to follow through on a preestablished approach to their ritual of negotiation.

It may appear that there's much greater flexibility on the buyer's side. To some extent that's true. But the buyer ultimately must be as disciplined in approach to his task as is the seller, whether or not he has a wider latitude in regard to any particular seller. Although a particular seller may not accurately identify the buyer's needs, the buyer has to remain alert to those. He has to know his priorities and meet them in time and on the best possible terms. The buyer can't afford to be ruled by caprice in handling his purchase responsibilities. Because this is so, some element of opportunity exists for any seller potentially able to supply a needed product or service.

TEAM NEGOTIATIONS

Because of the multiple factors involved, and because those are different on each side, it's important that team efforts in this type of negotiation be carefully orchestrated. This is particularly true on the selling side. All sales team members must be familiar with all the points of the sales proposal and with supporting data. Then those with specialized responsibilities—technical personnel, pricing analysts, quality control engineers, manufacturing consultants— must be careful to dovetail their presentations with the overall sales strategy. On the buyer's side, personnel need not coordinate as tightly in evaluation of the points of the presentation or in answering questions from the seller's side that bear on supply arrangements.

Sometimes you find the buyer's side balking at making a commitment because additional expertise is needed. Someone with very specific knowledge related to an aspect of utilizing the proffered goods/services has to be consulted first. That always means delay. At times it's a tactic for breaking off the negotiation.

The seller can't readily employ this kind of delaying tactic—he has to have his experts in place. Effective salesmanship requires ready response to questions raised and convincing reply to doubts expressed. It's always to the seller's advantage to find out the composition of the opposing team so that the sales team can be optimally prepared in any area where questions may arise. It is at times advisable for the seller to suggest to a buyer that a certain type of specialist be present on the buyer's team for evaluation of a particular sales point.

A Change in the Traditional Relationship

In several major areas of commerce and industry, the supply-demand ratios have so altered in recent years that a new type of buyer-seller relationship exists. This is one in which a seller has command over a commodity that is in short supply, creating more potential buyers than sellers for it. Under this circumstance, the factors in the more traditional situation either don't apply or work along different lines. A buyer who takes the traditional perspective, stressing needs without immediate, explicit regard for the seller's wants, can find himself bypassed. The potential for damage can be acute.

We're moving out of an age where the purchaser is always sure to have the edge in any buy-sell negotiation. Sometimes he will, but it's very clear that occasions will arise when he won't. That means buyers will have to become more conscious of negotiating skills that have heretofore seemed more applicable on the sales side. Where buyers working along a traditional line of relationship with sellers have shown themselves sensitive to the seller's needs, changeover to meet the needs of new circumstances should be fairly easily accomplished. In some cases, however, it may prove to an organization's advantage to employ sales personnel in a new buying capacity. Because they usually have a greater flexibility in dealing with a wide range of people, those with sales experience may prove more readily able to adjust to change than those with an old-line buyer's mentality.

NEGOTIATING INTERNATIONALLY

Obvious difficulties occur when dealing with individuals from another culture. This is as much so when you are dealing with a friendly foreigner as when you are dealing with someone who is antagonistic. Any language barrier can by itself create a frustrating impediment to clear understanding, and differences in cultural values add to the potential for confusion and misunderstanding. Nevertheless, the process of negotiation operates in an international context as readily as in any other. Somewhere beneath the differences that exist between the parties there has to be a range of shared perceptions—how the process works and what its value is. Otherwise agreements between nations or nationals of different countries would prove virtually impossible.

What are the underlying similarities that make negotiation a viable means of resolving issues across language and cultural barriers? What are the elements of difference that make negotiation more complex in an international context?

Process Similarities

The fact is that negotiation is a universally recognized ritual process for bringing parties to agreement. It is a means of developing cooperation and settling differences that is as old as history. It draws on a reservoir of faith present in all cultures that people can, if they want to, effectively communicate needs and desires to each other to peacefully bridge differences between them. It builds on the conviction that dialogue is possible between any individuals or groups of individuals, because ultimately all issues have as a common denominator the experience of human needs or desires. Although the expression of these is subject to cultural influences, their existence grows out of the shared human condition.

THE SAME RANGE OF PRECONDITIONS

The same preconditions for negotiating exist at one time or other in an culture. A quick review of what they are will illustrate the irrelevance of cultural differences when it comes to the reasons for negotiation.

A Need for Assistance. That's the precondition for any country requesting economic or military aid, as well as for any individual faced with a problem he wants help with.

A Common Threat. This is what's behind the formation of alliances on any level, whether it be NATO or just two people joining forces for security against sinister designs on the part of a third person.

A Possible Chance for Gain. A prime example here would be discussions aimed at developing an international consortium for stabilizing world commodity prices.

Desire for Influential Favor. This is what prompts lobbying efforts in every world capital, to mention but one prominent example of negotiation under this precondition.

A Sales Opportunity. The same considerations have to be weighed by every person trying to persuade a potential buyer to a purchase decision, whether the merchandise is armaments or phonograph records.

A Purchase Requirement. It's the same precondition whether you want industrial solvent or a guaranteed supply of betel nuts.

A Contract Renegotiation. Between countries it's treaty renegotiation and requires taking the same considerations into account.

A Desire to Disengage. Countries go through the process of pulling back from each other just the way people do, and every culture recognizes circumstances in which relationships come to an end, with a consequent need for some readjustment between the parties.

A Breakdown in Relations. It's the other side of the coin from disengagement; either or both parties want to reestablish a closeness previously enjoyed but now threatened or absent.

A Last-Ditch Salvage Effort. There are times when the situation looks pretty desperate and yet discussions offer some hope of producing a change for the better.

The preconditions that lead parties to negotiate exist at one time or other in all cultures. Any time you want to enlist the support or acquiescence of another party to achieve objectives you have, you rely on the basic human interaction that is negotiation. There is no other alternative, short of crass intimidation or actual use of force. And regardless of culture, these are simply not practical for eliciting cooperation that is genuine and self-sustaining. Even bribes are negotiated. Whether you're an American, an Arab, or a Hottentot, any experienced need to enlist the voluntary cooperation or support of another party pushes you to the bargaining table (or tent or stump). While the manner in which you address the opposite party will vary according to the cultural context, what you are doing will be essentially the same, subject to the same operative guidelines in any situation.

THE SAME RELIANCE ON PERSUASION

We could probably draw up an extended list of specific guidelines, but they all revolve around the prerequisites for success in the art of persuasion. These we've previously boiled down to four main considerations:

1. Getting the other party's interest;
2. Gaining the other party's understanding of what you are looking for from them;
3. Providing appropriate motivation so the other party sees a benefit for itself in any cooperative or supportive move it makes;
4. Winning an explicit commitment to follow through on the course of action desired.

Implicit in all this is adherence in each case to a standard of behavior that reflects respect and consideration for needs, which includes a sensitivity to your opposite's ego needs.

The Common Human Element

Further similarities grow out of the fact that negotiators bring their own human strengths and frailties to the process. Although we at times imagine Americans or Canadians altogether different creatures from, say, the Chinese or Japanese, the fact is they aren't. The selfless and the selfish exist in every society, as do the capable and the incompetent, the highly motivated and the indifferent. Although the manner in which personality affects the negotiation process will vary from culture to culture, you cannot escape the reality that it will have an effect.

UNIVERSAL FACTORS AFFECTING PERSONAL STYLE

In any culture, how substantive issues are resolved is affected by the ego needs and communication capabilities of the people involved.

Individual Tolerance Levels. Each negotiator has his own level of tolerance for frustration and reacts to frustration accordingly.

Intuition. Each negotiator relies to some extent on his own intuitive assessment of the situation at hand as well as on any "hard" data presented for consideration.

Intimidation. In any culture, attempts to force agreement through intimidation are likely to meet with increased resistance and/or resentment.

Argument. There is always a possibility that one party will attempt to debate issues rather than negotiate them. The danger always exists that energies will be directed to proving one side "correct" in its approach to differences between the parties.

Role-Playing. All negotiators to some extent assume the role of actor in their presentation of perspectives on the issues and in their efforts to advance their priorities.

Disposition to Cooperate. Whatever the cultural background, as negotiators see the possibility growing that their needs may be satisfied, they tend to become more cooperative and supportive.

Pragmatism. In any culture, the most successful negotiators are those with a strong pragmatic bent who recognize that opportunities for gain in a negotiation are greatest when linked to achievement of objectives on the other side.

Personal Style. Every negotiator has certain idiosyncracies, mannerisms, gestures, etc. that reflect ease or discomfort with what is happening during negotiation. An attentive opponent can observe these for some indication of the negotiator's reactions to how things are going.

At this point you may be wondering what peculiar problems might arise in an international context that you haven't already had to deal with in negotiations with fellow countrymen.

The Differences to Take into Account

Anytime you negotiate with someone from a different cultural background, you have to make adjustments in these areas:

THE SENSE OF PROTOCOL TO FOLLOW

Each society has its own protocol or rules of etiquette. There's no difficulty for you in applying your own sense of behavioral proprieties in a negotiating encounter with a fellow countryman. Both sides will tend to follow practices that are conventional in the society to which they belong and familiar to each for that reason. But in an encounter with a foreign national, you face someone whose sense of the formalities to observe in presenting and resolving issues arises from a different background.

Following your usual protocol with an opposite from another land can complicate things tremendously, even if your excuse for doing so is that it's easier for you. To begin with, implicit in a refusal to make any adjustment in your approach to the process is an assertion of superiority. In effect you are saying to the other side, "Our way of doing things is better than yours. You'll just have to adjust your behavior to our standards." Right away your opposite is going to feel put down and resentful.

One of the things Westerners—Americans in particular—have difficulty with when dealing with representatives from certain non-Western cultures is their lack of directness displayed throughout a negotiating exchange. Westerners like to think that directness is a prime asset in interpersonal exchange. They often regard an Oriental tendency to talk around issues with an impatience that is hard to conceal. What they fail to consider, however, is that the Oriental practice is based on a long-established tradition of regard for the ego needs in every interpersonal exchange. Their society's sense of protocol aims at minimizing embarrassment or humiliation that might otherwise result. Western directness, on the other hand, leads to frequent confrontation that often leaves damaged egos in clear view of all concerned.

A valuable consequence of the Oriental approach is the expression of disagreement in muted terms, allowing each side to retain its dignity, to concede issues gracefully, and thereby to hold doors as open as possible to future cooperative endeavor. From the Oriental perspective, the Western penchant for putting things bluntly is seen as coarse and devoid of respect for feelings on the other side.

A refusal to adapt to the protocol for interpersonal exchange established in another culture may amount not only to a sort of arrogance, but may be considered a personal affront as well.

The protocol established in other societies has its underlying rationale. Rarely if ever do formalities exist just for the sake of formality. To treat them as if they do is extremely shortsighted and potentially counterproductive.

ORIENTATION TO TIME

In North America and northern Europe, time is commonly regarded as a precious commodity. It ought not to be wasted; every effort should be directed toward utilizing it productively. In other cultures—we can point to the Latins as an example—this emphasis on productive use of time seems highly exaggerated. They tend to be less concerned that business be conducted according to the clock. After all, the most fundamental priority is the enjoyment of life. To subordinate that to the conduct of business seems to them a sad perversion of priorities. Reactions to efforts to establish and hold to a tight schedule of meetings are likely to be met with a certain amused sympathy. Outrage from a clock-oriented negotiator to the "unnecessary" delay in getting down to business is ultimately likely to engender only irritability, rather than a more cooperative compliance with schedules.

Changing Appointment Dates. In some countries, particularly in the Far East, it's not unusual to find a negotiating opposite requesting a change in the day or time of a scheduled meeting without apparent good reason. One reason for this is to exploit the most astrologically auspicious moment for a meeting. Pressure to hold to schedule in this case will be taken as a callous disregard of factors influencing chances for success of the meetings. That you don't take these factors into account does not mean they are not of serious concern to the other side.

Getting Down to Business in Meetings. North Americans and northern Europeans find it exasperating to go into meetings in other countries and find 75 percent of the time taken up with unbusinesslike social exchanges. They don't realize that in other cultures there may be no sharp distinction drawn between business and social life. Often the governing rule is "We only do busness with friends." The foreign businessman isn't content to work out a business deal without regard to who the other party is or whether any personal rapport is possible. This is true in many Third World countries and also traditional in Japan. The conversation may seem undirected social chatter to you, but it's an integral part of getting or losing business. How you respond on a personal level to what seem mere social niceties is as carefully weighed as you were proposing contract terms promising great opportunity for financial benefit.

PRIORITIES IN THE CONDUCT OF BUSINESS

These too differ from society to society. For example, a major American emphasis is on efficiency and productivity as standards for evaluating business performance. Although these are usually factors businessmen in other countries also take into account, they often do not understand why they should be stressed to the exclusion of other considerations.

There are those in other lands who share Mahatma Gandhi's criticism of Western industrial values as dehumanizing. Gandhi recommended an opposite approach: reliance on cottage industry characterized by production of articles of consumption through handicraft techniques rather than in industrial complexes. He believed this would guarantee all citizens more equal participation in the economic life of the country. To stress efficiency and productivity would only result in the individual being exploited as a laborer while giving him little share in the fruits of his labor. Elements of this philosophy continue to appeal to leaders in some Third World countries.

Other cultural attitudes influence priorities in the conduct of business outside industrialized North America and Western Europe to the extent that principles of efficiency, productivity, and profitability are often secondary considerations. Even between the United States and certain of the Western European nations—Sweden is a good example —one can observe a different emphasis in priorities affecting the conduct of business.

Don't take it for granted that the priorities paramount for you even in the broadest sense will or should be those of most importance to a counterpart from another country. Rather, make an effort to understand first what general priorities tend to be emphasized in the culture from which your opposite comes.

THE ELEMENT OF TRUST

The degree to which trust is directly expressed or remains implicit also varies from culture to culture. In some parts of the world a handshake following a discussion of broad issues suffices to commit two parties to a close cooperative relationship. In other parts of the world, any agreement must be spelled out in the most minute detail. The contracting party will not feel itself bound by a spirit of cooperation to provide support or services that have not explicitly been provided for in a document of agreement. Much of a negotiation with parties of this sort (the Russians are a prime example, but the Germans and the Japanese share this legalistic sort of approach to negotiations) revolves around the wording to be incorporated in the document that is being shaped. (Americans tend to be somewhat divided in their insistence on documentary precision. There is much more formalism evident on the East Coast than in the South or much of the Midwest or West.)

To be an effective negotiator with parties from another background, establish with certainty what form the final agreement must take in order to ensure the other party's full and continuing cooperation. That includes recognizing that in some instances an insistence on contractual formalism may be seen as implying the other side is not fully trustworthy.

ATTENTION TO DISTINCTIONS OF RANK

Americans, Canadians, and Australians in particular like to stress their democratic orientation. Although they require that anyone claiming to act as spokesman for an organization be authorized to do so, they automatically assume that any individual duly authorized to negotiate will be acceptable to and command the full respect of those with whom they are to deal. They project this assumption on people from other cultures, but this is often an erroneous supposition.

In many countries there is much more emphasis placed on the rank of the person authorized to negotiate important issues. Even Western Europeans have some sensitivity on this score. Some years ago the

British press expressed outrage at the patronage appointment of Nixon supporter Walter Annenberg as ambassador to the Court of St. James. The Yugoslavs were reported to be insulted when the American government sent only second-ranked officials to the funeral for Marshall Tito; other nations sent first-ranked leaders to pay their respects.

Not just any deputized representative will win the necessary respect and cooperation of a foreign government or organization when it comes to working out important agreements. It won't matter how talented that person may be; if it's a project or interaction involving prestige, the negotiator must be someone with established rank and/or prestige of his own. (Sometimes a talented individual can overcome initial resistance on that score. By all accounts, Walter Annenberg's dedication and ability won the respect necessary to ensure his functioning capably as ambassador.)

THE LANGUAGE BARRIER

We've saved going into detail on this for last because we wanted to emphasize the importance of factors not usually paid as much attention as language differences.

Obviously representatives speaking a different language must find a way of making themselves understood. That can be accomplished through interpreters or through both parties agreeing to use a language common to both.

In the latter case, some problems may arise because the understanding or nuance on either side is unequal. Language evolves in a cultural context and always to an extent reflects the idiosyncracies of the culture. Even when a foreigner has gained some facility in another language, he may not have fully grasped subtle shades of meaning attached to certain words or idiomatic constructions; his own cultural background will not have prepared him to be alert to these. This can even present problems when negotiators speak the same language, but come from different culture areas. The nuances of the American and British languages vary sufficiently so that confusion can arise even between these two English-speaking peoples. But the problems are differences of idiom and usually both parties recognize a need to achieve a common understanding.

There is often a tendency on one side to take it for granted that the opposition should assume the burden of working in a foreign language. Americans, for example, are notorious for their all-too-frequent insistence that negotiations will have to be conducted in English. They don't want to bother to learn other languages; at the same time they are quick to be amused at efforts by foreigners to express themselves in English. It does not seem to occur to them that this attitude reflects the same arrogance as a refusal to adjust their ideas of protocol to someone else's different cultural background.

We do not in this case, or in other areas where misunderstanding and confusion may arise, suggest that adjustments should be made only from your side. Some adjustment has to be made by each side. Both parties should be sensitive to the need to bridge cultural differences where these impede or confuse the negotiation process.

We do feel strongly that Americans should make a greater effort to consider the other side's cultural values when negotiating internationally. It's not only a matter of being more polite or respectful in an encounter with a foreign national. It's just as much a question of pragmatism. You still must motivate the other side to cooperation and you improve your chances for success when you are more sensitive to their needs and feelings. We've been emphasizing that point all along. When you negotiate you try to put to work every persuasive skill you have. To achieve that to the best effect you must show respect for your opposite's cultural background and a willingness to be more flexible in your effort to open communication between you.

Suggested Supplemental Reading

THERE is a wealth of good material published on the psychology of human behavior and communication, and helpful books on business relations are available as well. A little research in your local library will quickly uncover titles that will help you in each of these areas. The brief list that follows is intended to alert you to just a few volumes that we feel can prove especially helpful in honing your negotiation skills.

Argyle, Michael, *The Psychology of Interpersonal Behavior*, London: Penguin Books, 1978.

Bach, George, and Goldberg, Herb, *Creative Aggression*, New York: Doubleday and Company, 1974; Avon Books, 1975.

Bernie, Eric, *Games People Play*, New York, Ballantine Books, 1978.

Calero, Henry H., *Winning the Negotiation*, New York: Hawthorn/ E. P. Dutton, 1979.

_____, and Nierenberg, Gerard I., *How to Read a Person Like a Book*, New York: Hawthorn Books, 1971; Cornerstone Library, 1972.

_____, and Nierenberg, Gerard I., *Meta-Talk: A Guide to Hidden Meanings in Conversations*, New York: Trident Press, 1973.

Harris, Thomas, *I'm OK—You're OK*, New York: Harper & Row, Publishers, 1969; Avon Books, 1973.

Nirenberg, Jesse S., *Getting Through to People*, Englewood Cliffs: Prentice-Hall, Inc., 1963.

Olson, Robert W., *The Art of Creative Thinking*, New York: Harper & Row, Publishers, 1980.

Smith, Manual J., *When I Say No, I Feel Guilty*, New York: Dial Press, 1975.